The Latest
and
Greatest Read-Alouds

The Latest and Greatest Read-Alouds

Sharron L. McElmeel

Illustrated by Deborah L. McElmeel

1994
Libraries Unlimited, Inc.
Englewood, Colorado

LIBRARIES UNLIMITED, INC.
P.O. Box 6633
Englewood, CO 80155-6633

1-800-237-6124

Library of Congress Cataloging-in-Publication Data

McElmeel, Sharron L.
    The latest and greatest read-alouds / Sharron L. McElmeel ;
illustrated by Deborah L. McElmeel.
     xv, 210 p. 17x25 cm.
    Includes bibliographical references and index.
    ISBN 1-56308-140-7
    1. Oral reading. 2. Children--Books and reading. I. Title.
LB1575.5.M34 1993
372.41--dc20   93-39048
                                                CIP

Especially for Jack, who knew the value of reading aloud before it was the thing to do, and for the parents of my grandchildren, who are giving their children a love of reading.

Contents

Acknowledgments

First and foremost I must thank Nancy Jennings of O. G. Waffle Book-house in Marion, Iowa, for sharing wonderful new books for *The Latest and Greatest Read-Alouds*. She not only suggested titles but she shared copies of many books to be read and evaluated. In addition, I must thank the educators with whom I work. They help me to know when a book "works for them and their students." The many hours of research to find just the right books would not have been possible without the patience and assistance of my in-house staff—my family. They have provided first readings, illustrative material, and location assistance. Special thanks to Jennifer Jennings, who provided valuable research assistance in helping to verify bibliographic data for the many titles listed in this book, and to Slayton Thompson, founder and director of the Grant Wood Drum and Bugle Corp and the members of the Corp who cooperated by letting us photograph their visit to the Cedar Rapids Public Library. And finally, I am appreciative of the cooperation of the many publishing house publicists, marketing directors, and others in the publishing industry who suggested new titles to evaluate and in some cases provided review copies.

Introduction

The late Dr. Seuss, Theodor S. Geisel, often commented that when he went to his office to write he never left the room during the workday even if all he did was sit there. I am now in that position. What more can I say about reading aloud that hasn't already been said? In his *A Father Reads to His Children: An Anthology of Prose and Poetry* (Dutton, 1965), Orville Prescott commented that few children learn to love books by themselves. Someone has to show children the way to good books. He expressed the idea that reading aloud to children would help to show them the way. Jim Trelease addresses the same topic, motivation through reading aloud, in his book *The Read-Aloud Handbook* (Penguin, 1985). Reading aloud does much to lure students into the world of books. Many believe as I do that the single most important thing a teacher or parent can do to ensure the success of a child in school and life is to read aloud to that child. In past years, many people have written books about the benefits of reading aloud, including Prescott and Trelease. Their books also listed a multitude of titles that could be used as successful read-alouds, including many of the classics that have been tried and true for many years. Certainly books such as Wilson Rawls's *Where the Red Fern Grows* (Bantam, 1961), Sheila Burnford's *The Incredible Journey* (Bantam, 1961), or Scott O'Dell's *Island of the Blue Dolphins* (Houghton, 1960) belong on any list that includes classics, and in fact, these books are included in many lists of not-to-be-missed read-alouds. Consequently, I have not attempted to list those books within these pages, nor will I attempt to duplicate the listings made previously by Trelease and other read-aloud advocates. What I have attempted to do is to update the read-aloud suggestions by including books that have been published since 1988. The picture books listed in Chapter 1 are those that will contribute to the body of titles being read as general read-alouds in many early childhood classrooms. For each of those books, I have listed a brief annotation touching on the content and illustrative matter (a more lengthy annotation might have been longer than the text of the book!). In Chapter 2, which lists primarily novels suggested for read-alouds, I have tried to include complete annotations to help the user of *The Latest and Greatest Read-Alouds* to assess whether or not a specific book will fit into educational goals or is of enough interest to seek out for reading aloud. Suggested listening levels and read-alone levels are given in addition to further reading suggestions.

Reading aloud allows a specific title to be shared with a child or a group of children. A good read-aloud will often promote the reading of other books by the same author or will become the stimulation for reading a group of books tied together with a thematic thread. The "Further Reading" section that accompanies each book listed in Chapter 2 is included to facilitate the selection of read-alouds in a specific genre, correlate with curriculum objectives, or facilitate locating collaborative reading material. A separate listing at the end of the chapter arranges the titles by suggested listening levels; another listing provides an alphabetical list by title.

I have tried to focus on books with strong narratives—books that are important in the elementary years as the narratives correspond with the speaking patterns familiar to students and with the students' listening experiences. Reading aloud to a child will aid the development of that child's listening vocabulary, and familiarity with speech patterns aids in the development of the child's ability to read.

Oral reading and responses to those readings assist children in developing an appreciation for well-written literature and extend the listener's thinking skills. It is within the power of every parent, every teacher, library media specialist, or public librarian to give children a rich experience with literature. We must teach children to read, but more importantly we must help them want to read—and the very best way to do that is to give children *time to read and the inspiration to enjoy and learn*. Reading aloud to children will provide the inspiration, and time to read will help them learn.

SCOPE/PURPOSE OF THIS BOOK

The purpose of *The Latest and Greatest Read-Alouds* is to help parents and educators to locate books created by contemporary authors and illustrators and published since 1988. Many of the books listed will have 1990 or later copyrights. Much as children's literature update courses build on a basis of general knowledge, this book attempts to build on the reader's general knowledge of read-alouds that have become classics or that have been available for some time. This book updates that knowledge by listing the latest (more recent) titles that are emerging as great read-alouds. Chapter 1, "Reading

Early—Reading Often," lists more than 50 books suggested for reading to children ages 5-7. Many of the selections are appropriate for reading aloud to preschoolers and can also be used with intermediate-age children as discussion starters or in relation to a specific theme or unit of study. For example, Patricia Polacco's *Thunder Cake* might be used to introduce a school unit on weather folklore, or it might be used in the home when a child is afraid of a storm; in fact, making the Thunder Cake would be an excellent stormy day activity. Jon Scieszka's *The True Story of the Three Little Pigs by A. Wolf* is a natural for use when point of view is discussed as an author's technique. It is also a fun book to read just before eating barbequed pork sandwiches.

Because reading aloud can promote further reading of books by the author or on the theme, suggestions for further reading are also given for each title listed in Chapter 2, "The Next Step." Although some picture books are included in the "Further Reading" sections, the majority of books referred to in this chapter are generally longer than the standard 32-page picture book.

The 100+ books listed in Chapter 2 have been given one of six listening-level designations from early primary (ages 5-6; grades K-1) to intermediate accelerated (ages 10-11; grades 5-6). Basically the read-aloud level suggested is one level higher than the level at which the child might be expected to be able to read the material independently. In addition, the level listed for reading aloud is the *minimum age/grade* at which I would suggest the book be read aloud. Some books might, in individual circumstances, be appropriate for younger ages. Many books listed for specific age groups will be appropriate for older age groups as well as for the age group listed. The factors considered when the designation was determined included the pacing of the book, the appropriateness or interest of the content, vocabulary, and basic story plot/structure. Once all of these factors were considered, a suggested listening level (read-aloud level) and a read-alone level were given to each of the books included. The list in Chapter 2 is certainly not all-inclusive of the best books (of a longer length) to read aloud, but it does contain more than 100 of the *best* read-alouds published since 1988—*The Latest and Greatest Read-Alouds*. It is hoped that this list will just be a starter list to get those interested in updating their lists of read-alouds used with children. As a beginning step to locating additional read-alouds, search out additional titles authored by authors who appear on the lists in Chapters 1 and 2. Those authors who write with a strong narrative often exhibit that same characteristic in other books that they write. Once an awareness with literature begins to evolve, the searching for additional titles will become more spontaneous. It is hoped that the children being read to will begin to seek out books they would like to have shared with them. Choices of the titles selected for reading aloud should evolve as a joint decision. Sometimes it might be a choice of a specific title, but other times it might be a title based on genre or type of character (female, male, animal, etc.).

The suggestions I make throughout this book are, of course, books that I like and that I recommend for reading aloud, but my (or anyone else's) recommendations should not be the deciding factor. The single most important criterion for deciding on a read-aloud is whether or not *you*, the person who is reading aloud the book, enjoys it. In addition, consideration should be given to the audience who will be listening to the book. The enjoyment conveyed by the reader will be passed through to the listener through the shared experience. This book should help you locate novels that you will enjoy reading aloud to children; books that will extend their interest in reading and that they will enjoy hearing read aloud.

TIPS FOR READING ALOUD

When you read aloud consider the size of the group to whom you are reading. The reading style must fit your personality, but it must also fit the group/child you are reading to. If you are a parent reading at home to your own child or children, finding a comfortable, overstuffed chair to share or seating yourself close on a sofa are often the best choices. Simply stated: cozy and close. If the book has illustrations, be sure to share them. If you can do so comfortably, put your arm around your child and read aloud in a clear, energetic voice. Unique voices for each character are not necessary, but it is important to avoid reading in a monotone.

If you are reading to a larger group, the children should sit as close to the reader as possible. If children are allowed to daydream, draw pictures at their desks, or do worksheets, their half-hearted listening will reflect the idea that listening and reading are not so important. In fact, just the opposite is true. So, if at all possible, bring the listeners to a reading carpet or to a more intimate space where they will not be preoccupied with other activities and can give their full attention to the reading that is being done. If a reading carpet or other suitable area is not available, try moving all the desks to the edge of the room and arrange the chairs in a big circle in the center of the room. At first, taking the time to rearrange the furniture may seem disruptive but with a little practice the arrangement will come quickly and pay dividends. The effort will serve to highlight the importance of the activity. But regardless of the actual manner in which you accomplish the task, it is most important that you—parent or educator—do read aloud on a regular basis.

USING THIS BOOK

Titles suggested in Chapters 1 and 2 are arranged with the entries listed alphabetically by the author's last name. The list could be browsed for interesting titles that might appeal to you and the children with whom you intend to share the book or books. At the end of Chapter 1 is an alphabetical listing of titles with a reference to the author's last name as a cross-reference. At the end of Chapter 2 is both an alphabetical listing of titles with a cross-reference to the author's last name and the sequential entry number used within the chapter. In addition, there is a listing of the titles by suggested listening levels.

Chapter 3 includes 21 suggestions for moving beyond reading aloud and including other reading motivation techniques to help build a family/class-room of readers on our way to building a nation of readers.

Finally, the comprehensive index at the end of the book lists all titles, authors, and subjects related to the books suggested and other topics discussed within this book. That index should assist the user in locating read-aloud titles that will provide collaborative readings for thematic and curriculum units or titles that will focus on topics being discussed within the classroom or in the family. The index should also assist in providing a menu of balanced read-alouds.

Read, share, enjoy!

Chapter 1
Reading Early—Reading Often

The value of reading aloud to young children and the positive relationship of that activity to children who learn to read early is affirmed by several studies. Among the most significant studies is that of Dolores Durkin, who reported on her study in 1966.[1] In that study, Durkin stated that a common factor in the homes of children who learned to read early was a respect for books. All of Durkin's early readers had been read to as toddlers, and some had been read to as early as infancy. A similar pattern was noted by Margaret Clark in her study in Scotland.[2] Clark found that while the families she studied did not necessarily share a common level of economic wealth, the families did share a pattern of frequent use of the public library and a respect for the value of books and reading. Her study strengthened the belief that picture books should be standard read-aloud fare in every early primary classroom and in homes where there is a primary-aged child. Dorothy Butler presented a situation where books read aloud had a dramatic effect on the development of a multiply disabled girl. Doctors had diagnosed Cushla as severely retarded, but she was read to from the age of four months. She eventually learned to read well beyond her actual chronological age, much to the astonishment of her doctors. The story of Cushla's impressive discovery of the world is told in *Cushla and Her Books* by Dorothy Butler (Horn Book, 1980).

CONTINUING BENEFITS OF READING ALOUD

Not only is it commonly thought that reading aloud profoundly affects the early development of a child's reading attitudes and abilities, reading aloud seems to also have a long-range effect on the reading behavior of children. In an unpublished doctoral dissertation (Ohio State University, 1974), Judith Sostarich cites a comparative study of sixth-grade students. Sostarich identified active and nonactive readers within the total group. Even though both groups, in general, were able to read as well as the students in the other group, the active readers chose to read on their own often while those in the nonactive group seldom read on their own. Sostarich investigated the background of the students in each group and discovered a definite pattern: The active reading group had been frequently read to as toddlers, some as early as infancy. In some of those families, books were still being read aloud.

WHAT TO READ?

When choosing books to share with children, there seems to be as many sets of criteria as there are books. Donna E. Norton discusses the evaluation of books for children in her children's literature text, *Through the Eyes of a Child: An Introduction to Children's Literature*, third edition (Macmillan, 1990) as does Charlotte S. Huck and her coauthors in *Children's Literature in the Elementary School*, fifth edition (Harcourt, 1993). A simple guideline proposed by some whole language proponents suggests that books shared with young children should include the 3 Rs: rhyme, repetition, and rhythm. I prefer a simpler guide—if the book interests me, I read it to children. I never choose to read a book that I don't personally find interesting. There are simply too many books to waste my time or the children's time by reading something that doesn't bring a tear or a smile to my face—and most good books do. My definition of a good book to read, regardless of the age of child to whom I am reading, is whether or not the book (text/illustrations) evokes an emotional response. Those are the books I prefer to read to myself and those are the books I read to children. Readers of this book, *The Latest and Greatest Read-Alouds*, will not necessarily agree with all of the selections I have included in this chapter or in the following chapters. That is the way the world is. The list that follows is simply a starter list. The books included are merely suggestions—my suggestions. We are all different, and we will all have different responses to specific titles. I happen to like the books included on this list—I like them a lot. Some readers will make different choices and some listeners will ask to have different titles read over and over again. The one criterion should be that the read-aloud session leaves both the reader and the listeners with a positive experience.

The selections listed in this section are among the most recent titles that I now include in my list of "must reads." The purpose of this list is to highlight the latest read-aloud titles. A complete list of read-alouds should include tried and true favorites—classics by Steven Kellogg, Maurice Sendak, Tomie dePaola, and a host of other wonderful authors and illustrators of books for children. Many suggestions for additional picture book authors or illustrators to highlight and titles to read are included in other books that I have written, including the An Author a Month[3] series and the Bookpeople[4] albums.

When choosing books to read to children, keep in mind the child's or children's collective background of experience and depth of knowledge. Books about children are not necessarily for children. A child does not need to know every word that is read aloud to him or her as that is one of the goals of reading aloud—to stretch the listener's vocabulary. However, the words used must be used in a meaningful and logical context. If a book is to be read in one sitting, the length of the book will be a factor to consider. However, if the book can extend over two or more sessions, one must ascertain appropriate stopping points. When, with young listeners, a read-aloud is carried over to a second session, it is especially important that the previous reading session be summarized prior to beginning the second or subsequent readings. A simple question, "Can anyone tell me what has happened so far?," will often suffice to get the discussion started. After the discussion, move on to complete the next segment that will be read aloud.

When sharing a picture book with listeners, gather those to whom you are reading as close to you as possible. If you are reading to just one or two children, sit beside one another and hold the book together. If the group is larger, try to get all the children close enough that they can see the illustrations. Many picture books are now being published for educational use in a "big book" format. Although the concept has some merit, I have difficulty handling the large books. The binding is often not stiff enough to stand without bending. The various stands I have used do not, in general, solve the problem of how to handle the book and turn the pages. As a consequence, I generally use the regular-sized book. If the group is too large and seeing the illustrations is difficult, I often will read the story first and then go back and reread the story (or summarize the episodes if rereading would be too lengthy) while moving among the listeners to show the illustrations. With books that have a brief text, I sometimes reread the story a third time. I always make sure the book is available to students to browse through and enjoy independently after the oral reading. Be aware of the reaction of those to whom you are reading. Their level of interest will dictate much about how the read-aloud session is conducted. Maintaining eye contact with the audience and reading in an energetic manner will do much to keep the interest of listeners.

The list of titles that could be included on a read-aloud list could fill several books. The books on the following list have been selected because they are books that have a strong narrative, are energetically paced, and provide food for thought. Every classic was once a new book; the following list of suggestions are among the newest titles published—and many are sure to become classics. However, there is no magic list of books that all children must hear before they move on or pass out of childhood. The most important thing is that children are read to. Sharing literature and a love of reading is one of the most valuable gifts that any adult can pass on to children. And it's never too early (or too late) to start to share that gift.

NOTES

[1]Dolores Durkin, *Children Who Read Early* (New York: Columbia Teachers College Press, 1966).

[2]Margaret Clark, *Young Fluent Readers* (London: Heinemann Educational Books, 1976).

[3]*An Author a Month (for Pennies)* (1988); *An Author a Month (for Nickels)* (1990); *An Author a Month (for Dimes)* (1993); all published by Libraries Unlimited/Teacher Ideas Press.

[4]*Bookpeople: A First Album* (1990); *Bookpeople: A Second Album* (1990); *Bookpeople: A Multicultural Album* (1993); all published by Libraries Unlimited/Teacher Ideas Press.

Bookshelf—Picture Book Parade

A bercrombie, Barbara
Charlie Anderson

Illustrated by Mark Graham. McElderry, 1990. 32 pp. ISBN 0-689-50486-1.

A gentle story of a cat who travels between two homes, unbeknownst to each of the families in those homes. One family calls the cat Anderson; the other calls him Charlie. When his dual life is uncovered, the families—two girls and their mother, and a young couple—agree to share their pet. The parallel situation involving the two girls who have a home with their mother, and another with their father and stepmother, is not missed.

A lbert, Burton
Where Does the Trail Lead?

Illustrated by Brian Pinkney. Simon & Schuster, 1991. 32 pp. ISBN 0-671-73409-1.

A summertime family holiday on an island is illustrated by Pinkney's expressive scratchboard illustrations. The young African-American boy is depicted in a gentle New England island setting.

Aylesworth, Jim
The Folks in the Valley: A Pennsylvania Dutch ABC

Illustrated by Stefano Vitale. HarperCollins, 1992. 32 pp. ISBN 0-06-021672-7.

A rhythmic romp through the alphabet and a farm day. The simple pictures reflecting the motifs commonly associated with the Pennsylvania Dutch are rendered in warm colors edged in black. The paintings appear to have been painted on wood.

Aylesworth, Jim
Old Black Fly

Illustrated by Stephen Gammell. Holt, 1992. 32 pp. ISBN 0-8050-1401-2.

A rollicking poetic flight of a fly that goes from object to object—in alphabetical order. Boldly colored abstract illustrations help young listeners follow the action of the fly's adventures.

Balian, Lorna
Wilbur's Space Machine

Illustrated by Lorna Balian. Holiday House, 1990. 32 pp. ISBN 0-8234-0836-1.

An older couple, Wilbur and Olive, enjoy their peace and quiet until other people begin to invade their space. Wilbur devises a plan to give them all the space they need. He uses his "space" machine to inflate balloons that raise their home and yard into the sky. But, unbeknownst to the couple, one of their "invaders" has accompanied them on their journey.

Blundell, Tony
Beware of Boys

Illustrated by Tony Blundell. Greenwillow, 1992. 32 pp. ISBN 0-688-10924-1.

A boy outwits the hungry wolf who fancies him as his dinner by suggesting recipes on how to prepare him—after all, one wouldn't want to eat a boy raw! Of course, there are additional ingredients needed for the recipes, but when the wolf returns with the ingredients, the boy informs him that he has forgotten the salt. The final twist at the end will delight listeners who have been attentive to the ingredients requested by the boy. Blundell's cartoonlike artwork helps to move the story along.

Brett, Jan
Berlioz the Bear

Illustrated by Jan Brett. Putnam, 1991. 32 pp. ISBN 0-399-22248-0.

An animal orchestra is headed to a local village fair where they will perform. The bear's trouble with a buzzing sound in his instrument proves to be the distraction that causes their donkey-pulled cart to become stuck by the roadside. The efforts of many animals to help the stubborn donkey pull the cart out fail until the bee, who was the culprit behind the buzzing sound, flies out and stings the donkey into action. Beautifully detailed illustrations with borders present a second view of the preparations going on in the village while the orchestra is attempting to get to the celebration.

Brown, Marc
Arthur Meets the President

Illustrated by Marc Brown. Joy Street/Little, Brown, 1991. 32 pp. ISBN 0-316-11265-8.

Arthur's essay on making America great by helping others wins him the opportunity to meet the president of the United States. When Arthur forgets the words to his presentation his sister, D.W., saves the day by holding up cue cards. Another in the popular Arthur series by Brown.

B rowne, Anthony
Willy and Hugh

Illustrated by Anthony Browne. Knopf, 1991. 26 pp. ISBN 0-679-81446-9.

Another adventure of Willy, the Wimp/Champ. Willy finds a gorilla friend, Hugh, and they take care of each other. A library scene emphasizes the role of the library in their friendship.

B unting, Eve
Fly Away Home

Illustrated by Ronald Himler. Clarion, 1991. 32 pp. ISBN 0-395-55962-6.

A father and his child, Andrew, are homeless and live in an airport. In order to keep from being noticed they keep to themselves, change terminals each night, and sleep sitting up. They build a support system among other homeless people who also live in the airport. The expressive watercolors reflect the sadness of the situation but also allow a glimmer of hope to shine through.

B unting, Eve
The Wall

Illustrated by Ronald Himler. Clarion, 1990. 32 pp. ISBN 0-395-51588-2.

A father and his young son come to the Vietnam Veterans Memorial to locate the name of the grandfather the boy never knew. Himler's watercolors capture the impressive scenes.

B urningham, John
Hey! Get Off Our Train
Illustrated by John Burningham. Crown, 1989. 46 pp. ISBN 0-517-57638-4.

A boy and a dog take a dream journey, and at each stop they meet an endangered animal asking for sanctuary. The illustrations are clear and brilliantly executed.

B utler, Dorothy
My Brown Bear Barney in Trouble
Illustrated by Elizabeth Fuller. Greenwillow, 1993. unp. ISBN 0-688-10521-1.

The little girl and her bear, Barney, are as inseparable as ever. They go everywhere together and get into trouble together. Almost everything they do displeases someone. At last, Sunday comes and the quiet makes Barney bored, but the little girl tells him, "It's Monday again tomorrow." Readers will know just what she means.

C almenson, Stephanie
Dinner at the Panda Palace
Illustrated by Nadine Bernard Westcott. HarperCollins, 1991. 32 pp. ISBN 0-06-021010-9.

A very unusual assortment of animals comes to the Panda Palace to eat. One elephant arrives first, and eventually the numbers increase until a mother hen and her nine chicks arrive. But in this cumulative story, one tiny mouse arrives to make the total number of guests number 55. Everyone enjoys a good feast.

Carlstrom, Nancy White
Blow Me a Kiss, Miss Lilly

Illustrated by Amy Schwartz. Harper, 1990. 32 pp. ISBN 0-06-021012-5.

A story of intergenerational love and friendship that ends when Sara's best friend becomes ill and dies.

Cherry, Lynne
The Great Kapok Tree: A Tale of the Amazon Rain Forest

Illustrated by Lynne Cherry. Gulliver/Harcourt, 1990. 33 pp. ISBN 0-15-200520-X.

The animals of the rain forest convince a man not to chop down a kapok tree. Includes a message about the vanishing rain forests. The illustrations and endpapers enhance both the look and the information contained in the book.

Cole, Joanna
Don't Tell the Whole World!

Illustrated by Kate Duke. Crowell, 1990. 32 pp. ISBN 0-690-04809-2.

Farmer John's wife tells *everything*. When Farmer John finds a treasure in the field he knows that he must do something to keep her from telling. John sets up some preposterous situations (like fish growing in a tree) that he knows she will repeat to others. This way, when she tells about the treasure, nobody will believe her story any more than they would believe that the fish grew in trees or candy was in fields.

C ummings, Pat
Clean Your Room, Harvey Moon!
Illustrated by Pat Cummings. Bradbury, 1991. 32 pp. ISBN 0-02-725511-5.

When given the choice of cleaning his room or missing his favorite television programs, Harvey sets out to clean his room in a hurry. Illustrations show Harvey's technique—to stash all the toys and clothes under the blanket on the bed. Watch for the snakes among the shoelaces in Cummings's cheery illustrations.

d e Regniers, Beatrice Schenk
How Joe the Bear and Sam the Mouse Got Together
Illustrated by Bernice Myers. Lothrop, 1990. 32 pp. ISBN 0-688-09079-6.

A new edition of a 1965 title. After trying to find some activity they can share—both like to play ball but Joe likes to play football and Sam likes to play baseball—they discover eventually that they both like ice cream. So every day they meet at three o'clock and eat ice cream together. Myers's illustrations are cartoonish watercolors.

D emuth, Patricia Brennan
The Ornery Morning
Illustrated by Craig McFarland Brown. Dutton, 1991. 24 pp. ISBN 0-525-44688-5.

An ornery rooster promotes a barnyard strike when he refuses to crow. The other animals follow the rooster's lead, and soon there is no wool, no eggs, and no milk for Farmer Bill. The farmer decides to compromise in face of his predicament.

dePaola, Tomie
Tom

Illustrated by Tomie dePaola. Putnam, 1993. unp. ISBN 0-399-22417-3.

An autobiographical tale of Tom and Tommy (grandfather and grandson) and the special moments they share. Sometimes they are so loud Nana sends them to the basement. One day Tom shows Tommy a trick that really makes Tommy laugh—but Tommy's teacher does not think the trick is funny. Sometimes tricks are only for certain people. dePaola's illustrations are as brilliant as ever.

Dunphy, Madeleine
Here Is the Arctic Winter

Illustrated by Alan James Robinson. Hyperion, 1993. unp. ISBN 1-56282-336-1.

Information about the Arctic winter is built through a rhyming text that calls to mind the familiar "This is the house that Jack built" pattern. Reader/listeners learn that the "sun does not rise in this cold world of white" and that the sky is "dark day and night." Other verses introduce the animals of this region: caribou, wolf, hare, owl, bear, seal, fish, and whale. The final phrases focus on the sky that shines with the northern lights. The last page of the book gives more complete names for the animals that are part of the rhyme and includes the address of the National Audubon Society, where writers may obtain more information about the Arctic animals that need protection.

Fox, Mem
Possum Magic

Illustrated by Julie Vivas. Gulliver/Harcourt, 1990. 32 pp. ISBN 0-15-200572-2.

A reissue of a 1987 book first published in the United States by Abingdon. An invisible possum treks all over Australia with his grandmother in an attempt to find the food that will restore his visibility.

Galbraith, Kathryn O.
Laura Charlotte

Illustrated by Floyd Cooper. Philomel, 1990. 32 pp. ISBN 0-399-21613-8.

In this pleasant, gentle story, Laura's mother tells her child about her own stuffed elephant, made by the child's grandmother. The book is a family story that begs to be shared.

Grossman, Bill
The Guy Who Was Five Minutes Late

Illustrated by Judy Glasser. Harper, 1990. 32 pp. ISBN 0-06-022268-9.

A boy was born five minutes late and from that time on is five minutes late for everything in his life. Eventually he finds a princess who is also five minutes late and together they find true happiness—even if they are five minutes late for their wedding. The pastels are as zany as the events portrayed.

Hazen, Barbara Shook
Wally, the Worry-Warthog

Illustrated by Janet Stevens. Clarion, 1990. 32 pp. ISBN 0-89919-896-1.

Wally worries about everything, but his biggest worry is Wilberforce Warthog. But later his "worry" becomes his best friend. Wilberforce's image is given just enough bulk to justify the worry.

Henkes, Kevin
Chrysanthemum
Illustrated by Kevin Henkes. Greenwillow, 1991. 32 pp. ISBN 0-688-09699-9.

Chrysanthemum, a young mouse, loves her name until she starts school and is teased by her classmates. But when her teacher, Delphinium Twinkle, tells the class that she intends to name her expected baby Chrysanthemum, all the children want to be named after a flower.

Henkes, Kevin
Julius, the Baby of the World
Illustrated by Kevin Henkes. Greenwillow, 1990. 32 pp. ISBN 0-688-08943-7.

Lilly thinks her baby brother, Julius, is next to zero but comes to his defense when her cousin criticizes him. Lilly declares that her brother is "the baby of the world."

Hoffman, Mary
Amazing Grace
Illustrated by Caroline Binch. Dial, 1991. 26 pp. ISBN 0-8037-1040-2.

Grace wants more than anything to play the part of Peter Pan in the school play. But her classmates inform her that she can't be Peter Pan because she is a girl and because she is black. Grace's mother and grandmother let her know that she can be anything she wants to be. With her confidence reaffirmed, Grace wins the part of Peter Pan and plays it, to the delight of the audience. Realistic watercolor illustrations illuminate the action of the text.

Hopkinson, Deborah
Sweet Clara and the Freedom Quilt

Illustrated by James Ransome. Knopf, 1993. 32 pp. ISBN 0-679-82311-5.

A young slave, Clara, is sold away from her mother and taken to a nearby plantation. She is befriended by one of the kitchen slaves and taken from the fields and allowed to be a house slave. It is as a house slave that she learns to quilt. By using information she overhears, she is able to create a quilt with a map pattern—a map that shows the route to the North and to freedom. When Clara finishes the quilt and leaves for freedom, she leaves the quilt behind with her mentor, who is "too old to leave." Many other slaves use the quilt to show them the way to freedom.

Howard, Elizabeth Fitzgerald
Aunt Flossie's Hats (and Crab Cakes Later)

Illustrated by James Ransome. Clarion, 1991. 32 pp. ISBN 0-395-54682-6.

Two girls try on many hats at their Sunday tea party with their Aunt Flossie. Each of the hats holds a story that Aunt Flossie tells. Many of the stories reflect the history of African-Americans in Baltimore. Ransome's portraitlike oil paintings depict the mutually loving relationship between Aunt Flossie and her two great-nieces.

Kasza, Keiko
When the Elephant Walks

Illustrated by Keiko Kasza. Putnam, 1990. 32 pp. ISBN 0-399-21755-X.

A circular tale that begins with "when the elephant walks ... he scares the bear." The elephant's series of encounters ends when a mouse scares the same elephant who started the chain of events. Features bright, clear watercolors.

Kimmel, Eric A.
The Chanukkah Guest
Illustrated by Giora Carmi. Holiday House, 1990. 32 pp. ISBN 0-8234-0788-8.

Bubba Brayna mistakes a hungry bear for a hungry rabbi. She serves her guest the "best potato latkes in the village." A lively story filled with friendly illustrations.

Kimmel, Eric A.
Four Dollars and Fifty Cents
Illustrated by Glen Rounds. Holiday House, 1990. 32 pp. ISBN 0-8234-0817-5.

Widow Macrae tries to get the money she is owed by a shifty cowboy, Shorty Long. When he tries to trick her by having her notified that he is dead, she turns the story around and offers to bury him. His choice is to pay what he owes or be buried alive.

Kimmel, Eric A.
I Took My Frog to the Library
Illustrated by Blanche Sims. Viking, 1990. 32 pp. ISBN 0-670-82418-6.

Bridgett brings a series of unusual pets to the library. The pelican puts the dictionary in its pouch and the hyena and the elephant create their own form of havoc. In the end, Bridgett finds a different way to enjoy books with her animals.

Kroll, Virginia
Wood-Hoopoe Willie
Illustrated by Katherine Roundtree. Charlesbridge, 1992. unp. ISBN 0-88106-409-2.

After Willie's grandpa tells him about the different kinds of music that his ancestors made, Willie finds that he cannot leave the melodies alone. Finally, on an icy evening in December, Willie gets his chance to perform when his family meets to celebrate the fifth night of the Kwanzaa celebration. The drummer has been in a car accident and cannot play, so Willie's grandpa suggests that it is time to set the Wood-hoopoe free. Willie does not need to be asked twice. Soon he is beating the hollow wooden drums, the other musicians are joining in, and the butterfly dancers are dancing.

Lionni, Leo
Matthew's Dream
Illustrated by Leo Lionni. Knopf, 1991. 32 pp. ISBN 0-679-81075-7.

Back with his enchanting mice illustrated with torn paper collages and paint, Lionni tells the story of Matthew. When Matthew visits a museum, he knows that he must become a painter. A tale of finding a goal for a future life.

Martin, Bill, Jr.
Polar Bear, Polar Bear, What Do You Hear?
Illustrated by Eric Carle. Holt, 1991. 28 pp. ISBN 0-8050-1759-3.

A companion volume to Martin's and Carle's *Brown Bear, Brown Bear, What Do You See?* (Holt, 1967; 1992), this predictable text is just right for participatory reading. Great color-filled collages help move the rhythmic text onward.

Martin, Jacqueline Briggs
The Finest Horse in Town

Illustrated by Susan Graber. HarperCollins, 1992. 32 pp. ISBN 0-06-024151-9.

The author tells a story of her two great-aunts who ran a dry goods store in a little town in Maine. The only person who knows anything about the great-aunts is an old watchmaker, who remembers only that the women had the finest horse in town. The author muses about who might have cared for the horse while the aunts ran the store. The musings take the form of three episodes that might explain what might have occurred. Listeners will enjoy creating their own stories of who might have cared for the horse for the aunts.

Martin, Jacqueline Briggs
Good Times on Grandfather Mountain

Illustrated by Susan Gaber. Orchard, 1992. 32 pp. ISBN 0-531-05977-4.

A story of Old Washburn, who lives on Grandfather Mountain and has the incredible ability to view positively every event that occurs. For example, when his animals run away he realizes that he won't have to take care of them any longer, and he uses the wood from the fences to make musical instruments. When, in the final episode, a storm blows down his cabin, he sits on the porch and whittles a fiddle from the cabin wood. The music he makes attracts his neighbors, who help him rebuild his cabin, and it draws back the animals to his homestead. The final scene is a country-style dance where neighbors are gathered and enjoying a good time.

McDermott, Gerald
Tim O'Toole and the Wee Folk

Illustrated by Gerald McDermott. Viking, 1990. 32 pp. ISBN 0-670-80393-6.

A humorous tale of Tim O'Toole and his band of leprechauns. Features the bold, colorful collages that are typical of McDermott's award-winning books.

McPhail, David
Lost!

Illustrated by David McPhail. Joy Street/Little, Brown, 1990. 32 pp. ISBN 0-316-56329-3.

A bear travels to the big city and finds that he is lost. When a young boy befriends the bear, the boy agrees to accompany the bear on a long bus ride home to the forest. Once they get there the boy realizes that he is now lost in the forest. Together the boy and the bear return to the city.

Numeroff, Laura Joffe
If You Give a Moose a Muffin

Illustrated by Felicia Bond. Geringer/HarperCollins, 1991. 32 pp. ISBN 0-06-024405-4.

A circular, cumulative tale that begins with what first happens when a moose gets a muffin and then.... An innovation on the author's and illustrator's previous book *If You Give a Mouse a Cookie* (Harper, 1985).

Polacco, Patricia
Babushka's Doll

Illustrated by Patricia Polacco. Simon & Schuster, 1990. 40 pp. ISBN 0-671-68343-8.

Natasha demands that her grandmother drop her work whenever Natasha wants anything. Then her doll comes to life and begins to make demands on Natasha. She finally learns her lesson. Colorful folk-art illustrations make the story even livelier.

P olacco, Patricia
Chicken Sunday

Illustrated by Patricia Polacco. Philomel, 1992. 32 pp. ISBN 0-399-22133-6.

Two African-American boys conspire to buy a special Easter hat for their grandmother, who prepares wonderful chicken dinners. Depicts a loving, warm, intergenerational family relationship. Visually rich illustrations include actual photographs as part of the background images.

P olacco, Patricia
Mrs. Katz and Tush

Illustrated by Patricia Polacco. Bantam, 1992. 32 pp. ISBN 0-553-08122-5.

Larnel, an African-American boy, convinces his elderly neighbor, a Jewish widow named Mrs. Katz, to adopt a kitten. She agrees if he will promise to help her care for it. The cat, who has no tail, is named Tush. While they care for Tush, the two become good friends and learn about each other's culture and holidays. Larnel and Mrs. Katz find many areas of common experience in their people's history. A warm and skillfully told story of a unique friendship that bonds the families through generations.

P olacco, Patricia
Thunder Cake

Illustrated by Patricia Polacco. Philomel, 1990. 32 pp. ISBN 0-399-22231-6.

When a young girl becomes frightened of thunderstorms, her grandmother distracts her with preparations to make a "thunder cake." They finish the cake just as the storm arrives. The brilliantly colored illustrations, reminiscent of Russian folk art, depict the gentle relationship between grandmother and child.

Pulver, Robin
Mrs. Toggle's Zipper

Illustrated by R. W. Alley. Four Winds, 1990. 32 pp. ISBN 0-02-775451-0.

A hilarious and somewhat outrageous tale of a teacher's jacket zipper that gets stuck and cannot be loosened despite the efforts of almost everyone at school—from the school nurse to the custodian. Gloriously humorous illustrations.

Ray, Deborah Kogan
My Daddy Was a Soldier: A World War II Story

Illustrated by Deborah Kogan Ray. Holiday House, 1990. 40 pp. ISBN 0-8234-0795-0.

The loneliness of a young girl when her father goes off to war is depicted in serious black-and-white drawings. The text describes ration books, scrap metal drives, and victory gardens. A powerful view of a past era as seen through a child's eyes.

Ringgold, Faith
Tar Beach

Illustrated by Faith Ringgold. Crown, 1991. 32 pp. ISBN 0-517-58030-6.

Cassie, in a dream adventure, flies over her apartment building and views her apartment rooftop in Harlem. The story, illustrated by a story quilt, takes place in 1939 and reflects the African-American experience during that time period.

Robertus, Polly M.
The Dog Who Had Kittens

Illustrated by Janet Stevens. Holiday House, 1991. 32 pp. ISBN 0-8234-0860-4.

Eloise has seven kittens and her friend, Baxter, the basset hound feels left out. One day when Eloise leaves the kittens alone, Baxter is there to keep them company. From that day on, Baxter and Eloise share the parenting responsibilities until the kittens are ready for homes of their own. A gentle, warm story with attractive illustrations.

Say, Allen
Tree of Cranes

Illustrated by Allen Say. Houghton, 1991. 32 pp. ISBN 0-395-52024-X.

A young Japanese boy describes his first Christmas. From his sickbed, he watches as his mother decorates a small pine tree with silver paper cranes that she has carefully folded. She then tells her son about her American childhood and the holiday where people smile at one another and enemies make peace. Say's portrait-like illustrations are photographic in their rendering. The tale is based on Say's own childhood.

Scieszka, Jon
The Frog Prince Continued

Illustrated by Steve Johnson. Viking, 1991. 32 pp. ISBN 0-670-83421-1.

A brightly written description of the events that occur in the prince's household after the ending of the traditional "Frog Prince" tale. The illustrations represent the prince in an amphibious manner. The story is very humorous but will be more humorous to those who are familiar with the traditional "Frog Prince" tale. Wonderful story, wonderful illustrations.

Scieszka, Jon
The True Story of the Three Little Pigs by A. Wolf

Illustrated by Lane Smith. Viking, 1989. 32 pp. ISBN 0-670-82759-2.

Zany illustrations accompany the wolf's version of the traditional tale of "The Three Little Pigs." Could the wolf help it if he was borrowing a cup of sugar and accidentally sneezed? According to the wolf, he has been wrongly accused.

Steig, William
Doctor De Soto Goes to Africa

Illustrated by William Steig. HarperCollins/di Capua, 1992. 32 pp. ISBN 0-06-205002-8.

The famous Doctor De Soto is summoned to Africa to relieve the suffering of an elephant, Mudambo. When he arrives he is kidnapped by a monkey that Mudambo has insulted. Doctor De Soto is rescued and his wife services, the pair are paid 10,000 gold walulus. The story ends with Doctor De Soto and his wife contemplating their next adventure. Charming watercolors.

Van Laan, Nancy
Possum Come a-Knockin'

Illustrated by George Booth. Knopf, 1990. 32 pp. ISBN 0-394-82206-4.

A rhythmic trickster tale that has a possum knocking at the door while the humans and critters inside go about their business—except for the young child who knows that a possum has come a-knockin' at the door.

Woodruff, Elvira
Tubtime

Illustrated by Suçie Stevenson. Holiday House, 1990. 32 pp. ISBN 0-8234-0777-2.

When the O'Mally sisters blow bubbles in their bathtub, they find they are filled with magic—and animals, including an alligator. Just before their father arrives, the girls manage to get rid of all the animals, but then their father decides to try out one of the pipes. Iridescent watercolors fill the pages with bubbling images.

ALPHABETICAL LISTING OF PICTURE BOOKS BY TITLE
(author's last name is in parentheses)

Amazing Grace (Hoffman)
Arthur Meets the President (Brown)
Aunt Flossie's Hats (and Crab Cakes Later) (Howard)
Babushka's Doll (Polacco)
Berlioz the Bear (Brett)
Beware of Boys (Blundell)
Blow Me a Kiss, Miss Lilly (Carlstrom)
The Chanukkah Guest (Kimmel)
Charlie Anderson (Abercrombie)
Chicken Sunday (Polacco)
Chrysanthemum (Henkes)
Clean Your Room, Harvey Moon! (Cummings)
Dinner at the Panda Palace (Calmenson)
Doctor De Soto Goes to Africa (Steig)
The Dog Who Had Kittens (Robertus)
Don't Tell the Whole World! (Cole)
The Finest Horse in Town (Martin)
Fly Away Home (Bunting)
The Folks in the Valley: A Pennsylvania Dutch ABC (Aylesworth)
Four Dollars and Fifty Cents (Kimmel)
The Frog Prince Continued (Scieszka)
Good Times on Grandfather Mountain (Martin)
The Great Kapok Tree: A Tale of the Amazon Rain Forest (Cherry)
The Guy Who Was Five Minutes Late (Grossman)
Here Is the Arctic Winter (Dunphy)
Hey! Get Off Our Train (Burningham)
How Joe the Bear and Sam the Mouse Got Together (de Regniers)
I Took My Frog to the Library (Kimmel)
If You Give a Moose a Muffin (Numeroff)
Julius, the Baby of the World (Henkes)
Laura Charlotte (Galbraith)
Lost! (McPhail)
Matthew's Dream (Lionni)
Mrs. Katz and Tush (Polacco)
Mrs. Toggle's Zipper (Pulver)
My Brown Bear Barney in Trouble (Butler)
My Daddy Was a Soldier: A War World II Story (Ray)
Old Black Fly (Aylesworth)
The Ornery Morning (Demuth)
Polar Bear, Polar Bear, What Do You Hear? (Martin)
Possum Come a-Knockin' (Van Laan)
Possum Magic (Fox)
Sweet Clara and the Freedom Quilt (Hopkinson)
Tar Beach (Ringgold)

Thunder Cake (Polacco)
Tim O'Toole and the Wee Folk (McDermott)
Tom (dePaola)
Tree of Cranes (Say)
The True Story of the Three Little Pigs by A. Wolf (Scieszka)
Tubtime (Woodruff)
The Wall (Bunting)
Wally, the Worry-Warthog (Hazen)
When the Elephant Walks (Kasza)
Where Does the Trail Lead? (Albert)
Wilbur's Space Machine (Balian)
Willy and Hugh (Browne)
Wood-Hoopoe Willie (Kroll)

Chapter 2

The Next Step

During the primary years children are learning to read, and as their attention span increases they are able to listen to and enjoy longer stories. Introducing listeners to longer stories is the next step beyond the reading of picture books. As longer stories are introduced to this age level, an entire segment (chapter) should be completed each time. During the middle-grade years, reading skills of students are improving at widely varying rates, and the span of improvement among children of the same age group grows wider as each year passes. It is hoped that during this time they will be developing an enjoyment for independent reading by sharing book experiences with their classmates, parents, siblings, and others. In many cases, the child's interest

level will still be above his or her own reading level. A daily time during which the child is able to listen to books being read aloud will help satisfy the child's curiosity for stimulating information/literature, enhance memory, and build on the listener's prior knowledge. As a variety of genres are introduced and shared through reading aloud and discussions, children will build an understanding of author technique, chronological ordering and historical perspective, use of inference to make predictions, etc.

SELECTING BOOKS TO READ ALOUD

By choosing carefully the books used in your read-aloud sessions, you can do much to help children understand different viewpoints and attitudes of other cultures and groups of people. When selecting titles to read, an attempt should be made to present a balanced picture of the world—an unbiased view of people and their cultures. Sometimes that is difficult because minorities or cultures of other countries are underrepresented in the total list of books available. Books reflecting contemporary Native American or Hispanic cultures are difficult to find. The two things we can do are to continue to do the best job we can with the books that are available, and make our needs known to the editors at publishing houses. It is those editors who make the decisions about the books that are published.

As with the picture books listed in Chapter 1, the books featured in this chapter are among the more recent titles that I feel belong on any "must read" list. The purpose of this list is to highlight the latest read-aloud titles. Any comprehensive list of read-alouds should include classics by E. B. White, Katherine Paterson, Scott O'Dell, Ted Taylor, and all of the other wonderful authors of books for children. Many suggestions for authors who write for an older elementary audience and classic titles to highlight are included in other titles that I have authored, including Bookpeople[1] albums and other titles[2] focusing on using literature in the classroom.

When choosing books, the child's (or children's) background of experience and depth of knowledge must be taken into consideration. Situations must be realistic and believable and, in most cases, presented from a youthful point of view.

READING ALOUD—A FEW COMMENTS

If you are reading to just one or two children, sit beside one another. Be aware of the reaction of those to whom you are reading. Their level of interest will dictate much about how the read-aloud session is conducted. Maintaining eye contact with the audience and an energetic reading style will do much to keep the interest of your listeners. I personally believe that those who are listening must be encouraged to be active listeners. That means giving the reader his or her undivided attention—no doodling, doing study sheets, etc.

As with the picture book list, this list of books could go on and on. Even though there are some books that many of us would encourage youngsters to read and enjoy, there is much latitude for individual tastes and preferences. The most important thing is that children are read to and learn to enjoy reading. It is my hope that the books that are shared from this list will contribute to many children's joy in reading and that the read-aloud sessions will pass on to many children a love and interest in reading more and more books.

NOTES

[1]*Bookpeople: A First Album* (1990); *Bookpeople: A Second Album* (1990); *Bookpeople: A Multicultural Album* (1993); all published by Libraries Unlimited/Teacher Ideas Press.

[2]*Adventures with Social Studies (Through Literature)* (1991); and *McElmeel Booknotes: Literature Across the Curriculum* (1993); both published by Libraries Unlimited/Teacher Ideas Press.

Bookshelf—
Going Beyond Picture Books

1 Angell, Judie
Don't Rent My Room!

Angell, Judie. *Don't Rent My Room!* Bantam, 1990. 138 pp. ISBN 0-553-07023-1.
Listening Level: Early Intermediate (ages 8-9; grades 3-4)
Read-Alone Level: Intermediate (ages 9-10; grades 4-5)

Lucy Weber lives in New York City with her parents and younger brother. Her grandmother lives nearby. Lucy's parents happen upon a country inn and come to think that running an inn would be something they'd like to do. Lucy does not want to move to the cape in Massachusetts, and she definitely does not want to help run the Scottwood Inn, but that is exactly what she does all summer. Before the move, Lucy's grandmother tries to convince Lucy's parents that Lucy should stay in the city and live with her. But that discussion only ends in Lucy's parents agreeing that Lucy may choose to stay at Scottwood Inn or return to the city—but only after staying in Massachusetts for the summer. So the entire family moves to the cape and encounters the problems of running an inn, storms, and hired help that quits without notice. Lucy herself meets new friends and finds much to do in the small town. Two of the events that the family has to deal with are the presence of the ghost of the Scottwood Inn's founder, Mercer Scottwood, and the desire of 13-year-old Henry to quit school (like his friend Donald) and to work on Donald's uncle's fishing boat. But just as their efforts seem to be paying off, summer comes to an end and Lucy must decide whether she will stay or return to the city to live with her grandmother. Her decision comes as a surprise to her parents ... Lucy decides to return to New York City.

Decisions, Decisions

Parent's decisions can affect greatly the lives of other family members—in *What a Wimp!* by Carol Carrick (Clarion, 1983), Barney's parents' divorce indirectly causes Barney's confrontation with the school bully, Lenny. In *Rat Teeth* by Patricia Reilly Giff (Delacorte, 1984), a similar situation forces Radcliffe Samson to deal with shuffling between parents and attending a new school. But worst of all, the kids in the new town tease him by calling him "Rat-cliffe" and "Rat Teeth"—because of his rodent-like two front teeth. In Judy Delton's series featuring Angel, including *Angel in Charge* (Houghton, 1985), Angel must deal with many situations, including her mother's eccentric boyfriend, her mother's wedding, and later a new baby in the household. Younger readers will read about the effects of parents' decisions in *I'm Not Moving, Mama* by Nancy White Carlstrom (Macmillan, 1990); *When Grandpa Came to Stay* by Judith Caseley (Greenwillow, 1986); *I Hate My Sister, Maggie* by Crescent Dragonwagon (Macmillan, 1989); *Alone at Home* by Barbara Shook Hazen (Atheneum, 1992); *Chrysanthemum* by Kevin Henkes (Greenwillow, 1991); and *My New Mom and Me* by Betty Ren Wright (Raintree, 1981).

---

2 Avi

"Who Was That Masked Man, Anyway?"

Avi. *"Who Was That Masked Man, Anyway?"* Orchard, 1992. 170 pp. ISBN 0-531-05457-8.
Listening Level: Intermediate (ages 9-10; grades 4-5)
Read-Alone Level: Intermediate Accelerated (ages 10-11; grades 5-6)

Using dialogue exclusively, Avi has managed to tell the story of Franklin Delano Wattleson, and his best friend, Mario Calvino. The year is 1945 in Brooklyn, New York, where the boys live in a tenement settlement. The windows to their rooms face one another and often they lay a board between their windowsills and crawl back and forth across the alleyway to each other's room. Each of them listens to radio adventure series featuring the Lone Ranger, the Green Hornet, Buck Rogers, and all the other radio heroes. Franklin's family is renting out his older brother's room to a strange scientist-type boarder, Mr. Swerdlow. Franklin is determined to get Mr. Swerdlow out of his house; to get his wounded brother, Tom, back home and in his own room; and to help his sixth-grade teacher, Esmeralda Gomez, recover from the war death of her fiancé. Soon the answer to all of Franklin's goals seems to be to get Miss Gomez to meet his brother, Tom. He plots to cause enough trouble at school so that Miss Gomez will want to meet his parents. He will get her to come to his house, arrange for his parents to be gone, and will see to it that his brother answers the door. All goes well until Tom refuses to go to the door and instead attempts to crawl across the board (and across the alleyway) to reach Mario's room. When the board begins to crack, Tom finds himself hanging onto the windowsill while fire engines, police officers, and others crowd into the apartment to try and save him—while Franklin and Miss Gomez look on in startled amazement. Franklin's plot does eventually work out, but even in the end he does not abandon his secret investigation.

Super Heroes

In the fifties and sixties, the radio broadcast many adventures of heroes that might be remembered by those growing up in those times. The Lone Ranger, the Green Hornet, and Superman were all considered heroic champions of justice. Because these shows are no longer aired on the radio, the best way to introduce young readers to these super heroes is to bring in stacks of comic books that feature them. Use episodes in the comic books to create your own radio shows starring the super heroes of yesterday. Those who wish to read about the real heroes who lived during World War II might enjoy reading *As the Waltz Was Ending* by Emma Macalik Butterworth (Scholastic, 1982); *Rose Blanche* by Christopher Galloz and Roberto Innocenti (Creative, 1985); *Number the Stars* by Lois Lowry (Houghton, 1989); *The Angel with a Mouth-Organ* by Christebol Mattingley (Holiday House, 1984); and *Snow Treasure* by Marie McSwigan (Dutton, 1942, 1970).

---

3 Avi
Windcatcher

Avi. *Windcatcher.* Bradbury, 1991. 124 pp. ISBN 0-02-707761-6.
Listening Level: Early Intermediate (ages 8-9; grades 3-4)
Read-Alone Level: Intermediate (ages 9-10; grades 4-5)

Tony Souza was not looking forward to the summer—not if he had to spend it at his grandmother's house at Swallow's Bay. However, when he spotted the 12-foot sailboat, *The Snark*, the visit seemed more promising, and once he got his parents' permission to purchase the boat in return for his promise to take sailing lessons, he became more excited about going to the bay. But sailing was only to be part of the adventures Tony would have that summer. In 1777, a British ship, *The Swallow*, was said to have sunk in the waters surrounding the Thimble Islands in Swallow's Bay. The ship was thought to have been a payroll ship and when she went down, the payroll went down with it—perhaps a million dollars or more. Tony is interested in finding the treasure, if it does exist, but he is also interested in finding out what the man and woman in the motorboat are doing in the area. They are acting mysterious and seem not to want him anywhere around them. Once out in the island waters, Tony manages to spy on the couple but soon finds himself stranded on an island and lost. And when he is found, it is the mysterious couple who rescue him—and then want information, information about what he had seen. Only when Christine, her brother the harbormaster, and Tony's grandmother arrive in their motorboat does Tony feel that he is safe.

Sunken Treasure

Robert D. Ballard has discovered several sunken ships. He tells about some of his expeditions in his books *Exploring the Titanic* (Scholastic, 1988); *Exploring the Bismarck* (Scholastic, 1991); and *The Lost Wreck of the Isis* (Scholastic, 1990)—a book he coauthored with Rick Archbold. Color photographs and oil paintings help the reader see what Ballard and his crew found under the sea. Younger readers will enjoy reading about the *Titanic* and its sinking in Judy Donnelly's *The Titanic: Lost ... and Found*, illustrated by Keith Kohler (Random, 1987). Readers of all ages will enjoy Gail Gibbons's illustrated information book, *Sunken Treasure* (Crowell, 1988). In her book, Gibbons tells the story of the *Atocha*—a ship that sunk off the coast of Florida in 1622. Her many drawings illustrate the conventional steps actually taken by Mel Fisher as he searched for and salvaged the *Atocha*'s treasure beneath the sea. Gibbons further whets the reader's interest whenshe summarizes information about other famous treasure hunts: the *Mary Rose*, an English warship; the *Vasa*, a Swedish warship; the *Whydah*, a pirate ship; and the *Titanic*, a luxury liner.

---

4 Beatty, Patricia

Who Comes with Cannons?

Beatty, Patricia. *Who Comes with Cannons?* Morrow, 1992. 186 pp.
ISBN 0-688-11028-2.
Listening Level: Intermediate (ages 9-10; grades 4-5)
Read-Alone Level: Intermediate Accelerated (ages 10-11; grades 5-6)

After the death of her father during the Civil War, Truth Hopkins goes to live with her uncle and his family on their North Carolina farm. Truth and her uncle's family, the Bardwells, are Quakers. They do not believe that slavery should exist, but because of their pacifist beliefs, they also refuse to take up arms in the war. One day a runaway slave shows up at the Bardwell farm and Truth realizes that her uncle is hiding him from the slave catchers. Later her uncle asks Truth to accompany him as he delivers a load of hay to a neighbor. Truth discovers the secret of the wagon's real cargo and becomes aware of the dangerous Underground Railroad movement. Armed with this knowledge, Truth soon realizes how she can contribute to finding freedom for hundreds of slaves—without the use of a rifle.

The Underground Railroad

Faith Ringgold, the winner of the 1992 Coretta Scott King award for *Tar Beach* (Crown, 1991), has joined history, the Underground Railroad, and Harriet Tubman with fantasy in her picture book *Aunt Harriet's Underground Railroad in the Sky* (Crown, 1992). Another picture book dealing with the Underground Railroad is *Follow the Drinking Gourd* by Jeanette Winter (Knopf, 1988). Winter's story begins with a peg-leg sailor who teaches the slaves a song that assists them in finding the way North to freedom on the Underground Railroad. A similar theme runs through Deborah Hopkinson's *Sweet Clara and the Freedom Quilt*, illustrated by James Ransome (Knopf, 1993). Clara manages to use the cloth in her scrap bag to make a map of the land and the road to freedom—a freedom quilt—that circumvents detection by her master. In a book that will appeal to an intermediate audience, Joan Blos has recounted the efforts of Catherine Cabot Hill to help a runaway slave in *A Gathering of Days: A New England Girl's Journal, 1830-32* (Scribner's, 1979), and

Jean Fritz has focused on the discovery of an Underground Railroad station near a family farm in *Brady* (Puffin, 1987). Virginia Hamilton has also recounted a family story involving the Underground Railroad in her story "Carrying the Running-Aways" in *The People Could Fly: American Black Folktales* (Knopf, 1985). Hamilton continues to tell stories of African-Americans finding freedom in *Many Thousand Gone: African Americans from Slavery to Freedom* (Knopf, 1993). Both Hamilton collections of tales are illustrated by two-time Caldecott medalists Leo Dillon and Diane Dillon.

5 Bellairs, John
The Mansion in the Mist

Bellairs, John. *The Mansion in the Mist*. Dial, 1992. 170 pp. ISBN 0-8037-0845-9.
Listening Level: Intermediate Accelerated (ages 10-11; grades 5-6)
Read-Alone Level: Intermediate Accelerated+ (ages 10-11+; grades 5-6+)

Miss Eells decides to take a restful summer vacation with her brother, Emerson, and they invite Anthony Monday to go along with them to spend the time in an old house on a desolate island. It isn't long before Anthony explores the house and finds a large chest in a dusty bedroom. Once the chest is opened, Anthony discovers that the chest can transport him to another world. His experiences in the world of the Autarchs both frighten and excite him. More and more frequently Anthony crawls into the chest and is spun into the scary world. Soon Emerson, and later Miss Eells, find themselves accompanying Anthony into the maniacal world in a desperate search for the logos cube—and the power of the Autarchs—power that threatens to destroy the world as they know it.

Good Versus Evil

Anthony and Miss Eells appear in two other books, facing danger in each tale. In *The Treasure of Alpheus Winterborn* (Dial, 1978), the two search for treasure in the town of Hoosac. In *The Dark Secret of Weatherend* (Dial, 1984), Anthony and Miss Eells become involved in a more dangerous task. They are up against the demon, Anders Borkman, who wants to wipe out humans in order to produce a new pure race. Borkman casts spells on Anthony and Miss Eells, but they manage to outwit and conquer the demon—just as they conquer the evil forces in *The Mansion in the Mist*. Science fantasy stories seem to appeal most to the intellectually gifted, and those who enjoy Bellairs's tales are sure to enjoy the stories by Lloyd Alexander, William Sleator, and Madeleine L'Engle.

6 Berry, James
Ajeemah and His Son

Berry, James. *Ajeemah and His Son*. Willa Perlman/HarperCollins, 1992. 83 pp. ISBN 0-06-021043-5.
Listening Level: Intermediate (ages 9-10; grades 4-5)
Read-Alone Level: Intermediate Accelerated (ages 10-11; grades 5-6)

The year was 1807, and the slave trade was about to be shut down. The slave traders were making one last effort to reap all the cash they could by doing as much slave trading as possible before the laws forbade the trading on the slave market. Ajeemah and his son, Atu, are on their way to the home of Atu's bride-to-be, Sisi. Sisi brought sunshine wherever she went; she was a Sunday-born child. As a dowry, Ajeemah was taking Sisi's father two pieces of gold—gold that he had hidden in the soles of his sandals. Appearing to meet Sisi's father without a proper dowry was Ajeemah's idea of a practical joke. Once he had met her father he intended to reveal his hidden cache. But Ajeemah was never given a chance to play his joke. Ajeemah and Atu were taken by slave traders and forced aboard a crowded boat headed for Jamaica. Once in Jamaica father and son were separated. They never again saw or spoke to the families they left behind in Africa. Atu's bride-to-be never knew why Atu did not come. All of what Ajeemah and Atu knew was left behind. They were stripped of their family, their African names, and their freedom. Over the next decade, the slavery affected each in a different way. Atu does not survive, and Ajeemah "goes mad." It is only then that one of the house slaves, Bella, visits Ajeemah in the hospital and brings him hope. Once Ajeemah recovers, Bella and Ajeemah became more than friends. Thirteen years after he arrived in Jamaica, Ajeemah and Bella are married—he is now 49 years old. A year later they have a Sunday-born child and name her Sisi. The next 19 years are good to Ajeemah and Bella. Slaves are given their freedom, and although it is too late for many of them to return to their homeland, they are able to establish their own villages and enjoy a level of life that had previously been out of reach. When his daughter, Sisi, turns 19, in 1840, she marries. It was only now that Ajeemah decides to reveal his treasure, a treasure he had hidden and kept safe through all of his years of slavery. He had not used it to buy a freedom that had been taken from him (he refused to buy something that had been stolen from him). For 33 years he had kept the gold sheets secret from even Bella. But now was the time. He takes the sheets of gold from his pockets and holds them up in his hands and presents the African bride-gift, once intended for the African Sisi, to his Jamaican Sisi. Sisi had known little of her father's story. Her father's suffering, strength, and love are all part of this surprising gift of gold.

The African Experience in the Americas

The sanctioning of slavery in the Americas is one of the dark spots on the continents' shining history. The sufferings of the Africans forced into slavery are well documented. Young readers must not forget this portion of history so that it will not be repeated. Three picture books that detail efforts of slaves to regain their freedom are *Aunt Harriet's Underground Railroad in the Sky* by Faith Ringgold (Crown, 1992); *Follow the Drinking Gourd* by Jeanette Winter (Knopf, 1988); and Deborah Hopkinson's *Sweet Clara and the Freedom Quilt* (Knopf, 1993). An illustrated story by William H. Hooks, *The Ballad of Belle Dorcus* (Knopf, 1990), tells the story of a free woman, Belle Dorcus, and her love for Joshua, a slave. When the plantation owner decides to sell Joshua, Belle Dorcus visits a conjure woman in an attempt to keep Joshua with her. Lengthier tales of slaves that intermediate students will enjoy hearing or reading include *Anthony Burns: The Defeat and Triumph of a Fugitive Slave* by Virginia Hamilton (Knopf, 1988); *This Strange New Feeling* by Julius Lester (Dial, 1982); and *To Be a Slave* by Julius Lester (Dial, 1968).

---

7 Blume, Judy
Fudge-a-Mania

Blume, Judy. *Fudge-a-Mania*. Dutton, 1990. 147 pp. ISBN 0-525-44672-9.
Listening Level: Primary (ages 6-7; grades 1-2)
Read-Alone Level: Primary Accelerated (ages 7-8; grades 2-3)

Fudge, first introduced in *Tales of a Fourth Grade Nothing* (Dutton, 1972) and *Superfudge* (Dutton, 1980), drives his brother, Peter Hatcher, crazy. Fudge's latest plan is to *marry* Peter's archenemy, Sheila Tubman [from *Otherwise Known as Sheila the Great* (Dutton, 1972)]. If that were not bad enough, Peter's parents decide to share a summer vacation cabin with the Tubmans. Now Peter will have to put up with his obnoxious little brother *and* Sheila, the Cootie Queen. Fudge (actually his name is Farley) is up to his usual mischief, but the story takes an interesting twist when Peter's grandmother meets Sheila's grandfather and things begin to happen. Before Peter knows it the Hatchers and the Tubmans are part of the same family.

Books by Judy Blume

Judy Blume has been a popular author of books for young readers for more than two decades. In addition to the books about Fudge, Peter, and Sheila, Blume writes books for a variety of other age levels. Her books for primary students include *The Pain and the Great One* (Bradbury, 1974); *The One in the Middle Is the Green Kangaroo* (Dell, 1981), and *Freckle Juice* (Four Winds, 1971). Older intermediate readers will enjoy *Blubber* (Bradbury, 1974), *Iggie's House* (Bradbury, 1970), *Are You There God? It's Me, Margaret* (Bradbury, 1970), *Deenie* (Bradbury, 1973), *Starring Sally J. Freedman as Herself* (Bradbury, 1977), *Just as Long as We're Together* (Orchard, 1987), and *It's Not the End of the World* (Bradbury, 1972). Middle school readers will enjoy *Tiger Eyes* (Bradbury, 1981).

---

8 Brittain, Bill
The Ghost from Beneath the Sea

Brittain, Bill. *The Ghost from Beneath the Sea.* Illustrated by Michele Chessare. HarperCollins, 1992. 129 pp. ISBN 0-06-020827-9.
Listening Level: Intermediate (ages 9-10; grades 4-5)
Read-Alone Level: Intermediate Accelerated (ages 10-11; grades 5-6)

Three friends, Tommy, Books, and Harry the Blimp, spent many hours and much energy to save the historic Parnell House from destruction. After their successful campaign, Alonzo Peace financed a restoration project and the town was able to maintain the house as a museum. It was also the home for the children's ghost friends. While he was fighting in the American Revolution, Horace Parnell had his head cut off. Esmeralda "Essie" fell from the deck of a Mississippi riverboat and drowned in 1857. Now their home is threatened with destruction again when Hiram Fixx shows up claiming that he owns Parnell House because his great-great grandfather won the deed to it in a card game on the ill-fated *Titanic*. Fixx intends to turn the three acres surrounding the mansion into an amusement park. He also intends to move or take down the house, until he discovers the ghosts; then he decides to make them part of the amusement park. The children must prove the deed a fake or the game a fraud. Quite unexpectedly, a new ghost shows up, and it is none other than Ellsworth Parnell himself—the man who gambled away the Parnell family home. Through their investigative efforts, Tommy, Books, and Harry uncover the flaw in Fixx's claim. It seems that Fixx's great-great grandfather cheated Ellsworth. They had gambled with poker and the collective show of hands indicated that there were five 10s in the deck, making the deal a misdeal and the winnings invalid. So the Parnells retained possession to the home and consequently the city's claim was the only one valid.

Ghostly Tales

The first story involving Tommy, Books, Harry, and the ghosts was Bill Brittain's *Who Knew There'd Be Ghosts?* (HarperCollins, 1986). In that story the children successfully saved the Parnell House from destruction and made friends with Horace and Essie. Other tales involving ghost friends include the Blossom Culp books written by Richard Peck: *Blossom Culp and the Sleep of Death* (Delacorte, 1987); *The Dreadful Future of Blossom Culp* (Delacorte, 1983); *The Ghost Belonged to Me* (Delacorte, 1975); and *Ghosts I Have Been* (Delacorte, 1977). Blossom Culp lived in 1914 and was transported into the 1980s. She is amazed at the things she encounters in her new environment. Lila McGinnis has written about a ghost who is displaced from a house destroyed to make way for the town's new library. While the library is being built the ghost takes up residence in a nearby home. That is how Otis, the ghost, meets Albert. The problems they encounter are told in *The Ghost Upstairs* (Hastings House, 1982). Later, in *The Ghost Alarm* (Hastings House, 1988), ghosts take up residence in the newly constructed library. Pam Conrad wrote a strange tale of two girls—one in the past and one in the present—who move back and forth in each other's lives. The tale, *Stonewords: A Ghost Story* (Harper, 1990), is compelling and fascinating. C. S. Adler's *Ghost Brother* (Clarion, 1990) tells the story of Wally and his older brother, who is killed in an accident. The brother returns as a ghost to encourage Wally to be less timid and cautious. In *A Ghost in the House* (Scholastic, 1991), Betty Ren Wright focuses on a relationship between a great-aunt and her young teenage niece as they become aware of ghostly occurrences in their old house. *Seven Strange and Ghostly Tales* by Brian Jacques (Philomel, 1991) includes "The Lies of Henry Mawdsley" and "The Sad History of Gilly Bodkin," who has yearned for a taste of candy for more than 300 years.

9 Brooke, William J.
Untold Tales

Brooke, William J. *Untold Tales*. HarperCollins, 1992. 144 pp. ISBN 0-06-020271-8.
Listening Level: Intermediate (ages 9-10; grades 4-5)
Read-Alone Level: Intermediate Accelerated (ages 10-11; grades 5-6)

"Happily ever after" takes on a new meaning in these interwoven tales of "The Frog Prince," "Sleeping Beauty," and "Beauty and the Beast." Imagine what would happen if the Queen wanted the frog back after she turned him into a prince. And how did Prince Charming know the real beauty to kiss—what if he kissed the wrong sleeping beauty? And what if the author insisted on a cameo role in each of the stories? Those familiar with the traditional tellings of these tales will find the most humor in these twisted tales that bring a sense of the contemporary to age-old stories.

Fractured Tales for Twisted Readers

The reader does not really have to be twisted to enjoy the many fractured versions of traditional fairy tales. Brooke has written one previous volume of fairy tales—*A Telling of the Tales: Five Stories* (Harper, 1990). In *A Telling of the Tales*, Brooke muses about what might happen if Cinderella did not want to try on the glass slipper or if Sleeping Beauty did not believe that she had been asleep. And what would happen if Paul Bunyan (a man known for chopping trees) and Johnny Appleseed (a man known for planting trees) met in the forest? Heavily illustrated books that bring a humorous twist or viewpoint to traditional tales include Jon Scieszka's *The True Story of the Three Little Pigs by A. Wolf* (Viking, 1989) and *The Frog Prince Continued* (Viking, 1991). Other elaborations on classic tales include John W. Ivimey's *The Complete Story of the Three Blind Mice* (Joy Street, 1990) and Jim Aylesworth's *The Complete Hickory Dickory Dock* (Atheneum, 1990).

---

10 Brown, Margaret Wise

Under the Sun and the Moon and Other Poems

Brown, Margaret Wise. *Under the Sun and the Moon and Other Poems.*
Illustrated by Tom Leonard. Hyperion, 1993. 32 pp. ISBN 1-56282-
354-X.
Listening Level: Primary (ages 6-7; grades 1-2)
Read-Alone Level: Primary Accelerated (ages 7-8; grades 2-3)

Nineteen nature poems tell of butterflies fluttering in the tall grasses,
rabbits bounding across flower-filled meadows, and geese gliding across the
morning sky. The illustrations, reminiscent of early American folk art, show
the life that the poetry describes. The collection of poetry includes "Apple
Trees," "From a Hornet's Nest," and "I Dreamed of a Horse."

Margaret Wise Brown and Other Poets of Note

During her lifetime (1910-1952), Margaret Wise Brown
achieved acclaim as a poet. The collection cited above is newly
discovered poetry that has not been published previously. However, much of her writing is being reissued in newly illustrated
editions for a new generation of readers. Among new works being
reissued for the younger reader are *Goodnight Moon* (HarperCollins, 1947; 1991); *The Runaway Bunny* (HarperCollins, 1942;
1991); and *A Child's Good Night Book* (Addison, 1943; Harper-
Collins, 1992). Brown's favorite *Little Fur Family*, illustrated by
Garth Williams, was first published in 1946, reissued in 1951,
and reissued once more by HarperCollins in 1991. The book tells
of a "little fur family, warm as toast, smaller than most." The
family lives in a "warm wooden tree."

Margaret Wise Brown also wrote under the pseudonym
Golden MacDonald. Use the catalog in your school or public
library to locate other books under the names Brown or MacDon-
ald. You may also want to locate poetry collections by Lee
Bennett Hopkins, Karla Kuskin, Eve Merriam, and Myra Cohn
Livingston.

11 Bulla, Clyde Robert
Charlie's House

Bulla, Clyde Robert. *Charlie's House.* Illustrated by Teresa Flavin.
Knopf, 1993. 93 pp. ISBN 0-679-83841-4.
Listening Level: Intermediate (ages 9-10; grades 4-5)
Read-Alone Level: Intermediate Accelerated+ (ages 10-11+; grades
5-6+)

Charlie Brig is 12 years old and alone in eighteenth-century England. An acquaintance he meets "befriends" him and helps him sign on to a ship bound for America. During the trip he realizes that he has been sent to Philadelphia as an indentured servant. His original master is very good to him but loses him to a relative who is less than kind or humane toward his indentured servants. Charlie is sent to work on the plantation with the slaves and is treated no differently. Not able to endure the thought of spending years in this cruel man's service, Charlie runs away to freedom. After days of running he finds a haven on a little-known island inhabited by runaway slaves. This may be just the place for Charlie to build the house he has dreamed of building in America.

Early Americans

Although indentured servants were thought to be better off in comparison to slaves, many were forced into a lifetime of servitude. Bonded to others for seven years, they often were charged for goods, food, etc., during those years—and thus were always in debt to their masters. Other times the person holding an indentured servant's bond was cruel and abusive to the servant. In many ways their plight resembled that of the African-Americans. The basic difference was pointed out by Drogo, an African-American Charlie meets during his flight to freedom—as Charlie grew older, few would recognize him as belonging to someone else, but the African-American slaves could easily be found because of the color of their skin. Paul Fleischman wrote about a similar arrangement in *Saturnalia* (Zolotow/HarperCollins, 1990). *Saturnalia* describes the experiences of William, a Narragansett Indian, who is working as an apprentice in Boston in 1681.

12 Bunting, Eve
Coffin on a Case

Bunting, Eve. *Coffin on a Case*. HarperCollins, 1992. 105 pp. ISBN 0-06-020273-4.
Listening Level: Intermediate (ages 9-10; grades 4-5)
Read-Alone Level: Intermediate Accelerated (ages 10-11; grades 5-6)

Coffin and Pale Detective Agency is operated by Henry Coffin's father and his partner, Mr. Pale. Twelve-year-old Henry is their junior associate, who sometimes works with them on real cases. Today, however, Pale is away on business and needs to have Mr. Coffin leave the office and come to help. But before Mr. Coffin leaves, a very nice-looking young woman comes to the agency asking for help in finding her mother. Mr. Coffin has to decline taking her as a client because he has to leave town and Henry is not licensed to work on his own. Nevertheless, Lily Larson calls Henry at home and asks if he would consider helping her. He cannot resist the offer, so together, they find some clues that lead them to thieves who have stolen a rare jade statue from a museum. Unfortunately, Lily's mother accidentally came across the thieves as they were returning with the statue, and she was taken captive and held in a dark cellar until the thieves could travel out of the country. Henry manages to follow the same trail and is taken captive and put into the same cellar. But he has a plan to lure one of the captors back to the cellar doorway so that he can push her in and lock the door while he makes his escape. Meanwhile, Lily is making her way to the police station to notify them. After a scary chase during which Henry must hide underwater in the slimy, green pool, the police arrive to rescue Henry, Lily's mother, reclaim the jade statue from the bottom of the pool (where Henry had hidden it), and take the two thieves into custody. And Henry—he gets a lot of press coverage and learns, to his relief, that Lily is still his friend.

More Mysteries to Solve

Henry Coffin is a 12-year-old detective who successfully solves a case or two. Several authors have written mystery series that will appeal to a similar group of readers. Under the name Gertrude Warner, Whitman Publishers have published dozens of Boxcar Children Mysteries. Some recent titles include *The Haunted Cabin Mystery* (Whitman, 1991); *The Animal Shelter Mystery* (Whitman, 1991); *The Deserted Library Mystery* (Whitman, 1991); and *The Old Hotel Mystery* (Whitman, 1991). Books for early intermediate readers include those titles within the Cam Jansen mystery series by David A. Adler and his Fourth Floor

Twins series of books, which also feature young sleuths. Some titles in Adler's series include *Cam Jansen and the Mystery at the Haunted House* (Viking, 1992); *Cam Jansen and the Mystery of Flight 54* (Viking, 1989); *The Fourth Floor Twins and the Disappearing Parrot Trick* (Viking, 1986); *The Fourth Floor Twins and the Sand Castle Contest* (Viking, 1988); and *The Fourth Floor Twins and the Fortune Cookie Chase* (Viking, 1986). In addition to these titles, other mysteries that will appeal to young readers include the Encyclopedia Brown series by Donald J. Sobol (Lodestar/Dutton) and the Sebastian (Super Sleuth) series by Mary Blount Christian, which features a canine sleuth and is published by Macmillan.

13 Byars, Betsy
Bingo Brown's Guide to Romance

Byars, Betsy. *Bingo Brown's Guide to Romance*. Viking, 1992. 115 pp. ISBN 0-670-84491-8.
Listening Level: Intermediate (ages 9-10; grades 4-5)
Read-Alone Level: Intermediate Accelerated (ages 10-11; grades 5-6)

Bingo Brown is back again in another adventure—this time with Melissa, the "lost love" of his life. Melissa had lived in town but had moved a year ago to Bixby, Oklahoma. While she was in Oklahoma, Bingo wrote her letters, but he hadn't heard from her for three months. He wasn't sure why it was, but perhaps it was because he had sent her a special letter—a photocopied letter. He had written such a special letter that he wanted to keep a copy so he photocopied the letter, and then he accidentally sent her the photocopy instead of the original copy. She had not written since. Now she was back home— Wentworth, a friend of Bingo's, had seen her in the Winn Dixie food store. After getting up the courage to go see her at her cousin's, Bingo wasn't any further ahead in his quest to win Melissa's heart. Throughout the episodes, Bingo writes and answers his advice questions for his *Guide to Romance* or more completely his *"Guide to Romance, a Record of the Personal Ups and Downs of Bingo Brown. Dedicated to My Brother, Jamie, as a Guide and Comfort to Him When He Finds Himself, as He Surely Will, upon the Roller Coaster of Life."*

More Bingo Brown Tales and Other Stories by Betsy Byars

Bingo Brown has starred in at least three other books by Betsy Byars: *The Burning Questions of Bingo Brown* (Viking, 1988); *Bingo Brown and the Language of Love* (Viking, 1990); and *Bingo Brown, Gypsy Lover* (Viking, 1989). Other popular protagonists, including Cracker Jackson, are featured in Byars's other books. Those books include *Cracker Jackson* (Viking, 1985); *Glory Girl* (Viking, 1983); *The Two-Thousand Pound Goldfish* (Harper, 1982); *The Midnight Fox* (Viking, 1968); *Computer Nut* (Viking, 1984); and *Trouble River* (Viking, 1969). Early intermediate readers will enjoy *The House of Wings* (Viking, 1972); *Seven Treasure Hunts* (HarperCollins, 1991); *Wanted: Mud Blossom* (Delacorte, 1991); and *Cybil War* (Viking, 1981).

---

14 Byars, Betsy
Coast to Coast

Byars, Betsy. *Coast to Coast.* Delacorte, 1992. 164 pp. ISBN 0-385-30787-X.
Listening Level: Intermediate (ages 9-10; grades 4-5)
Read-Alone Level: Intermediate Accelerated (ages 10-11; grades 5-6)

Birch's grandfather is facing a move to a retirement community. Selling many of his personal belongings does not bother him as much as selling his prized antique plane, a Piper Cub. Birch is very close to her grandfather and convinces him to take one last flight in his plane—with her in the other seat. Once they took a short trip, it was only a little more difficult to convince him to take his dreamed-of trip across the United States and to take Birch along. Once convinced, Grandfather leaves a note for his daughter, Birch's mother, and the two of them set off from Charleston, South Carolina, across Alabama, Mississippi, and Texas. The two adventurers fly across the Colorado River, over the Joshua Tree National Monument, and across the San Gabriel Mountains. They finally land in California. Along the way Birch is able to reflect on the poems her grandmother had written before her death. There is a particularly puzzling poem written on the day Birch was born. At first Birch thinks that the short poem refers to the birth of a child who died and that she has replaced (through adoption). When she finally gets the courage to ask her grandfather, he explains that the poem refers to the birth of Birch's twin, who died shortly after birth. Birch and Grandfather weather many adventures, and

Birch has many new experiences, including a first date with a very handsome young man who helps tie down their plane when they are forced to land because of strong winds.

Airplanes • Airplanes

Betsy Byars, herself a pilot, often does her writing in a log cabin near her home in Clemson, South Carolina. Much of her summer is spent flying. For 35 years she flew with her husband, Ed, as the pilot, but she obtained her own pilot's license December 19, 1984. In March of 1987, she and her husband flew a 1940 J-3 Cub from coast to coast and back. That flight was the basis for *Coast to Coast*. Other writers have researched airplane flights and have used that research to write books. *The Glorious Flight: Across the Channel with Louis Blériot, July 25, 1909* by Alice Provensen and Martin Provensen is an account of this historical flight. The Provensens' illustrations, in addition to the text, present many historical and background details of the times. Russell Freedman's book, *The Wright Brothers: How They Invented the Airplane* (Holiday House, 1991), details the Wright Brothers' development of the airplane. The Wright Brothers' own photographs illustrate Freedman's book.

---

15 Carris, Joan
Howling for Home

Carris, Joan. *Howling for Home*. Illustrated by Judith Mitchell. Little, Brown, 1992. 62 pp. ISBN 0-316-13017-6.
Listening Level: Primary (ages 6-7; grades 1-2)
Read-Alone Level: Primary Accelerated (ages 7-8; grades 2-3)

Written from Beau's point of view, this title tells of the trials of living in a family of people who just don't understand. Beau is a Bernese mountain dog and is used to having wide-open spaces on which to roam. Now he is left alone in the laundry room, and instead of the hearty food he is used to, he is given dry, tasteless dog food. He doesn't have any real jobs like herding cattle or guarding the homestead—and now he has to wear a noisy, nasty collar around his neck. When it becomes too much for him he sets out to find his old home. Only then does Beau realize where he really belongs. He returns to his new home with sore feet and a new sense of loyalty.

Dog Tales

The most read story of animal travel is probably the classic tale of the journey of three animals told in *The Incredible Journey* by Sheila Burnford (Bantam, 1961; 1990). Other animal stories for intermediate readers include the classic tales by Jim Kjelgaard, such as *Big Red* (Holiday House, 1973) and *Outlaw Red* (Holiday House, 1953), and Zachary Ball's *Bristle Face* (Holiday House, 1991). Walter Farley has written more than a dozen titles featuring the Black Stallion in titles such as *The Black Stallion Legend* (Random, 1983) and *The Black Stallion Mystery* (Random, 1957). Primary-aged readers will enjoy reading the novels *Hot Fudge* by James Howe (Morrow, 1990) and *Snot Stew* by Bill Wallace (Holiday House, 1989).

---

16 Christian, Mary Blount
Sebastian (Super Sleuth) and the Impossible Crime

Christian, Mary Blount. *Sebastian (Super Sleuth) and the Impossible Crime.* Illustrated by Lisa McCue. Macmillan, 1992. 64 pp. ISBN 0-02-718435-8.
Listening Level: Early Intermediate (ages 8-9; grades 3-4)
Read-Alone Level: Intermediate (ages 9-10; grades 4-5)

Sebastian, a four-footed sleuth, is determined to help his human, Detective John Quincy, solve the crime that couldn't have happened. The city's art museum is holding a reception with all of its dignitaries present. They are to unveil a newly discovered piece of art that supposedly was hidden away when the Germans invaded France during World War II. The police chief has set up security that could not possibly be penetrated: guards at each open door; alarms for the emergency exits; and specially coded "dots" that activate an alarm if the item passes through the security doors. Nothing seemed to have been overlooked, but during a five-second blackout, the celebrated painting disappears. The police chief is terribly embarrassed and promises to have the case solved in 48 hours or he'll fire his detectives—and that means Sebastian's human, Detective Quincy. Sebastian knows he must get to work immediately, yet he cannot reveal his involvement. Because Sebastian thinks in terms of humans but is really a dog, he must find a way to solve the crime while letting the humans think they have solved it. Sebastian, as in his other books, does solve the crime—this time the mysterious case of the crime that couldn't have occurred.

Sebastian (Super Sleuth)

Mary Blount Christian has written several mysteries featuring the super sleuth canine who helps his master solve crimes. Early intermediate and intermediate readers who need shorter books to read will enjoy the other books in Christian's series: *Sebastian (Super Sleuth) and the Battling Bigfoot* (Macmillan, 1990); *Sebastian (Super Sleuth) and the Bone to Pick Mystery* (Macmillan, 1983); *Sebastian (Super Sleuth) and the Clumsy Cowboy* (Macmillan, 1985); *Sebastian (Super Sleuth) and the Crummy Yummies Caper* (Macmillan, 1983); *Sebastian (Super Sleuth) and the Egyptian Connection* (Macmillan, 1988); *Sebastian (Super Sleuth) and the Hair of the Dog Mystery* (Macmillan, 1982); *Sebastian (Super Sleuth) and the Mystery Patient* (Macmillan, 1992); *Sebastian (Super Sleuth) and the Purloined Sirloin* (Macmillan, 1986); *Sebastian (Super Sleuth) and the Santa Claus Caper* (Pocket, 1989); *Sebastian (Super Sleuth) and the Secret of the Skewered Skier* (Macmillan, 1984); *Sebastian (Super Sleuth) and the Stars-in-His-Eyes Mystery* (Macmillan, 1987); and *Sebastian (Super Sleuth) and the Time Capsule Caper* (Macmillan, 1989). Several other authors have written mystery series that will appeal to a similar group of readers. The most popular mystery series include: Miss Mallard Mysteries by Robert Quackenbush (Simon & Schuster); the Sebastian Barth Mysteries by James Howe (Atheneum); the Boxcar Children Mysteries by Gertrude Warner (Whitman); the Cam Jansen mysteries by David A. Adler (Viking); the Fourth Floor Twins series by David A. Adler (Viking); and the Encyclopedia Brown series by Donald J. Sobol (Lodestar/Dutton).

17 Christopher, Matt
Centerfield Ballhawk

Christopher, Matt. *Centerfield Ballhawk.* Illustrated by Ellen Beier. Little, Brown, 1992. 59 pp. ISBN 0-316-14079-1.
Listening Level: Primary (ages 6-7; grades 1-2)
Read-Alone Level: Primary Accelerated (ages 7-8; grades 2-3)

José Mendez is the best fielder on the Peach Street Mudders baseball team. During baseball season he finds it hard to think of anything but baseball; in fact, he even forgets the warning his father gave him about playing ball in the front yard. This time he manages to hit a baseball through a window in Mrs. Dooley's new car, and as a result his father grounds him from playing baseball for two weeks. He uses this new free time to figure out how to pay for Mrs. Dooley's window and hopes that he won't forget how to play ball in the next two weeks. José's father used to be a minor league player, and José really wants to live up to being like his father. Matters only seem worse when his older sister, Ellen, seems to be a natural hitter on her newly formed softball team. José has the idea that a new bat might help him become a better hitter, so he finds a way to earn money to buy one. Later, though, José comes to realize that his father is proud of him just the way he is and that he doesn't need to be a great hitter—in fact, his father tells him that he is a natural outfielder and has made catches like he was never able to make. José finds out that there is more about him to like than the fact that he may or may not be a great ball player.

Sport Books

Matt Christopher is noted for the many books about sports that he has written. He has written at least three other Springboard Books for primary accelerated or early intermediate readers: *The Hit-Away Kid* (Little, Brown, 1988); *The Lucky Baseball Bat* (Little, Brown, 1991); and *The Spy on Third Base* (Little, Brown, 1988). He has also written many books for intermediate readers (see list accompanying entry below for Christopher's *Takedown*). A writer of sports stories for intermediate readers is Dean Hughes. His books in the Angel Park All-Stars series deal with three nine-year-old rookies on a Little League team. The series follows the boys through the team's tryouts, slumps, recoveries, and triumphs. Some of the titles are *All Together Now* (Knopf, 1991); *Big Base Hit* (Knopf, 1990); and *Up to Bat* (Knopf, 1991). Readers who are more advanced may find titles by Thomas Dygard of interest. His titles include *Halfback Tough* (Morrow, 1986); *Rebound Caper* (Morrow, 1983); and *Tournament Upstart* (Morrow, 1984).

---

18 Christopher, Matt
Takedown

Christopher, Matt. *Takedown.* Illustrated by Margaret Sanfilippo. Little, Brown, 1990. 147 pp. ISBN 0-316-13930-0.
Listening Level: Early Intermediate (ages 8-9; grades 3-4)
Read-Alone Level: Intermediate (ages 9-10; grades 4-5)

It had been years since Sean had seen his biological father, who had left shortly after divorcing Sean's mother years ago. Now he has to fit into a new family. He had a stepfather and a bigger but younger stepbrother, Carl. Carl constantly teases Sean about his small size. Sean's only consolation is his skill at wrestling. His own father had been a wrestler, and the sport helped him to stay close to his father's memory. With the help of an assistant wrestling referee, Clint Wagner, Sean improves and comes to feel that he could really beat his nemesis from a rival school, Max "the Octopus" Rundel. Max is a bully who not only beats Sean on the wrestling mat, but engages Sean in his own version of a wrestling match whenever he encounters Sean on the street. In the end, Sean's wrestling practice serves him well and also brings his stepbrother, Carl, to his side, along with Sean's new stepfather.

More Stories by Matt Christopher

Matt Christopher has been writing sports stories for more than two decades. His many popular stories include *Baseball Pals* (Little, Brown, 1956; 1990); *Centerfield Ballhawk* (Little, Brown, 1992); *Dirt Bike Racer* (Little, Brown, 1979); *Dirt Bike Runaway* (Little, Brown, 1983); *The Dog That Called the Signals* (Little, Brown, 1982); *The Dog That Pitched a No-Hitter* (Little, Brown, 1988); *The Dog That Stole Football Plays* (Little, Brown, 1980); *Football Fugitive* (Little, Brown, 1979); *Fox Steals Home* (Little, Brown, 1978); *Great Quarterback Switch* (Little, Brown, 1984); *Hockey Machine* (Little, Brown, 1986); *Ice Magic* (Little, Brown, 1987); *The Kid Who Only Hit Homers* (Little, Brown, 1986); *The Lucky Baseball Bat* (Little, Brown, 1991); *Red-Hot Hightops* (Little, Brown, 1987); *Return of the Home Run Kid* (Little, Brown, 1992); *Skateboard Tough* (Little, Brown, 1991); *Soccer Halfback* (Little, Brown, 1978); *The Spy on Third Base* (Little, Brown, 1988); *Supercharged Infield* (Little, Brown, 1985); *Tackle Without a Team* (Little, Brown, 1989); and *Tight End* (Little, Brown, 1981).

---

19 Christopher, Matt
Undercover Tailback

Christopher, Matt. *Undercover Tailback*. Illustrated by Paul Casale. Little, Brown, 1992. 145 pp. ISBN 0-316-14251-4.
Listening Level: Early Intermediate (ages 8-9; grades 3-4)
Read-Alone Level: Intermediate (ages 9-10; grades 4-5)

The Kensington Kudzus football players make a good showing in their orange uniforms with white numbers—a good showing, that is, until they get on the football field. The other teams seem to know what the Kudzuses are going to do before they do it. Parker Nolan knows something is strange, but he can't prove it. One day he sees someone in a gray sweatshirt coming out of the coach's office with a camera in his hand. Later Parker finds the team playbook open on the coach's desk. Unfortunately, Parker is known for telling lies, so even when he tells his teammates what he has seen, no one believes it. Parker is sure the mysterious person was taking pictures of the playbook and passing them on to the Kudzus's opponents. Parker and his friend, Joni Anderson, stake out the coach's office in an effort to catch the culprit in the act. Their efforts are fruitless until other clues lead Parker to suspect a team member. Parker and Joni plan a strategy to force the thief to show his hand, even though the plan puts Parker's position on the team in jeopardy. During the game with the Piranhas everything seems to be going wrong. The Piranhas know every move before it happens. In an effort to foil the Piranhas's advantage, the Kudzuses repeat plays and give their other signals in code. Their plan works and in the end the culprit is exposed. Parker decides to break his pattern—his pattern of telling lies.

Sports Heroes

Matt Christopher's stories are mysteries, problem novels, and basically interesting tales—all with a large dose of sports information. Another author who interweaves sports terminology and exciting accounts of sports events is Thomas J. Dygard, who has written *Halfback Tough* (Morrow, 1986), *Outside Shooter* (Morrow, 1979), *Quarterback Walk-On* (Morrow, 1982), and *Tournament Upstart* (Morrow, 1984). Dygard's books will appeal to the more mature intermediate reader. Books for younger readers include *Bobby Baseball* by Robert Kimmel Smith (Delacorte, 1989) and *Trading Game* by Alfred Slote (Lippincott, 1990).

---

20 Cleary, Beverly
Muggie Maggie

Cleary, Beverly. *Muggie Maggie.* Illustrated by Kay Life. Morrow, 1990. 70 pp. ISBN 0-688-08553-9.
Listening Level: Primary (ages 6-7; grades 1-2)
Read-Alone Level: Primary Accelerated (ages 7-8; grades 2-3)

Maggie absolutely refuses to write in cursive. She doesn't want to write it and she doesn't care if she learns to read it. After all, she probably won't ever need to read or use cursive because *she uses the computer.* And besides, Maggie points out, the handwriting of grown-ups who use cursive is often very messy. The real reason Maggie does not want to learn to write in cursive may be because her classmates laughed at her first efforts—making "Maggie" look more like "Muggie." Whatever the real reason, Maggie will not back down—that is, not until her teacher, Mrs. Leeper, devises a foolproof plan.

More Books by Beverly Cleary

Beverly Cleary has been writing books for more than 40 years. She was born in McMinnville, Oregon, April 12, 1916, and for the first six years she lived on a farm near Yamhill. Later the family moved to Portland, and she attended Fernwood Elementary. She grew up and became a librarian and for a long time she thought about writing books. Eventually she began to write about the kind of children she had gotten to know as a librarian in Yakima, Washington. The first story was *Henry Huggins* (Morrow, 1950). Later she wrote about Ramona (the pest) and Beezus Quimby, Otis Spofford, Ellen Tibbits, a cat named Socks, a scraggly dog named Ribsy, and Ralph S. Mouse. *Ramona and Her Father* (Morrow, 1977) and *Ramona Quimby, Age 8* (Morrow, 1981) were both Newbery Honor books. Beverly Cleary was awarded the Newbery Award in 1984 for *Dear Mr. Henshaw* (Morrow, 1983). *Dear Mr. Henshaw* is a story about a young reader, Leigh Botts, who writes letters to the author, Boyd Henshaw, and then records events that take place in his life in his own diary. *Strider* (Morrow, 1991) continues Leigh's story.

---

21 Cleary, Beverly
Strider

Cleary, Beverly. *Strider.* Illustrated by Paul O. Zelinsky. Morrow, 1991. 179 pp. ISBN 0-688-09900-9.
Listening Level: Primary Accelerated (ages 7-8; grades 2-3)
Read-Alone Level: Early Intermediate (ages 8-9; grades 3-4)

Leigh Botts first appeared in *Dear Mr. Henshaw* (Morrow, 1983). His correspondence with Boyd Henshaw changed Leigh's life. Now Leigh is 14 years old and is writing in his diary again. He still lives with his mom in a rundown "cottage" in Pacific Grove. His parents are divorced, and Leigh feels abandoned by his father, a trucker who is often on the road for long stretches at a time. One day while walking on the beach with his friend, Barry, they find a hungry and abandoned dog. Leigh coaxes the dog to come home with him, and they are soon inseparable friends. At first Leigh begins to run as a way to exercise Strider, but before long he is not only exercising Strider but is *running*. Eventually Leigh begins to come out of his inner self and gets involved at school. He joins the track team and finds himself a winner. He not only wins for himself, but he is able to focus on his running as a competition with himself. His running also gives him a focus for some of his writing, and his grades actually improve. Strider is the force that helps Leigh come out of his inner self and motivates him to step out of his cottage and look at life in a new way.

Writing in Diaries

Both *Dear Mr. Henshaw* and *Strider* are written in diary entry form. Other authors have used similar techniques to present stories that intermediate students will enjoy. Read any of the Adventures of Henry Reed books by Keith Robertson (Viking). One of the first titles, *Henry Reed's Journey* (Viking, 1963), introduces Henry Reed and his best friend, Midge. Other books that model diary or journal writing include Joan Blos's *A Gathering of Days: A New England Girl's Journal, 1830-32* (Scribner's, 1979); Barbara Brenner's *On the Frontier with Mr. Audubon* (Coward, 1977); Jean Craighead George's *My Side of the Mountain* (Dutton, 1959) and *On the Far Side of the Mountain* (Dutton, 1990); Marilyn Sachs's *Dorrie's Book* (Doubleday, 1975); and a picture book titled *Three Days on a River in a Red Canoe* by Vera B. Williams (Greenwillow, 1981).

---

22 Clifford, Eth
Harvey's Wacky Parrot Adventure

Clifford, Eth. *Harvey's Wacky Parrot Adventure*. Houghton, 1990. 112 pp. ISBN 0-395-53352-X.
Listening Level: Primary Accelerated (ages 7-8; grades 2-3)
Read-Alone Level: Early Intermediate (ages 8-9; grades 3-4)

Uncle Buck's good friend, Captain Corbin, is thought to have hidden a treasure in Uncle Buck's house. When Harvey and his pesky cousin, Nora, show up for the holidays, they suddenly find themselves in the midst of a search for the treasure—and they are not the only ones looking. A strange Mr. Singh, claiming to be an Indian Sikh and a friend of Captain Corbin, shows up at Uncle Buck's house bearing news of the captain's death; though Mr. Singh seems to have convinced Uncle Buck of his sincerity, he is viewed suspiciously by Harvey and Nora. Uncle Buck's house was, in 1859, part of the Underground Railroad system, so when Harvey and Nora discover a secret tunnel and evidence that someone has been in the tunnel recently, they begin to put pieces of evidence together and realize that Captain Corbin must not be dead but is somewhere nearby. When the treasure is found, Mr. Singh's true identity is revealed and Harvey and Nora realize that they were closer than they thought—too close.

Traveling on the Underground Railroad

During the Civil War, the Underground Railroad was a series of "safe houses" that sheltered slaves on their journey North to freedom. Many of the houses had secret passages and rooms where slaves hid until it was safe to move on during the dark of night. Details of how one section of the Underground Railroad was traveled is part of a true story told by Virginia Hamilton in her story "Carrying the Running-Aways" in *The People Could Fly: American Black Folktales* (Knopf, 1985). The Underground Railroad is also an element in Jean Fritz's historical novel *Brady* (Coward, 1960; Puffin, 1960); F. N. Monjo's picture book *The Drinking Gourd*, illustrated by Fred Brenner (Harper, 1970); and in the version retold and illustrated by Jeanette Winter, *Follow the Drinking Gourd* (Knopf, 1988).

---

23 Clifford, Eth
Will Somebody Please *Marry My Sister?*

Clifford, Eth. *Will Somebody* Please *Marry My Sister?* Illustrated by Ellen Eagle. Houghton, 1992. 122 pp. ISBN 0-395-58037-4.
Listening Level: Intermediate (ages 9-10; grades 4-5)
Read-Alone Level: Intermediate Accelerated (ages 10-11; grades 5-6)

The time period is the early 1920s, but it is the characters who take center stage. Abel lives with his grandmother and two older sisters in a small apartment over Grandmother's bakery and coffee shop. Abel and his sisters came to live with their grandmother after their parents were killed in a car accident. However, the apartment has only two bedrooms. Abel is forced to sleep on the couch so his one older sister can have a room to herself so she can study to become a doctor; Abel's other sister shares a room with Grandmother. Abel desperately wants a room of his own, but it seems the only way to get one is to convince someone to marry one of his sisters. Anne is the younger of his two sisters, and although she is seeing someone she would like to marry, Grandmother says that a younger sister cannot marry before her older sister. It is against *the rules*. So it seems that Abel's only chance is to find someone to marry Ruth. Ruth is a medical doctor, one of the first female physicians in the city, and is not really interested in getting married. Abel consults with Hilda, the daughter of a local matchmaker. Hilda has a deal with her father that may mean she could go to a camp during the summer. Hilda really wants to go to camp so that she can ride horses. Her dad has promised to send her if she can get someone to marry a man from one of his prospect lists. So together Abel and Hilda set out to find a suitor for Ruth. They go through the lists and identify several possibilities, then invite the prospects to dinner at their apartment. Although each of the suitors invited to dinner is met cordially by Ruth, none of them interests her enough to establish a relationship. Through believable coincidences Ruth meets another young doctor, who invites her to meet with a doctor's group that meets socially. In the meantime, Grandmother meets a man who proposes to her, Anne (the younger sister) does marry her fiancé, Bruce, Ruth is offered a position (with room and board) at a local hospital, and Abel gets his own room. Will Grandmother marry Mr. Fox? Maybe she will and maybe she won't—she says she likes things just like they are.

More Books by Eth Clifford

Eth Clifford is noted for her fast-moving stories. Although many of them are set in contemporary times, others are set in the past. Among some of Clifford's more popular titles are *The Dastardly Murder of Dirty Pete* (Houghton, 1981); *Flatfoot Fox and the Case of the Missing Eye* (Houghton, 1990); *Harvey's Horrible Snake Disaster* (Houghton, 1984); *Harvey's Marvelous Monkey Mystery* (Houghton, 1987); *Harvey's Wacky Parrot Adventure* (Houghton, 1990); *Help! I'm a Prisoner in the Library* (Houghton, 1979); *I Hate Your Guts, Ben Brooster* (Houghton, 1989); *I Never Wanted to Be Famous* (Houghton, 1986); *Just Tell Me When We're Dead* (Houghton, 1983); *Sacred Silly* (Houghton, 1983); and *Summer of the Dancing Horse* (Houghton, 1991). Intermediate readers will be the main audience for books by Eth Clifford.

24 Conford, Ellen
Can Do, Jenny Archer

Conford, Ellen. *Can Do, Jenny Archer*. Illustrated by Diane Palmisciano. Little, Brown, 1991. 58 pp. ISBN 0-316-15356-7.
Listening Level: Primary Accelerated (ages 7-8; grades 2-3)
Read-Alone Level: Early Intermediate (ages 8-9; grades 3-4)

There is a schoolwide can-collecting contest. The school is attempting to earn enough money to buy a video camera, and the person who collects the most cans will be allowed to use the camera and direct a class movie. Jenny is excited because she knows that she would make a great director. She searches all over for cans. But then one of her collection schemes fails and she almost loses her best friend, Beth. However, Beth is a true friend, and even though she is mad at Jenny, she secretly helps her in her quest to win the contest. When Jenny loses the contest to a much younger can collector (he got the cans from his aunt's pet kennel), the news of Beth's help makes Jenny feel like a real winner even though she has lost the contest.

More Jenny Archer

Ellen Conford has featured Jenny Archer in five other junior novels: *Case for Jenny Archer* (Little, Brown, 1988); *Jenny Archer, Author* (Little, Brown, 1989); *Jenny Archer to the Rescue* (Little, Brown, 1990); *A Job for Jenny Archer* (Little, Brown, 1988); and *What's Cooking, Jenny Archer?* (Little, Brown, 1989).

---

25 Conrad, Pam
Stonewords: A Ghost Story

Conrad, Pam. *Stonewords: A Ghost Story*. Harper, 1990. 130 pp. ISBN 0-06-021315-9.
Listening Level: Intermediate (ages 9-10; grades 4-5)
Read-Alone Level: Intermediate Accelerated+ (ages 10-11+; grades 5-6+)

Left by her mother to live with her grandparents, Zoe finds herself longing for her mother to return. Zoe's grandparents surround her with love and gentleness but cannot fill the emptiness Zoe feels. It isn't long before Zoe finds a playmate—Zoe Louise. At first Zoe's grandparents feel that the playmate is imaginary, but soon there is evidence that young Zoe Louise may actually exist. When Zoe shows up with a doll, a gift from Zoe Louise, Zoe's grandparents cannot reconcile the events with reality. During their playtimes together, Zoe Louise often refers to events of the past—and soon it is clear that she does live in the past and that, years before, something dreadful has happened to her. Even worse, time begins to run out for Zoe Louise, and Zoe must discover what has caused her friend's death *before* it happens. But even if she does, can Zoe change the course of events that occurred in the past?

More Books by Pam Conrad

Since she first started writing in 1981, Pam Conrad has written *Prairie Songs* (Harper, 1985), a story about a young woman who loves the solitude of the Nebraska prairie, and Emmeline, a doctor's wife who finds the harsh life of the prairie unbearable. Grandchildren hear the story of *My Daniel* (Harper, 1989) from the mouth of an old woman who tells of her own beloved teenage brother's death at the time (before the turn of the century) of the frenzied hunt for dinosaur remains in Nebraska. *Pedro's Journey: A Voyage with Christopher Columbus (August 3, 1492-February 14, 1493)* (Boyds Mill, 1991) brings to life the story of the crew of the *Santa Maria* from the journal of one of the ship's boys. Conrad's writing for younger readers includes a picture book, *The Tub People* (Harper, 1989), and books for the primary or early intermediate readers. Among those books are *Seven Silly Circles* (Harper, 1987), the story of Nicki, who is embarrassed by the marks on her face made by rubber-tipped arrows, and *Staying Nine* (Harper, 1988), a story that focuses on a few days in the life of a 9-year-old who refuses to have her birthday and to turn 10. Pam Conrad has also written for an older audience: *Holding Me There* (Harper, 1986) tells of 14-year-old Robin and her meddling in the life of a boarder in her mother's home; *What I Did for Roman* (Harper, 1987) details the search of 16-year-old Darcie for the father about whom she knows little; and *Taking the Ferry Home* (Harper, 1988), a story that speaks of the friendships and tragedies that occur in the life of 16-year-old Ali (the child of a recovering alcoholic) and Simone, an insecure youngster in the family of an active alcoholic.

26 Coville, Bruce
Jeremy Thatcher, Dragon Hatcher

Coville, Bruce. *Jeremy Thatcher, Dragon Hatcher.* Illustrated by Gary A. Lippincott. Jane Yolen/Harcourt, 1991. 148 pp. ISBN 0-15-200748-2.
Listening Level: Intermediate (ages 9-10; grades 4-5)
Read-Alone Level: Intermediate Accelerated (ages 10-11; grades 5-6)

Jeremy Thatcher has always lived in Blodgett's Crossing, but the day he ducks into a shop to avoid meeting Mary Lou Hutton, he discovers Elives's Magic Shop. The discovery changes his life forever. The owner of the shop is an older man who is reluctant to sell Jeremy anything—he seems especially reluctant to sell Jeremy the beautiful marbled ball. But suddenly Mr. Elives changes his mind and lets Jeremy buy the ball for only a quarter. That is when Jeremy's adventures begin—and the dragon Tiamet enters his life. Strangely, when he went to the library searching for a book telling him how to raise a dragon, the librarian, Miss Priest, opened her desk drawer and pulled out just the book that he needed, *On the Nature (and Disappearance) of Dragons* by S. H. Elives. Only Jeremy can see the dragon (or dragonlet), but that is enough to put Jeremy in some awkward situations. For example, Jeremy's creativity seems to be enhanced by the presence of the dragon. When Tiamet must return to her own world, Jeremy seems listless, and his desire to draw is greatly diminished. Then just as Miss Priest had predicted, "Midsummer Night will break your heart, All Hallow's Eve may patch it," the night of Halloween brings Jeremy a renewed vision of life—a vision through Tiamet's eyes. And with this renewed vision, Jeremy "took out some paper and began to draw."

Tales from Mr. Elives's Magic Shop

Bruce Coville first wrote of Mr. Elives's Magic Shop in *The Monster's Ring* (Knopf, 1982). *Jeremy Thatcher, Dragon Hatcher* is not a sequel to *The Monster's Ring*, but each of the stories gets its start in the magic shop. His third Magic Shop novel, *Jennifer Murdley's Toad* (Harcourt, 1992), is one of the funniest novels he has ever written (according to Coville himself). His next Magic Shop book will be titled *The Skull of Truth*.

---

27 Danziger, Paula
Not for a Billion Gazillion Dollars

Danziger, Paula. *Not for a Billion Gazillion Dollars*. Delacorte, 1992.
121 pp. ISBN 0-385-30819-1.
Listening Level: Early Intermediate (ages 8-9; grades 3-4)
Read-Alone Level: Intermediate (ages 9-10; grades 4-5)

Matthew Martin's summer looks like it will be a bummer. His parents will not buy him the computer program that he really wants and his best friend, Jill "Jil!" Hudson, has to go to the lake with her parents while her mother awaits the birth of her baby. The only thing that will make the summer better is if Matthew can think of a way to earn money to buy the computer program he wants, but he already owes almost everyone in his family and class. And money-making schemes are difficult to devise. His plan to wash car windshields does not work out the way he had thought, and baby-sitting is too dangerous. It is only when Jil! comes home early and joins Matt do they come up with a plan—doing what they do best—creating cards and posters on the computer.

More Stories About Matthew

Paula Danziger first introduced Matthew and his friend, Jil!, in *Everyone Else's Parents Said Yes* (Delacorte, 1989). Other stories about the two friends include *Make Like a Tree and Leave* (Delacorte, 1990) and *Earth to Matthew* (Delacorte, 1991). In *Everyone Else's Parents Said Yes*, sixth-grader Matthew Martin harasses his older sister and barrages the girls in his class with embarrassing practical jokes. Only when the girls retaliate with threats to disrupt his birthday party does he realize the consequences that will result from his obnoxious behavior. *Make Like a Tree and Leave* finds Matthew and his friends involved in more outrageous antics. They cover one of their classmates with cast bandages for their Egyptian project, successfully simulating a mummy, but find that they have problems when they try to remove the cast. *Earth to Matthew* depicts Matthew's life as both hilarious and embarrassing—and further complicated by his crush on "Jil!."

28 Dicks, Terrance

Sally Ann on Her Own

Dicks, Terrance. *Sally Ann on Her Own*. Illustrated by Blanche Sims. Simon & Schuster, 1992. 62 pp. ISBN 0-671-74512-3.
Listening Level: Primary Accelerated (ages 7-8; grades 2-3)
Read-Alone Level: Early Intermediate (ages 8-9; grades 3-4)

Sally Ann, a rag doll, is the newest toy to join the stuffed animals at Mrs. Foster's day care center. She's just in time to hear the bad news. Two men have come to Mrs. Foster to inform her that her day care center is breaking several rules and that fixing up the old house will cost a lot of money. The very next day Mrs. Foster gets a letter in the mail from a real estate company. The company is offering to buy the old house, and Mrs. Foster is thinking of selling. The toys do not wish to lose each other as friends. But more importantly, they do not wish to lose the humans who keep them "alive" when the humans are not around. They must do something to keep from being tossed on some closet floor. During the day they listen and gather all the information that they can. That night Sally Ann comes up with a plan, but to make it work she has to reveal that she can talk. She visits Mrs. Foster in her bedroom and speaks to her. Sally Ann tells her that she thinks the two men are imposters and are trying to scare Mrs. Foster into selling her home so that they can buy it cheap. Sally Ann tells Mrs. Foster how to find out if the men are tricking her or not. Even though Sally Ann hopes that Mrs. Foster will think their conversation is a dream, Sally Ann wants Mrs. Foster to remember enough of the conversation to do something about the two men. However, Mrs. Foster is so busy the next day she forgets all about "the plan" until Sally Ann gets up the nerve to speak to her again—this time in the daylight. Spurred to action, Mrs. Foster helps the police get the evidence on the phony inspectors, Tinpot and Tring. Mrs. Foster manages to keep her day care center, and the toys all cheer Sally Ann for her determined efforts to save the center. Now they can all get on with their real job of playing with the children.

> ### Toy Animals Come to Life
>
> Toy animals that come alive and have adventures of one sort of another include Don Freeman's picture books about Corduroy and Jane Hissey's Old Bear series. Freeman's books include *Corduroy* (Viking, 1968); *A Pocket for Corduroy* (Viking, 1978); and *Corduroy's Christmas* (Viking, 1992). Hissey's Old Bear titles include *Best Friends: Old Bear Tales* (Philomel, 1989); *Little Bear Lost* (Philomel, 1989); *Little Bear's Trousers* Philomel, 1988); *Jolly Snow* (Philomel, 1991); and *Jolly Tall*

(Philomel, 1990). The reading level of each of Hissey's picture books is generally in the early intermediate level (ages 8-9; grades 3-4). Older students will enjoy reading A. A. Milne's Winnie-the-Pooh books and the many illustrated versions of Margery Williams's *The Velveteen Rabbit*. A particularly attractive illustrated version of Williams's tale is that of David Jorgensen (Knopf, 1985). Jorgensen's version is available as a videocassette from American School Publishers and as a book and audiocassette package. Meryl Streep narrates the classic tale on both the videocassette and the audiocassette.

29 Duffey, Betsy
A Boy in the Doghouse

Duffey, Betsy. *A Boy in the Doghouse*. Illustrated by Leslie Morrill. Simon & Schuster, 1991. 96 pp. ISBN 0-671-73618-3.
Listening Level: Primary (ages 6-7; grades 1-2)
Read-Alone Level: Primary Accelerated (ages 7-8; grades 2-3)

This is the tale of a boy and his dog. George gets a new dog, Lucky, and plans to teach him a lot of things. The two most important things are to teach Lucky not to bark and not to make puddles in the house. If George and Lucky are unsuccessful, Lucky will have to go. Meanwhile, Lucky sees things in a different way. He has a new home, a new doghouse, and a new boy to teach new things to. Lucky will have to work fast: The boy has a lot to learn. It isn't too long before Lucky teaches George one thing—to sleep with him in the doghouse. There are many more things for Lucky to teach George. There was the problem with the puppy food—it was dry food and the people ate ham. Lucky finally gets George to feed him some ham—dog heaven. Lucky also realizes that he has to figure out how to handle the puddle problem—and to stop the boy from throwing the cans at him. If he could just get these problems solved, life would truly be perfect. Lucky thought training people was very difficult and George thought training dogs was very difficult—yet they had done it.

Dog Tales

Betsy Duffey has written two books about Lucky. The sequel to *A Boy in the Doghouse* is *Lucky in Left Field* (Simon & Schuster, 1992). In *Lucky in Left Field*, George is excited that the Expos have a new coach; maybe now they will win a game. Lucky doesn't care about winning as long as he gets to play baseball. Readers may be interested in knowing that Betsy Duffey is the daughter of well-known author Betsy Byars. Other tales primary students will enjoy reading are the Henry and Mudge books by Cynthia Rylant, one of which is *Henry and Mudge Take the Big Test* (Bradbury, 1991); the stories about Clifford, the big red dog, by Norman Bridwell (Scholastic); and individual titles, such as *Bingo, the Best Dog in the World* by Catherine Siracusa (Harper, 1991) and *Three Names* by Patricia MacLachlan (Harper, 1991). Intermediate students will enjoy *Strider* by Beverly Cleary (Morrow, 1991).

30 Duffey, Betsy
Wild Things

Duffey, Betsy. *Wild Things*. Illustrated by Susanna Natti. Viking, 1993. 72 pp. ISBN 0-670-84347-4.
Listening Level: Primary (ages 6-7; grades 1-2)
Read-Alone Level: Primary Accelerated (ages 7-8; grades 2-3)

Every night somebody or something is getting into the neighborhood trash cans. Evie and Megan, first introduced in Duffey's *Puppy Love*, set out to find out who or what is raiding the cans. Matt and Joe want to be allowed to join the girls' pet patrol club. They insist that the culprit is Evie's dog, and if they are correct, the two boys want Evie and Megan to allow them to be in the club. The girls suspect that the boys themselves may be the responsible parties; however, the mischief maker turns out to be neither the dog nor the boys. The plot surrounds the search for the responsible party and the boys' quest to become members of the girls' club.

More Mysteries

Wild Things is the second title in Duffey's Pet Patrol series, designed for those who are just beginning to read chapter books. The first Pet Patrol title was *Puppy Love* (Viking, 1992). In that title, the two fourth-graders, Megan and Evie, find a box full of puppies on their doorstep. The puppies' appearance on the doorstep is a mystery, but the task does not involve solving that mystery as much as it becomes a search for homes for the four puppies. Those who enjoy reading Duffey's books will probably enjoy the titles in Stephen Roos's series, The Pet Lovers Club. One of those titles, *The Pet Lovers Club: Crocodile Christmas* (Delacorte, 1992), is cited in a separate entry in this chapter. Older readers will enjoy reading the animal mysteries by James Howe. Howe's mysteries feature Bunnicula and his animal detective friends.

Patricia Elmore has written some mysteries that will appeal to a slightly older reader. *Susannah and the Blue House Mystery* (Dutton, 1980) is an intriguing and exciting mystery that involves an old man, a wealthy antique dealer, who dies and leaves no trace of the inheritance that he has bequested to the little girl next door. *Susannah and the Poison Green Halloween* (Dutton, 1982) involves Susannah and Lucy's search for clues to lead them to the culprit who has poisoned Halloween candy. In *Susannah and the Purple Mongoose Mystery* (Dutton, 1992), Susannah and her detective friends attempt to find out who deliberately set fire to Miss Quigley's house.

31 Eisenberg, Lisa
Leave It to Lexie

Eisenberg, Lisa. *Leave It to Lexie*. Viking, 1989. 123 pp. ISBN 0-670-82844-0.
Listening Level: Primary Accelerated (ages 7-8; grades 2-3)
Read-Alone Level: Early Intermediate (ages 8-9; grades 3-4)

Lexie Nielsen does not think she fits into her family. Everyone has a talent—she has none. Her oldest sister, Karen, is a straight A student and actually enjoys working in the high school library reshelving books. Daniel is a sports star, and Lexie's parents, according to Lexie, let him get away with murder. Now that Lexie's other sister, Faith, is in junior high, she is very moody and not at all fun to be around. And to top it all off, Lexie's mother is working on a master's degree in counseling and has come to believe that all of their problems can be worked out if they just talk about them.

The room Faith and Lexie share is the center of contention with the two girls; Faith's half of the large L-shaped room is immaculate while Lexie's half is piled high with shirts, towels, stuffed toys, and almost everything else Lexie has had since she was a toddler. Faith is determined to make Lexie clean the room, but then her energies are focused on Lexie's failure to have an act for the Girl Scout talent show. The show is just two weeks away and Lexie does not know what she is going to do. Lexie is the only one in the family who enjoys her father's tradition of asking a riddle at the end of the evening meal. Daniel, Faith, and Karen seem to think the riddles are corny—but Lexie usually won the nickel he offered to the first one to solve his riddle. If she didn't know the answer, she figured it out. Riddles like "What reindeer would you find in your kitchen sink?" were easily answered. Comet. But others were more difficult. The Nielsens had played the riddle game almost every night since Lexie could remember. But the riddles were the least of Lexie's problems now. The scheduled date for the talent show is coming closer, but Lexie is no closer to figuring out an act to perform. The only thing that takes her mind off her dilemma is a silly book, *Two-Thousand-and-Two Whacky Wriddles for Weirdos*. Lexie cannot think of any talent that she has—until she realizes that being able to answer riddles is a talent. Lexie's act is an overwhelming hit.

Riddles • Riddles • Riddles

Lisa Eisenberg, the author of *Leave It to Lexie*, grew up enjoying riddles. She has collected some of her favorite riddles in books she coauthored with Katy Hall. Enjoy solving a riddle or two by reading Eisenberg's and Hall's *Buggy Riddles* (Dial, 1986); *Fishy Riddles* (Dial, 1983); *Snakey Riddles* (Dial, 1990); and *Spacey Riddles* (Dial, 1992). All have illustrations by Simms Taback. And don't miss Marc Brown's *Spooky Riddles* (Random, 1983)—they are the funniest. More mature thinkers will enjoy the challenge of Alvin Schwartz's *Unriddling: All Sorts of Riddles to Puzzle Your Guessery* (Lippincott, 1983). My favorite is the visual riddle on page 3.

32 Fairman, Tony

Bury My Bones but Keep My Words: African Tales for Retelling

Fairman, Tony. *Bury My Bones but Keep My Words: African Tales for Retelling*. Illustrated by Meshack Asare. Holt, 1991. 191 pp. ISBN 0-8050-2333-X.
Listening Level: Early Intermediate (ages 8-9; grades 3-4)
Read-Alone Level: Intermediate (ages 9-10; grades 4-5)

These 13 tales come from Africa: Kenya, Egypt, Botswana, Gambia, Nigeria, South Africa, and Namibia. They are meant for retelling. The collection includes tales about clever people and people who are arrogant and foolish. There are suspenseful stories about evil spirits and tales about gentle maidens. The retellings emphasize the songs, movements, sights, and sounds of the African setting. Fairman includes a brief paragraph about storytelling, and within that paragraph gives suggestions for helping students to become storytellers. Tale #11 is "Omutugwa," a tale from Kenya. Omutugwa is a servant girl who works for one of those women who do not take care of their home or families. The home was always very tidy, thanks to Omutugwa, who did all of the work. The mother and two grown daughters did nothing in the household. One night they attended a dance given by the chief's son. The dance was fantastic; there was Congolese music. The next night Omutugwa asks to go to the dance but is told that she must stay at home and pick up stones from the millet. But hundreds of birds fly in and help with the task and Omutugwa is able to attend the dance. When the dance is nearing its end, Omutugwa announces that she must leave and she runs away, leaving her shoe behind. The rest of the story continues much like the familiar Brothers Grimm version of the "Cinderella" tale. In the end Omutugwa becomes the wife of the chief's son—and they "walk off into the moonlight, following the call of *Igasi-yi-hano*." Other tales in the collection include "The Good Herdboy," "Hare and the White Man," and "The Wise Little Girl."

Stories from Storytellers

Storytelling is a common element in many cultures. Richard Chase has collected many tales from the Appalachian Mountain region of the United States in *The Jack Tales* (Houghton, 1943) and *Grandfather Tales* (Houghton, 1948). Virginia Hamilton retells many tales of African-Americans in *The People Could Fly: American Black Folktales* (Knopf, 1985). Hamilton continues to tell stories of African-Americans finding freedom in *Many Thousand Gone: African-Americans from Slavery to Freedom* (Knopf, 1993). Adèle Geras retells many tales from the Jewish tradition in *My Grandmother's Stories: A Collection of Jewish Folk Tales* (Knopf, 1990).

33 Fox, Paula

Amzat and His Brothers: Three Italian Tales Remembered by Floriano Vecchi

Fox, Paula. *Amzat and His Brothers: Three Italian Tales Remembered by Floriano Vecchi*. Illustrated by Emily Arnold McCully. Orchard, 1993. 67 pp. ISBN 0-531-05462-4.
Listening Level: Primary Accelerated (ages 7-8; grades 2-3)
Read-Alone Level: Early Intermediate (ages 8-9; grades 3-4)

These are three folktales retold from the Italian tradition. One tale tells of Olimpia and Cucol, the poor mother and son who never take baths. The villagers consider them stupid, but they find a way to outwit three wicked thieves and become the owners of a palace. When they discover the joys of bathing, they become very popular. The second adventure concerns Mezgalten, the tiny rooster who joins up with a ewe, a donkey, a dog, and a one-eyed cat to outwit a wolf who stalks them. Reminiscent of "The Bremen Town Musicians," this tale has humor and shows ingenuity. The final tale has Amzat and his pleasant wife turning the tables on his two greedy brothers, who attempt to cheat Amzat out of his inheritance.

More Folktales

Virginia Haviland has collected many tales from around the world. The books in her series, Favorite Fairy Tales Told in ..., are available in many libraries. Specific Haviland titles include *Favorite Fairy Tales Told in Sweden* (Little, Brown, 1966) and *Favorite Fairy Tales Told in Czechoslovakia* (Little, Brown, 1966). A compilation of tales from various countries are included in *Favorite Fairy Tales Told Around the World* (Little, Brown, 1985). Other collections that include several tales appropriate for reading aloud are *The Whistling Skeleton: American Indian Tales of the Supernatural*, originally told by George Bird Grinnell and edited by John Bierhorst (Four Winds, 1982); *The People Could Fly: American Black Folktales* by Virginia Hamilton (Knopf,

1985); *The Firebird and Other Russian Fairy Tales*, edited by Jacqueline Onassis (Viking, 1978); and *Bo Rabbit Smart for True: Folktales from the Gullah* by Priscilla Jaquith (Philomel, 1981).

34 Fox, Paula
Monkey Island

Fox, Paula. *Monkey Island.* Orchard, 1991. 151 pp. ISBN 0-531-05962-6.

Listening Level: Intermediate (ages 9-10; grades 4-5)

Read-Alone Level: Intermediate Accelerated (ages 10-11; grades 5-6)

Clay once had a very nice home with his father and mother. He attended school regularly and did all the things other 11-year-old boys did. But then his father loses his job as an advertising director and cannot get another one. His mother is able to borrow money from a friend for computer training and gets a night job. Everything seems to be fine until Clay's father goes away, unable to deal with his wife having the only job in the family and with the idea of a new baby coming. Without his father, Clay and his mother face difficult times but manage to get along until his mother's pregnancy forces her to stop working. They move to a hotel room provided by social services. One morning Clay wakes up to find his mother gone. For days he waits for her to return and then he takes to the streets. He was a homeless child in a big city. A young man, Buddy, and Calvin, an older man, befriend Clay and keep him safe, even from the "Stump People" who roam the city parks waiting to harass the homeless people in them. Clay, Buddy, and Calvin spend weeks together until Calvin gets into some whiskey and ends up in the hospital, and Clay contracts pneumonia. While being treated for his illness, Clay is visited by social workers who find him a foster home with the Biddles. The Biddles are kind and loving, but it is his mother and his baby sister or brother that Clay really wants.

The Homeless

Monkey Island focuses on the plight of a young man who is deserted by his parents and left all alone in the world. With no place to go and no place to sleep, he finds himself in the cold of the night with only the hard cement on which to sleep. A young man, Buddy, and his older friend, Calvin, notice Clay and eventually help him find a place to be. Not all children and families are as lucky as Clay. In *Fly Away Home* by Eve Bunting, illustrated by Ronald Himler (Clarion, 1991), a homeless boy lives in an airport with his father. They move from terminal to terminal to avoid being noticed. The boy's only hope is represented by a bird who finally leaves the airport and finds its freedom. In *The Leaves of October* (Atheneum, 1991), Karen Ackerman has written about a nine-year-old girl, Libby, and her younger brother, who try to make ends meet while they are with their unemployed father in a shelter. Their goal of having a real home together seems to be shattered when Libby's father accepts a job that means that she and her brother must go to a foster home—at least for a time.

35 George, Jean Craighead
On the Far Side of the Mountain

George, Jean Craighead. *On the Far Side of the Mountain.* Dutton, 1990. 170 pp. ISBN 0-525-44563-3.
Listening Level: Intermediate (ages 9-10; grades 4-5)
Read-Alone Level: Intermediate Accelerated (ages 10-11; grades 5-6)

In *My Side of the Mountain*, Sam Gribley had run away to live off the land. In this sequel, Sam continues to live in the wilderness with his peregrine falcon, Frightful, and his energetic younger sister, Alice. Sam's efforts to survive in his mountain home are interrupted when Frightful is illegally confiscated and Alice disappears. In order to find his sister and track down the location of Frightful, Sam finds that he must leave his mountain home and follow a trail across the rocky mountain terrain—to the far side of the mountain. The trail brings Sam into danger and to discovery, but it also brings him to the hardest decision of his life. The adventure includes an Arab sheik; a "hacker" who, it turns out, has stolen Frightful; and a chase to keep them from killing or selling Frightful, a valuable peregrine falcon.

Through the Woods and by a Brook—
Adventure in the Out-of-Doors

Younger readers or those wishing to know more about living with nature will enjoy reading Jim Arnosky's *I Was Born in a Tree and Raised by Bees* (Bradbury, 1988). In this book, Crinkleroot, the narrator, shows young naturalists how to share the excitement of the seasons in the woods. Readers will also enjoy Arnosky's earlier titles: *Crinkleroot's Book of Animal*

Tracking (Bradbury, 1989), which gives a wealth of tips for reading animal tracks and encourages readers to learn to track animals; and *Crinkleroot's Guide to Walking in Wild Places* (Bradbury, 1990). In *Crinkleroot's Guide to Walking in Wild Places*, Crinkleroot leads the way on a summer walk along a brook and through the woods.

Those wishing to read about more adventures in the out-of-doors will enjoy James Houston's *The Falcon Bow: An Arctic Legend* (McElderry, 1986). In Houston's book, Kungo returns to his adoptive parents and soon sets out once again to help the starving coastal Inuit people prove that the inland Indians have intentionally set fires to drive caribou away from the Inuit, thus destroying the Inuit's access to their food supply. Exciting episodes pit survival against elements of nature.

A tale of illegal activities and murder involves a peregrine falcon and illegal bird traders in *The Falcon Sting* (Bradbury, 1988), written by Barbara Brenner for older middle school readers. Marina, a smart high schooler, and Nick, a sometimes wild young man, meet and find that they share a mutual love of falcons. As their relationship grows they share Marina's secret knowledge of a rare peregrine falcon nest and the handicaps of Nick's past. They soon find themselves drawn into helping solve a sting operation against illegal bird traders and a murder in the Arizona desert.

36 Geras, Adèle
My Grandmother's Stories:
A Collection of Jewish Folk Tales

Geras, Adèle. *My Grandmother's Stories: A Collection of Jewish Folk Tales*. Illustrated by Jael Jordan. Knopf, 1990. 96 pp. ISBN 0-679-80910-4.
Listening Level: Early Intermediate (ages 8-9; grades 3-4)
Read-Alone Level: Intermediate (ages 9-10; grades 4-5)

This book features 10 stories, Grandmother's stories, inspired by a button box in a bedroom, an embroidered shawl in the parlor, freshly baked strudel in the kitchen, and other ordinary treasures in Grandmother's apartment. Grandmother's stories include one about King Solomon teaching a miser to be generous, a clever peasant outwitting the Czar, and Chief Sage keeping his shoes from getting muddy by wearing them on his hands. Grandmother tells stories about a rabbi, a ghost bride, and about a kvetch who meets an angel.

Stories Told

Other grandmothers and older friends tell their stories in Sharon Bell Mathis's *The Hundred Penny Box* (Viking, 1975) and Eth Clifford's novel *The Remembering Box* (Houghton, 1985). Clifford used some of her own mother's stories in *The Remembering Box*, in which a grandmother and a young Jewish boy share her memories of days gone by. Mathis's story tells of the love between Michael and his great-great-aunt, Dew, an aged black woman. Aunt Dew is 100 years old and keeps a boxful of pennies, one for each year of her life. Michael loves to count them while Aunt Dew tells him a story behind each one of them. Each of the stories relates to her life or to historical events.

37 Getz, David
Almost Famous

Getz, David. *Almost Famous.* Holt, 1992. 182pp. ISBN 0-8050-1940-5.
Listening Level: Early Intermediate (ages 8-9; grades 3-4)
Read-Alone Level: Intermediate (ages 9-10; grades 4-5)

Ten-year-old Maxine Candle is sure that she will be an inventor when she grows up. In fact, she is almost famous now. She has a four-year-old brother with a heart murmur and she often tries to invent something to help him. She knows that her inventions would work if she could just meet the right person and perhaps if she could become famous. One way to become famous is to get on the "Phil Donohue" show. She writes letter after letter trying to convince Phil that she should be invited to be on a panel of almost-famous inventors. Meanwhile, she receives in the mail the rules for the Children's Invention Contest. Maxine thinks the letter is from Donohue and decides that she must enter the contest. Because the very first rule says that the invention must be made by partners, Maxine sets out to find a partner. Her first choice is Toni, but Toni is not interested in Maxine. As the story progresses, the reader finds out that Toni lives with her grandmother in a poor section of town. Toni does not do well in school, and last year she hung around with girls who stole and got into a lot of trouble. Now she seems rebellious and uninterested in school. In reality she is really good at math and doesn't need to listen to the teacher's explanations in order to complete all of the problems. Eventually Maxine and Toni do become friends and decide to work on an invention, but their problem now is that their teacher doesn't think the contest is as important as learning the "basics." Maxine, through her persistence, does convince Mr. Seligram to hold a classroom contest. But then Maxine and Toni become disillusioned when none of their invention ideas work. They brainstorm a list of problems that they have and attempt to generate a solution. Their only problem is that Maxine's brother, Wat, cannot relax during his heart tests, and he cannot take naps at school because he is scared and has bad dreams. Toni's grandmother has a similar problem. She has bad dreams and sometimes is worried about what is to become of Toni. In the middle of one night the idea comes to Toni: She and Maxine should design a pillow that smells sweet and has soft sounds (talking) in the pillow. Then, whenever Toni's grandmother or Wat would lay their head on the pillow, they would hear the comforting sounds of someone talking. Toni goes out to a pay telephone to call Maxine at home; Maxine gets up to answer the phone and then just stays up to make the pillow. The next day they test their pillow on Wat and then enter the pillow in the classroom contest. Their invention wins! Later the pillow is used to keep Wat from being restless during his heart check—and the family finds out that his murmur had not gotten worse. Even Grandmother sleeps better. She does not have the pillow, but she does have the certificate that says Toni and Maxine have won the contest for inventors. She has it framed and hung on the wall. Although all of Toni's problems are not solved—she still doesn't know what has happened to her mother—it does appear that Toni and Maxine are in for a long friendship.

Coping with Adversity

Toni's life with her grandmother in a poor section of town, her rebellious attitude, and her choice of friends have caused her to seem different from other girls and boys at her school. The other children seem to have more stable lives, have less turmoil in their homes, and they and their friends seldom get into trouble. Toni doesn't seem to fit in, and her classmates often tease her and make her life more difficult. Some of those situations are present in *Daphne's Book* by Mary Downing Hahn (Clarion, 1983). Daphne was the new girl in school, she had no friends, and she seemed different than the other boys and girls. Her classmates often called her "Daffy Duck" and laughed at her because her clothes were not like theirs. The problem is that Daphne's parents are dead and she is living with her paternal grandmother. Daphne's younger sister, Hope, is also living with them. However, Daphne's grandmother often acts strange and is getting worse and worse. She really cannot care for the girls. Through a school project, Jessica is forced to work with Daphne and soon they are friends. Daphne does her best to keep her problems from Jessica, but Jessica soon finds out what is going on and even though she has promised Daphne not to tell, she cannot keep from telling her mother. Jessica hopes that her mother will find some way to help Daphne. In Cynthia Voigt's *Homecoming* (Atheneum, 1981) and *Dicey's Song* (Atheneum, 1982), Dicey and her siblings are left alone and must make their way to their grandmother's home. *Homecoming* details the children's efforts to reach their grandmother and *Dicey's Song* continues their story once they arrive at their grandmother's. Dicey has many of the same problems as Daphne and Toni. The books by Hahn and Getz will appeal to the intermediate reader while the books by Voigt will also challenge most intermediate readers.

38 Gorman, Carol
Die for Me

Gorman, Carol. *Die for Me*. Avon Flare, 1992. 138 pp. ISBN 0-380-76686-8 (paperback).
Listening Level: Intermediate (ages 9-10; grades 4-5)
Read-Alone Level: Intermediate Accelerated (ages 10-11; grades 5-6)

Holly had had the same group of friends since elementary school—Holly, Monica, Jessica, Carmen. There were some guys too: Tom, Kent, and others. But then Holly is killed, and her friends are very uneasy. It seems that whoever murdered Holly is among them, and they have been warned that there will be more murders. At a party Jessica uses a Ouija board to decode a frightening message. Monica receives a threatening note. Everyone is suspect and no one seems to know whom to trust and whom not to trust. For a while Kent is a prime suspect, but Jessica doesn't believe he could be a murderer. Carmen uncovers what she believes to be a blackmailing scheme by Holly. Maybe that is why she was killed. But who was she blackmailing? Then Carmen is found dead in a ravine. At first it is not clear if the death is murder or an accident. Carmen could have fallen from the bridge, but she could have been pushed too. Which was it? And then it was Monica. The blackmailing scheme isn't exactly what it seemed at first. Somehow Tom figured out the code to get into the school's computers; because Holly had worked in the school office, she often had access to them. Once Holly had been brought in on the scheme, she made it a business to change grades for a fee or to retaliate by lowering the grades of those who irked her. Did the grades have something to do with the deaths? One evening Jessica's parents go out for their anniversary and Jessica becomes frightened at home. She decides to go into hiding at her parents' remote cabin at Turtle Lake. The only problem is the murderer follows her to the cabin and confronts her. But Kent has also followed Jessica to the cabin and manages to restrain the murderer, Talley Johnson, and deliver her to the authorities. The murders had nothing to do with the changed grades. It turns out that Talley, who had moved to town during their high school years, had been in town once before, as the ugly, chubby second-grader, Susan Johnson. Nine years had passed and Talley/Susan had moved back to town, intent on punishing those who had taunted and teased her, making her life miserable. Jessica did not deserve to die, but she was too smart and had figured out too much of the scheme to live.

More Books by Carol Gorman

Chelsey and the Green-Haired Kid (Houghton, 1987; Archway, 1987) by Carol Gorman pairs up two unlikely friends: Chelsey, a spunky girl in a wheelchair, and Jack the green-haired kid. Together they seek to convince the police that the accident that they both witnessed was not an accident at all—and to do that they must uncover the murder. Older intermediate students and middle school readers will enjoy another very scary tale that takes place in *Graveyard Moon* (Avon, 1993). The darkness of the graveyard makes it clear that none but the dead are safe, especially when the moon beams a lighted path through the darkness.

---

39 Gormley, Beatrice
Ellie's Birthstone Ring

Gormley, Beatrice. *Ellie's Birthstone Ring*. Illustrated by Karen Ritz. Dutton, 1992. 101 pp. ISBN 0-525-44969-8.
Listening Level: Early Primary (ages 5-6; grades K-1)
Read-Alone Level: Primary (ages 6-7; grades 1-2)

Ellie is almost seven and looking forward to her birthday in two weeks. On Saturday she is allowed to walk to the variety store with her fourth-grade friend, Ruth. While Ellie is at the store she finds a birthstone ring priced at $3.15. Instead of buying candy she decides to save her money to buy the ring. Even though Ruth is not her own age, Ellie decides to invite her to her birthday party. Later she begins to feel sorry that she has asked Ruth. Whenever Ellie sees Ruth at school or whenever Ruth is with her friend, Christine, Ruth acts like Ellie is a baby. When Christine makes fun of the birthstone ring Ellie has bought, Ruth does not say anything to make Ellie feel better. Why does Ruth act so differently when Christine is around? Is Ruth trying to make fun of her too? Finally, Ellie's birthday arrives and so do the three six-year-old friends that Ellie has invited for the sleep-over. Then the doorbell rings and it is Ruth—her present for Ellie is something that "goes on your wrist, and it has a guess-what-color jewel for guess-what-month." Ruth doesn't plan on staying overnight, but it is clear that Ellie and Ruth will have a friendship—but it may not be the same kind of friendship that Ellie has with her second-grade friends, Caroline, Bonnie, and Nina. Now those three were the Pioneer girls, and they would have a lot of fun playing Pioneers and Fairies after the movie—after Ruth had gone home.

Friends and Friendship

Among the most famous friends in books for early primary readers are Frog and Toad in the series written by Arnold Lobel and the hippopotamus friends, George and Martha, in the series written by James Marshall. But human friends can be found in Elizabeth Winthrop's Best Friends Club books. Lizzie and Harold are best friends and appear in a number of books, including *Best Friends Club: A Lizzie and Harold Story* (Lothrop, 1989). Two best friends, Mimi and Mandy, call themselves M & M. Stories about M & M are written by Pat Ross and include *M & M and the Super Child Afternoon* (Viking, 1987) and *M & M and the Halloween Monster* (Viking, 1991). James Howe has written about Pinky and Rex in several short chapter books, including *Pinky and Rex and the Spelling Bee* (Atheneum, 1991) and *Pinky and Rex Go to Camp* (Atheneum, 1992). Steven Kellogg's *Best Friends* (Dial, 1986) is one title about two friends who find their friendship becomes more difficult when something they both want is involved. Intermediate readers will enjoy the tales about Angel and her friends in a series of books by Judy Delton: *Angel in Charge* (Dell, 1990), *Angel's Mother's Wedding* (Dell, 1987), and others; as well as the stories about Hobie Hanson and his friends by Jamie Gilson. Gilson's titles include *Hobie Hanson, Greatest Hero of the Mall* (Lothrop, 1989) and *Double Dog Dare* (Lothrop, 1988).

---

40 Greenwald, Sheila
Here's Hermione: A Rosy Cole Production

Greenwald, Sheila. *Here's Hermione: A Rosy Cole Production.* Joy Street/Little, Brown, 1991. 94 pp. ISBN 0-316-32715-8.
Listening Level: Primary (ages 6-7; grades 1-2)
Read-Alone Level: Primary Accelerated (ages 7-8; grades 2-3)

From the time she saw Pomona, the biggest rock star of the times, Hermione knew she wanted to be famous—famous like Pomona. And to be famous, Hermione had to have a gimmick, something memorable. Hermione just knew that her life would change once she became famous. With her music recital just a few days away, Hermione is determined to find a way to get the attention she needs. Rosy Cole offers to be her manager. Hermione's first attempt at achieving fame has her forming a band with two of her friends; dressed as the famous composer Bach, the three friends become "Hermione Wong and the Bach Rockers." Their publicity manager will add the tag line "A Rosy Cole Production." Their first gig results in a disaster—and the disbanding of the band. Next Hermione cooks up a plan to use the upcoming music recital to kick off her journey to fame. Not wanting to jinx her plan, Hermione does not let Rosy in on it. This plan, too, ends in disaster, but not everything is lost—the famous cello player, Joseph Pitkin, is to pay a visit at Rosy's house. Hermione finds the road to fame is right in front of her and has been there all the time.

More Rosy Cole

Sheila Greenwald has written several spoofs on fads and fashions and adolescent and preadolescent behavior in her books featuring Rosy Cole and her friends. Primary-aged readers will be able to read *Rosy Cole's Great American Guilt Club* (Atlantic, 1985) and *Here's Hermione: A Rosy Cole Production*, while intermediate readers will be able to read *Rosy's Romance* (Joy Street/Little, Brown, 1989); *Write On, Rosy!* (Joy Street/Little, Brown, 1988); *Give Us a Great Big Smile, Rosy Cole* (Little, Brown, 1981); *Valentine Rosy* (Little, Brown, 1984); and *Rosy Cole Discovers America* (Joy Street/Little, Brown, 1992). Each of the books features the humorous, havoc-raising heroine, Rosy Cole.

---

41 Greer, Gery, and Bob Ruddick
Jason and the Aliens Down the Street

Greer, Gery, and Bob Ruddick. *Jason and the Aliens Down the Street.* Illustrated by Blanche L. Sims. HarperCollins, 1991. 94 pp. ISBN 0-06-021761-8.
Listening Level: Primary Accelerated (ages 7-8; grades 2-3)
Read-Alone Level: Early Intermediate (ages 8-9; grades 3-4)

When Jason follows the dog he is training into the yard of his neighbor, he doesn't expect to encounter an alien from space, but that is exactly what happens. Before Jason knows it, he is being invited on a secret mission with Cooper "Coop" Vor and his pet, Lootna, Coop's talking cat. Coop is an Intergalactic Troubleshooter and needs an assistant. In just minutes Jason finds himself in Coop's spaceship, flying off into space to recapture a stolen energy crystal from Grugg the Awful and return it to its rightful owner, the

Star King of Zarr. When the three travelers—Coop, Jason, and Lootna—arrive on the planet Urkar, they find that Grugg the Awful has surrounded his home with many guards. The crystal rests in a box upon which Grugg the Awful rests his feet. In an effort to steal back the crystal, the three make themselves invisible with a special battery-operated belt. All goes well until the batteries run out on Coop's pack and he slowly becomes visible. Through an ingenious idea of Jason's, Coop is able to convince the guards and Grugg that he is a magician who will turn Grugg's nose green with purple warts unless he is let go. But before they can all leave, Jason's and Lootna's invisibility begins to give out too. If they are caught they are sure to be thrown into the slime pit.

Aliens

Those readers who enjoy the first story about Jason and the aliens are sure to enjoy the further adventures of the Intergalactic Troubleshooting Team as told in *Jason and the Lizard Pirates* (HarperCollins, 1992). Early intermediate students who read slightly below the level of these books may enjoy reading about aliens and outer space in *Aliens for Breakfast* (Random, 1989) or *Aliens for Lunch* (Random, 1991) by Jonathan Etra and Stephanie Spinner. In *Aliens for Breakfast*, Richard Bickerstaff is eating Alien Crisp cereal when a pink creature climbs up the side of his bowl. This title and the sequel, *Aliens for Lunch*, are wacky, offbeat offerings just right for students needing transitional reading material. Each is approximately 64 pages long.

More mature intermediate readers will enjoy *Aliens in the Family* by Margaret Mahy (Scholastic, 1986). In this adventure fantasy an alien boy named Bond becomes the "bond" between stepsiblings who are having difficulty adjusting to one another. Fans of stories that mix a contemporary setting with science fiction will enjoy this 192-page novel.

---

42 Hahn, Mary Downing
The Dead Man in Indian Creek

Hahn, Mary Downing. *The Dead Man in Indian Creek.* Clarion, 1990. 130 pp. ISBN 0-395-52397-4.
Listening Level: Intermediate (ages 9-10; grades 4-5)
Read-Alone Level: Intermediate Accelerated (ages 10-11; grades 5-6)

George Evans was dating Parker Pettengill's mother. Parker did not particularly care for him and neither did Parker's German shepherd, Otis. Parker's best friend, Matthew Armentrout, tries to stay neutral, but Evans did seem to show up in strange places. When the two friends decide to camp overnight by Indian Creek, they do not expect to find a dead man's body—and they do not expect to see Evans nearby. From the moment they report the death to the police the two boys have a funny feeling about Evans and his presence on the bridge. But for their suspicions to be believed by the police they must uncover more evidence. Bit by bit they begin to piece together new information—information that leads to the murderers. But the trouble for them begins when they explore Evans's Olde Mill Antique Shoppe and stumble on the scary secret of the antique dolls.

Illegal Goods and Smuggling

Matt and Parker find themselves in a lot of trouble when they uncover a plot to smuggle drugs to dealers. Other books that deal with illegal smuggling include *Three Stuffed Owls* by Keith Robertson (Viking, 1954); *River Rats, Inc.* by Jean Craighead George (Dutton, 1979); and *A Watery Grave* by Barbara Corcoran (Atheneum, 1982). However, one of the most exciting books about smuggling goods is *Snow Treasure* by Marie McSwigan (Scholastic, 1958). *Snow Treasure* is a tale based on the heroic efforts of Norwegian children to smuggle nine million dollars in gold past the Nazi sentries during World War II. The gold was stashed in a cave near a bay where a waiting ship hid from the soldiers. The children's task was to take the gold bricks, brick by brick, on their sleds or on their backs past the enemy soldiers. Their movements had to seem effortless even though they were carrying a heavy weight lest the soldiers suspect what they were doing. *Snow Treasure* is a tale of courage, wit, and grim determination.

43 Hall, Lynn
Here Comes Zelda Claus and Other Holiday Disasters

Hall, Lynn. *Here Comes Zelda Claus and Other Holiday Disasters.*
Harcourt, 1989. 149 pp. ISBN 0-15-233790-3.
Listening Level: Early Intermediate (ages 8-9; grades 3-4)
Read-Alone Level: Intermediate (ages 9-10; grades 4-5)

Zelda Marie Hammersmith finds herself in trouble often, and in these vignettes her trouble begins on Halloween when she makes her arrival by flying through the air, in a bat costume, and manages to tear the light fixture from the ceiling. The next four chapters tell of the turmoil Zelda causes during a Thanksgiving family gathering when she gives her namesake and great-grandmother, Zee, a ride on a sleigh pulled by a cow; her outrageous efforts to obtain the $69.95 needed to buy her mother a fancy nightgown for Christmas; her plans to surprise her teacher, Mrs. Green—and the turmoil caused by a rebellious cupid; and finally death (on Good Friday), the funeral, and resurrection of her beloved guinea pig, Mr. Batman.

More Zelda and Other Unique Individuals

Zelda Hammersmith manages to get herself into many other situations that cause concern for others. She appears in Hall's books *In Trouble Again, Zelda Hammersmith?* (Harcourt, 1987) and *Zelda Strikes Again!* (Harcourt, 1988). Those students who enjoy reading about Zelda will also enjoy reading about Angel in the books by Judy Delton and Anastasia in the books by Lois Lowry. Angel is an ingenious individual who manages to rollick her way through episode after episode. In *Angel's Mother's Baby* (Houghton, 1989), the fifth book in Delton's series, Angel finds out that her mother is pregnant. Anastasia is a very determined and energetic girl who manages to create a number of schemes that end up creating havoc. In the ninth book in Lois Lowry's Anastasia series, *Anastasia at This Address* (Houghton, 1991), 13-year-old Anastasia answers an ad in the personals column of her father's magazine—and later she discovers her SWM (single white male) pen pal at the wedding of a friend. Delton's Angel series will appeal to the same readers who find Zelda interesting reading. A slightly more able reader will find humor in Lowry's Anastasia books.

---

44 Hamilton, Virginia
Cousins

Hamilton, Virginia. *Cousins*. Philomel, 1990. 125 pp. ISBN 0-399-22164-6.
Listening Level: Intermediate (ages 9-10; grades 4-5)
Read-Alone Level: Intermediate Accelerated (ages 10-11; grades 5-6)

Cammy sometimes wishes that her too smart, too pretty, too spoiled cousin, Patty Ann, would evaporate like people sometimes do in science fiction stories. Everyone in town loves Patty Ann—even Cammy most of the time. But the day that Cammy got her wish—that was the day Elodie (L.O.D.) almost drowned and Patty Ann saved her, but Patty Ann could not save herself. Ms. Devine was the only adult around that day and the whole town blamed her. She moved away. A lot of the townspeople thought that Patty Ann's spirit was inside L.O.D.'s body. Cammy sometimes thought so too. Sometimes Cammy thought Patty Ann sat on the side of her bed. Then there was Grandmother Tut—she was in a care center and Cammy was full of love for her. Sometimes Cammy did not understand what was happening. At last, though, Grandmother Tut shows her how to understand.

Who's to Blame?

Cammy had a difficult time coming to grips with the death of her cousin. Even though she could have done nothing to prevent the tragedy, she blamed herself for being there because the girls should have never gone near the swollen Little River. A similar sense of guilt plagues Joel in Marion Dane Bauer's Newbery honor title, *On My Honor* (Clarion, 1986). Joel feels that his friend, Tony, drowned because they violated their parents' trust and went into the treacherous Vermillion River. Joel does not realize, until it is too late, that his friend cannot swim. For slightly younger readers, books that share similar emotions include Katherine Paterson's *Bridge to Terabithia* (Crowell, 1977) and Patricia Hermes's *Nobody's Fault* (Harcourt, 1981). In each of these stories a loved one dies as the result of an accident and one of those left behind is filled with guilt for the death.

45 Hamm, Diane Johnston
Second Family

Hamm, Diane Johnston. *Second Family*. Scribner's, 1992. 118 pp.
ISBN 0-684-19436-8.
Listening Level: Intermediate (ages 9-10; grades 4-5)
Read-Alone Level: Intermediate Accelerated (ages 10-11; grades 5-6)

Mr. Torkelson ("Mr. T") has been alone since his wife died. Now a mother and her 12-year-old son are scheduled to arrive to live with him. Rodney will attend the grade school across the street and his mother will attend the university. The home-sharing agency will help them negotiate the division of household tasks, etc., but none of them could foresee the challenges facing Mr. T, Catherine (Rodney's mother), and Rodney. Rodney is a typical 12-year-old with attitudes and behaviors that show the effects of his parents' divorce, his move from California to Washington State, and the changes his mother has made to take her away from the rejection she has felt. First, Rodney shoplifts in an effort to convince his mother that he should not be in Washington. All of his energy seems focused on getting back to California, but his dad doesn't seem to want him. Rodney's attitude is less than amicable toward his classmates and his school situation, and the other students do not go out of their way to include him or make friends with him. In fact, there are several instances where Rodney is the object of their teasing and insults. The final incident occurs when one of the boys calls Rodney's mother a name and says that she is trying to be a man. Rodney punches the boy and gets a suspension warning. Mr. T is able to discuss the situation with Rodney, but he is of little real comfort to Rodney—only his mother can do that. Finally, at the end of the book, Mr. T and Rodney and his mother feel like they are a family, but Catherine has decided to quit school and return to California, much to Rodney's delight. Their only regret is that now they will be leaving Mr. T behind. But their presence has made him more aware of things he could be doing to keep from being lonely. And perhaps his friendship with Mrs. Lacy will grow. But before Rodney leaves with his mother he wants to learn how to make Mr. T's peanut butter cookies—and that's just what they do on their last Saturday together.

Families Together

Another title that has a similar theme is Kristi Holl's *No Strings Attached* (Atheneum, 1988). The title is a sequel to *Just Like a Real Family* (Atheneum, 1983). In *Just Like a Real Family*, June's class decides to visit a nursing home where each student will adopt a "grandmother" or "grandfather." June is paired with grouchy old Mr. Cooper. Throughout the story, June and Mr. Cooper share a relationship that goes from adversarial to uneasy to uncomfortable. At the end of the story it seems that June and Mr. Cooper are actually friends, but it isn't until the beginning of *No Strings Attached* that June and Mr. Cooper begin to become a real family. It seems that Mr. Cooper has a home but is not able to stay in it alone. June and her mother are being threatened with eviction and will soon have no place to stay. A solution to both of their problems is for June and her mother to move into Mr. Cooper's home and share it with him; he would then be allowed to go home to his own house. Other types of adjustments must be made in titles that focus on a grandmother or grandfather sharing a home with a younger family. One of those titles, *War with Grandpa* by Robert Kimmel Smith (Delacorte, 1984), focuses on Peter's feelings when his grandfather comes to live with Peter's family. Peter adores his grandfather but resents having to give up his own bedroom. At the urging of his friends, Peter declares "war" on his grandfather. Grandfather does not prove to be easy prey. After several hilarious episodes an amicable surrender is brought about. The story is one of love and human dignity.

46 Helfman, Elizabeth
On Being Sarah

Helfman, Elizabeth. *On Being Sarah.* Illustrated by Lino Saffioti. Whitman, 1993. 173 pp. ISBN 0-8075-6068-5.
Listening Level: Intermediate (ages 9-10; grades 4-5)
Read-Alone Level: Intermediate Accelerated (ages 10-11; grades 5-6)

Sarah is confined to a wheelchair, the result of cerebral palsy. She cannot walk or talk, but she can think and enjoy jokes, people, and life in general. Sarah's story is told from her vantage point as she details her changing relationship with her family—Amy, her sister who is two years older; her mother, who dotes on Sarah and her special needs; and her father, who seems distant but has always given Sarah the things she has needed most. Sarah's father is the one who figures out a way to get a van so that it would be easier for Sarah to go places with her family. The electric wheelchair is his idea and so is the surprise she receives at the end of the story. Her sister, Amy, is supportive but has her own feelings of being left out. Sarah's mother shows her own love in many ways and tries hard not to do too much for Sarah. Throughout the story Sarah's use of the Blissymbols to communicate is an important element. As this book is read aloud, those reading will want to duplicate the Blissymbols on a chart or overhead transparency so that listeners can see the symbols referred to in the story. The story focuses on Sarah's first year in a classroom in a regular junior high school, her growing-up years, and her budding friendship with Johnny, who also has cerebral palsy. In addition to being a gentle story of growing up, the story will do much to help those without physical challenges in their life appreciate, understand, and accept those who are challenged on a daily basis.

Physical Challenges of Cerebral Palsy

Elizabeth Helfman introduced teachers to Charles Bliss's system of using symbols as an international means to communication when she wrote *Signs and Symbols Around the World* (Lothrop, 1967). Since then many people with difficulty communicating orally have found a means of communication by using a Bliss board. Sarah was unable to speak because of her cerebral palsy, but many others are able to speak but still face challenges due to their unique situation. *Golden Daffodils* by Marilyn Gould (Harper, 1982) is a story about Janis and her first year in regular school. Janis has difficulty walking, speaking, and writing, but that does not stop her from doing her best and showing that she has abilities similar to others. Her friendship with Barney helps her through that first difficult year. In the sequel to *Golden Daffodils*, *The Twelfth of June* (Harper, 1986), Janis and Barney continue their friendship and develop a relationship outside of school.

---

47 Hildick, E. W.
The Case of the Weeping Witch

Hildick, E. W. *The Case of the Weeping Witch*. Macmillan, 1992. 160 pp. ISBN 0-02-743785-X.
Listening Level: Intermediate (ages 9-10; grades 4-5)
Read-Alone Level: Intermediate Accelerated (ages 10-11; grades 5-6)

Jack P. McGurk and his friends are investigators. McGurk and the members of his organization—Joey "Recorder-of-the-Truth" Rockaway, Willie "Sniffer" Sandowsky, Brains "Measurer" Bellingham, Wanda "Climber" Grieg, and Mari "Speaker" Yoshimura—often met to discuss the goings-on in their community. But one particular afternoon the investigators were preoccupied with some of the information that had come up about their town during a discussion at school about life in their community 300 years ago. People had been accused of witchcraft right in their town. The members of the McGurk organization begin to chart the features they possess that might have marked them as witches in 1692. They then happen onto a set of six walkie-talkies that help them transport themselves through time. Their first trip was recorded in *The Case of the Dragon in Distress* (Macmillan, 1991), and now they are traveling again—this time instead of traveling eight centuries back in time, they will only be traveling 300 years. They had learned that a citizen of their town, Hester Bidgood, age 13 and an "investigatrix," had been accused 300 years ago of being a witch. Somewhat mysteriously, McGurk and his gang travel back in time and find themselves in the midst of Hester's trouble. They assist a friend of Hester's in releasing her during the drowning test for witches and help to expose Master Peabody, who is a professional witch-hunter. Peabody conspires with others in the community to find and punish witches. With the help of the McGurk organization and their walkie-talkies from the twentieth century, Hester is saved and Master Peabody and his cohorts are banished from the community; in fact, they are escorted to Boston and sent back to England that very day. And just as mysteriously as the detectives had found themselves in the seventeenth century, they now find themselves back in their own twentieth-century beds and back in school the next day. It is during a classroom discussion that the gang learns that Hester had later married Robert MacGregor, and when she had inherited a large tract of land from her benefactor (whom they had met during their time travels), Hester had donated it to the community to build a home for senior women. That home, the Hester MacGregor Residential Homes for Seniors, is now a group of bungalows and still stands in the community.

McGurk Mysteries

Brisk detective stories featuring McGurk and the members of his organization have the gang solving mysteries that stretch their investigative powers. *The Case of the Wandering Weathervanes* (Macmillan, 1988) has these middle school investigators using sound deductive reasoning to solve the disappearance of several weather vanes. *The Case of the Purloined Parrot* (Macmillan, 1990) involves cat rustlers who have been kidnapping pets—and, of course, McGurk and the others in his organization manage to solve the case. *The Case of the Muttering Mummy* (Macmillan, 1986) has the McGurk organization investigating a mystery in a local museum. The group of successful detectives eventually come to possess some used walkie-talkies that they believe are capable of sending them through time. Their first mystery fantasy case is *The Case of the Dragon in Distress* (Macmillan, 1991). Malfunctioning walkie-talkies take the McGurk detectives back to the Middle Ages, where they manage to find themselves at the mercy of an evil princess. When they are sent to the dungeon they find Prince Geoffrey and other nobles who have been enslaved without the king's knowledge. The McGurk organization members manage to use their wits to save their friends and their own heads. Other mystery series that will appeal to the intermediate reader include the Green Street Mysteries by Dana Brenford (Crestwood House); the Sabastian Barth Mysteries by James Howe (Atheneum); the Fourth Floor Twins series by David A. Adler (Viking); and the mysteries featuring private eye P. J. Clover by Susan Meyers (Lodestar/Dutton). A slightly younger group of readers will enjoy the Encyclopedia Brown series by Donald J. Sobol (Bantam or Scholastic) and the Cam Jansen series by David A. Adler (Viking).

48 Hooks, William H.
The Ballad of Belle Dorcus

Hooks, William H. *The Ballad of Belle Dorcus.* Illustrated by Brian Pinkney. Knopf, 1990. unp. ISBN 0-394-84645-1.
Listening Level: Primary Accelerated (ages 7-8; grades 2-3)
Read-Alone Level: Early Intermediate (ages 8-9; grades 3-4)

Pinkney's crosshatch illustrations illuminate this tale of a free issue black woman, Belle Dorcus, who falls in love with Joshua, a slave. When Joshua's master (and Belle's white father) is killed in an accident, the master's son sells off some of the plantation and eventually begins to sell the slaves. When the new master announces that he intends to sell Joshua, Belle seeks the help of a conjure woman. Belle must agree to give up Joshua in order to keep him. At first Joshua is transformed into a tree on the plantation, but at night his human form is restored and he and Belle spend many hours together. Eventually the master commands that a new smokehouse be built, and by coincidence the slaves choose the Joshua tree to fell for the lumber. From the beginning the smokehouse seems to howl whenever slaves enter it for the stores held inside. The master orders the smokehouse moved out into the woods, and it is then that after months of despair Belle discovers how she can again visit with her Joshua. In an eerily poignant tale that combines the devastating effects of slavery and supernatural elements, this tale demonstrates the pain of being black during the slave days.

To Be a Slave

The Ballad of Belle Dorcus is just one of many stories told about slavery. Stories by Julius Lester are excellent choices for sharing with intermediate and older students. *This Strange New Feeling* (Dial, 1982) by Julius Lester recounts the stories of three couples who experienced both slavery and the desire to escape. The first two stories are vignettes—one tells of Ras, who escapes, is recaptured, and attempts to escape once again; and the other tells of the slave, Maria, wife of the free black, Forrest. When Forrest is accidentally killed, his wife is sold to pay his debts. The final story is of William and Ellen Craft's flight to the North and freedom. Ellen poses as a "white gentleman" traveling with "his" personal slave (William). They do reach the North and freedom but eventually the Crafts must flee again—this time from slave hunters who come North. These are compelling stories set in one of America's most complex times. The story of the escape of William and Ellen Craft is also told in Florence B. Freedman's *Two Tickets to Freedom: The True Story of Ellen and William Craft, Fugitive Slaves*, illustrated by Ezra Jack Keats (Simon & Schuster, 1971; Bedrick, 1990). Another story collection compiled by Lester, *Long Journey Home: Stories from Black History* (Dial, 1972), includes six more stories of the black experience. The stories are loosely based on historical fact. In *To Be a Slave*, illustrated by Tom Feelings (Dial, 1968), Lester tells stories in the words of slaves. Virginia Hamilton retells several shorter stories about how slaves gained their freedom in the chapter "Carrying the Running-Aways: And Other Slave Tales of Freedom" in *The People Could Fly: American Black Folktales*, illustrated by Leo Dillon and Diane Dillon (Knopf, 1985), and in a companion title by Hamilton, *Many Thousands Gone: African Americans from Slavery to Freedom*, illustrated by Leo Dillon and Diane Dillon (Knopf, 1993).

49 Hooks, William H.
Moss Gown.

Hooks, William H. *Moss Gown.* Illustrated by Donald Carrick. Clarion, 1987. 48 pp. ISBN 0-89919-460-5.
Listening Level: Primary Accelerated (ages 7-8; grades 2-3)
Read-Alone Level: Early Intermediate (ages 8-9; grades 3-4)

In the heart of the swamp country in the South, an old man has three daughters. Each professes her love for him, but when Candace expresses her love by saying, "Father, I love you more than meat loves salt," she is chastised and sent away. Believing that his other two daughters, Grenadine and Retha, love him most, the old man gives them all of his land. They then order Candace off their land. Eventually Candace ends up in the household of a young master. When the master gives three festive balls, all who have a ball gown are invited to attend. Candace (now known as Moss Gown) does not have a gown except for the one given to her by the gris-gris woman—a tall, slender black woman, with catlike green eyes. It turns out that this gown is magic and surprises everyone by showing off Candace's beauty and helping her capture the fancy of the young master. As in the more familiar versions of the "Cinderella" tales, the enchanted golden gown fades as the Morning Star fades. The young master, depressed because he cannot find the woman from the ball, refuses to eat for days. Only when Moss Gown shows up with a plate of food does he agree to eat. At first he thinks he is dreaming, but during the evening they talk for hours. When the Morning Star fades, Moss Gown's beautiful gown once again turns into rags and moss, but this time she does not flee and he realizes that she is indeed the woman of his dreams. They marry and her father, who has been put out by her greedy sisters, comes to her and her new husband's home and is welcomed. Together the three of them live happily ever after.

Cinderella Tales

Almost every culture has its own version of the Cinderella tale. *Moss Gown* is one version based on stories told orally in the tidewater section of eastern North Carolina. Appalachian storytellers from western North Carolina tell a version of the story called *Rush Cape.* Because Spanish moss did not grow in the Appalachian Mountains, the heroine of the story is given a cape of rushes. The following list of Cinderella versions—including parodies—are appropriate as read-alouds for all age groups.

Cinderella Tales and Poems

Climo, Shirley. *The Egyptian Cinderella.* Illustrated by Ruth Heller. Crowell, 1989. (picture book)

Cole, Babette. *Prince Cinders.* Putnam, 1988. (picture book)

Ehrlich, Amy. *Cinderella.* Illustrated by Susan Jeffers. Dial, 1985. (picture book)

Grimm, Jacob, and Wilhelm Grimm. *Cinderella.* Illustrated by Nonny Hogrogrian. Greenwillow, 1981. (picture book)

Huck, Charlotte. *Princess Furball.* Illustrated by Anita Lobel. Greenwillow, 1989. (picture book)

Livingston, Myra Cohn. "Look Cinderella." In *A Song I Sang to You.* Harcourt, 1984. (poem)

Louie, Ai-Ling. *Yeh-Shen: A Cinderella Story from China.* Illustrated by Ed Young. Philomel, 1982. (picture book)

Murphy, Shirley Rousseau. *Silver Woven in My Hair.* Illustrated by Alan Tiegreen. Atheneum, 1977. (novel)

Myers, Bernice. *Sidney Rello and the Glass Sneaker.* Macmillan, 1985. (picture book)

Perrault, Charles. *Cinderella.* Illustrated by Marcia Brown. Scribner's, 1954. (picture book)

———. *Cinderella.* Illustrated by Paul Galdone. McGraw, 1978. (picture book)

Silverstein, Shel. "In Search of Cinderella." In *The Light in the Attic.* Harper, 1981. (poem)

Steptoe, John. *Mufaro's Beautiful Daughters: An African Tale.* Illustrated by John Steptoe. Lothrop, 1987. (picture book)

Vasilisa the Beautiful. Translated by Thomas P. Whitney. Illustrated by Nonny Hogrogrian. Macmillan, 1970. (picture book)

Viorst, Judith. "... And Then the Prince Knelt Down and Tried to Put the Glass Slipper on Cinderella's Foot." In *If I Were in Charge of the World and Other Worries.* Atheneum, 1981. (poem)

Vuong, Lynnette Dyer. *The Brocaded Slipper and Other Vietnamese Tales.* Illustrated by Vo-Dinh Mai. Addison, 1982. (picture book)

50 Howard, Ellen
The Cellar

Howard, Ellen. *The Cellar.* Illustrated by Patricia Mulvihill. Karl/Atheneum, 1992. 52 pp. ISBN 0-689-31724-7.
Listening Level: Early Primary (ages 5-6; grades K-1)
Read-Alone Level: Primary (ages 6-7; grades 1-2)

Faith is the youngest child in the family. Her two brothers do many adventurous things like sliding down the cellar door and walking barefooted in the pasture to bring the cows up to be milked. Faith tries to slide down the cellar door, but she gets scared and ends up landing on the ground with a bruised leg, torn pants, and hurt feelings. When she tags along with her brothers to get the cows, she is teased because "Baby Faith is wearing shoes." When she takes them off she finds that her feet are too tender to let her keep up with her brothers. In the final episode, Faith volunteers to go to the cellar to get the ripe red apples for the family's evening treat. She feels very brave until her brother "accidentally" slams the cellar door shut, putting out the lamp she is holding and forcing her into darkness. She shows him and her family that she is brave and emerges from the blackness full of triumph. It is her brother who must apologize and who finds that his own behavior is somewhat immature. Faith's experience happened many years ago, but it is very similar to fears experienced by young people today.

Fears • Fears • Fears

Older primary readers or early intermediate readers will enjoy reading *Skinnybones* by Barbara Park (Knopf, 1982). This is the story of a boy who fears playing baseball against a team that has the new kid as one of its members. T. J. Stoner is a great baseball player, and the pitching duel he proposes to Alex has Alex trying to figure out any way to get out of the contest gracefully. In the picture book *Spiders in the Fruit Cellar* by Barbara M. Joosse and illustrated by Kay Chorao (Knopf, 1983), Elisabeth is also frightened of what she would find in the cellar. Beatrice Schenk de Regniers includes a fun-to-read-aloud poem, "I'm Scared," in her book *The Way I Feel ... Sometimes* (Clarion, 1988).

---

51 Howe, James
Return to Howliday Inn

Howe, James. *Return to Howliday Inn*. Illustrated by Alan Daniel. Atheneum, 1992. 156 pp. ISBN 0-689-31661-5.
Listening Level: Early Intermediate (ages 8-9; grades 3-4)
Read-Alone Level: Intermediate (ages 9-10; grades 4-5)

The Monroe family is leaving for another vacation and Chester, Harold, and Howie are returning to Chateau Bow-Wow, the boarding kennel dubbed by Chester as "Howliday Inn." During this visit to Howliday Inn, the animal friends are greeted by a new group of temporary residents. Hamlet, a Great Dane, is despondent as he believes his master, Archie, does not intend to return for him. The yuppie puppies, Bob and Linda, seem to have an ample supply of gourmet treats but also plenty of worries to occupy their thoughts. But the troublemakers seem to be Felony and Miss Demeanor, who fancy themselves as real *cat* burglars. And then there is The Weasel, who tries much too hard to make an impression. When Hamlet's life is threatened, Chester, Harold, and Howie organize a breakout. The spooky goings-on are sure to spook even the most stable reader.

Chateau Bow-Wow

Bunnicula, the vampire rabbit; Chester, a self-assured cat; Howie, a dachshund with a most unusual howl; and Harold, a shaggy, reluctant, part Russian Wolfhound, are featured in several books by James Howe. *Bunnicula: A Rabbit Tale of Mystery*

(Atheneum, 1979) is a talking animal story featuring Harold and his fellow pet, Chester. Three sequels followed: *Howliday Inn* (Atheneum, 1982); *The Celery Stalks at Midnight* (Atheneum, 1983); and *Return to Howliday Inn*. *The Celery Stalks at Midnight* discusses the possibility that vegetables throughout the neighborhood may have been "vampirized" by Bunnicula, a rabbit who acts mysteriously. Easier-to-read titles by James Howe, which also feature Bunnicula and his buddies, include *Hot Fudge* (Morrow, 1990); *The Fright Before Christmas* (Morrow, 1988); *Scared Silly: A Halloween Treat* (Morrow, 1989); and *Creepy-Crawly Birthday* (Morrow, 1991).

52 Hoyt-Goldsmith, Diane
Hoang Anh: A Vietnamese-American Boy

Hoyt-Goldsmith, Diane. *Hoang Anh: A Vietnamese-American Boy.* Photographs by Lawrence Migdale. Holiday House, 1992. 32 pp. ISBN 0-8234-0948-1.
Listening Level: Early Intermediate (ages 8-9; grades 3-4)
Read-Alone Level: Intermediate (ages 9-10; grades 4-5)

Hoang Anh Chau tells of his Vietnamese family's life in San Rafael, California. Hoang Anh's parents managed to escape from Vietnam with their four young children. They and 24 other refugees fled on Hoang Anh's father's fishing boat. After two days and two nights the family reached Malaysia safely. They were sent to a crowded refugee camp. Hoang Anh was born in that camp, and then a few months later a church in Oregon sponsored the family and they all emigrated to the United States. Now the family lives in San Rafael, where Hoang Anh's father fishes for a living. Much of the food the family eats at home is similar to the food they would have eaten in Vietnam. Hoang Anh's favorite American food is pizza. Hoyt-Goldsmith uses Hoang Anh's own words to describe his family's life in America and then concludes with Hoang Anh's description of activities during the three-day New Year (Tet) celebration.

Expanding Cultural Views

Intermediate readers will enjoy Jamie Gilson's novel *Hello, My Name Is Scrambled Eggs* (Lothrop, 1985). The book was written after Gilson was introduced to some Cambodian and Vietnamese refugees. One of the women Gilson met had just come to the United States after the fall of Saigon. On her first day in America she went to a baton-twirling contest and an ice-cream social. Gilson decided her experiences would become part of the story she would write. The story would also include Harvey and his hometown of Pittsfield. Gilson began to wonder how Harvey would deal with someone who did not know about hot dogs, Halloween, or snow. The result is the fictionalized story of Tuan Nguyen, who comes to America with his family when a church group sponsors them. Norma J. Livo and Dia Cha have collaborated to compile a collection of stories in *Folk Stories of the Hmong: Peoples of Laos, Thailand, and Vietnam* (Libraries Unlimited, 1991). This book contains a description of Hmong history, culture, and folklore, including 16 pages of full-color photographs of Hmong dress and needlework, along with 27 tales. The collection, designed for high school or adult readers, will provide select stories that will be appropriate as read-alouds in elementary classrooms.

53 Hurwitz, Johanna
Class President

Hurwitz, Johanna. *Class President*. Illustrated by Sheila Hamanaka. Morrow, 1990. 85 pp. ISBN 0-688-09114-8.
Listening Level: Early Intermediate (ages 8-9; grades 3-4)
Read-Alone Level: Intermediate (ages 9-10; grades 4-5)

Lucas and Julio have been friends since kindergarten. In fact, many of their friends will be in the same fifth-grade class. But the class probably won't be the same. Mrs. Upchurch had retired in June, and their new teacher was going to be Ernesto Flores. On the first day of school Mr. Flores tells the class about some of the things that the class will be doing during the school year. One of those activities will be to elect a class president. The election shapes up as a close contest between class clown, Lucas Cott, and onetime teacher's pet, Cricket Kaufman. Julio (now pronounced by Mr. Flores with an "h" sound as it is in Spanish) pledges to support Lucas, but soon finds that he has supporters of his own. During the beginning weeks of the school year, Julio had encouraged his classmates to hold a bake sale to pay for Arthur Lewis's broken glasses and persuaded the principal to reconsider his ban on soccer at recess. In addition, Julio had successfully suggested that a class vote decide how the money from the bake sale be spent once it was learned that Arthur's glasses would be replaced free of charge. In fact, it is Arthur who decides to nominate Julio. The vote is swayed to Julio's side when Lucas requests that his name be taken out of nomination and that those who had intended to vote for him consider voting for Julio instead. All the boys and several of the girls vote for Julio, who wins the election. Julio's family would be *very* proud that Julio had run for fifth-grade class president and won. He could hardly wait to get home to tell them!

School Stories

Lucas Cott first appeared in Hurwitz's book *Class Clown* (Morrow, 1987); Cricket Kaufman first appeared in Hurwitz's *Teacher's Pet* (Morrow, 1988). In *Class President*, they appear as rivals in the class election for president. Primary-aged readers will enjoy other stories that take place in the classroom. One of the more popular series of stories is Harry Allard's Miss Nelson series: *Miss Nelson Is Missing* (Houghton, 1977); *Miss Nelson Is Back* (Houghton, 1982); and *Miss Nelson Has a Field Day* (Houghton, 1985). James Marshall's illustrations add to the humor in Allard's stories. Those students who are ready to begin on chapter books will be interested in Patricia Reilly Giff's junior novels in the Kids of the Polk Street School series; the New Kids at the Polk Street School series; and the Polka Dot mysteries. All Polk Street School and Polka Dot mystery titles are published by Dell. These same readers will enjoy Giff's titles about Ronald Morgan, a very normal second-grader. Titles in that series include *Happy Birthday, Ronald Morgan!* (Viking, 1986) and *Ronald Morgan Goes to Bat* (Viking, 1988). Other easy-to-read school stories include *The Day the Teacher Went Bananas* by James Howe (Dutton, 1984); *See You in Second Grade!* by Miriam Cohen (Dell, 1989); *The Teacher from the Black Lagoon* by Marc Thaler (Scholastic, 1989); and *First Grade Jitters* by Robert Quackenbush (Lippincott, 1982). Books for intermediate readers include Jamie Gilson's *4B Goes Wild!* (Lothrop, 1983) and *Thirteen Ways to Sink a Sub* (Lothrop, 1982), as well as the humorous books by Louis Sachar: *Sideways Stories from Wayside School* (Knopf, 1978); *There's a Boy in the Girls' Bathroom* (Knopf, 1987); and *Wayside School Is Falling Down* (Lothrop, 1989).

54 Hurwitz, Johanna
"E" Is for Elisa

Hurwitz, Johanna. *"E" Is for Elisa.* Illustrated by Lillian Hoban.
Morrow, 1991. 85 pp. ISBN 0-688-10439-8.
Listening Level: Early Primary (ages 5-6; grades K-1)
Read-Alone Level: Primary (ages 6-7; grades 1-2)

Elisa is four years old, and even though she knows she is getting more
and more grown up, her older brother, eight-year-old Russell, teases her. Elisa
enjoys riding her tricycle in the park, but she'd rather be at Cub Scouts like
Russell. Russell is smart; Elisa wonders if she will ever be like him. Russell
lets Elisa know that he doubts if she'll ever grow up, so Elisa sets out to prove
that she *is* growing up. But her plan to show Russell is filled with disaster. In
the final chapter of the book Russell jumps off the table; so does Elisa. Russell
jumps from the top of his bed; so does Elisa. Then Russell climbs to the top
of his dresser and jumps. At first Elisa is scared but then she climbs up, and
before Russell can stop her she jumps too. They both land in a heap, but Elisa's
arm hurts all over. The rest of the afternoon is spent at the medical center. And
for the first time in her life Elisa has done something that Russell has
not—Elisa has broken her arm. After a discussion of the consequences of
jumping off furniture, Elisa's parents take a picture of her cast to send to her
grandparents. Elisa has been very brave that day.

More Russell and Elisa

Before Elisa got her own book she appeared in four titles
featuring her eight-year-old brother, Russell. Those titles, all by
Hurwitz, are *Rip-Roaring Russell* (Morrow, 1983); *Russell Rides
Again* (Morrow, 1985); *Russell Sprouts* (Morrow, 1987); and
Russell and Elisa (Morrow, 1989).

55 Hurwitz, Johanna
Hurray for Ali Baba Bernstein

Hurwitz, Johanna. *Hurray for Ali Baba Bernstein.* Illustrated by Gail Owens. Morrow, 1989. 104 pp. ISBN 0-688-08241-6.
Listening Level: Primary (ages 6-7; grades 1-2)
Read-Alone Level: Primary Accelerated (ages 7-8; grades 2-3)

In an earlier book, *The Adventures of Ali Baba Bernstein*, David Bernstein decided that he did not like his name, and after reading *The Arabian Nights*, he changed it to "Ali Baba." Six episodes in that book introduced readers to this zany and humorous character. Now six new stories are collected in this episodic sequel. Ali Baba finds a solution to his problem when he doesn't have his library card for his class trip to the public library, helps solve the case of Kelly's Deli, becomes king for a day, meets Santa Claus (or does he?), stays home alone while his mother is out, and helps Roger find the missing circus tickets.

Ali Baba and More

As a third-grader, David Bernstein found that there were 17 David Bernsteins in the Manhatten phone book and 3 Davids in his classroom. So he decided to change his name to Ali Baba Bernstein (*The Adventures of Ali Baba Bernstein* [Morrow, 1985]). Ali Baba is a fourth-grader in the sequel. Primary students who enjoy the antics of Ali Baba will enjoy reading about Russell in Hurwitz's *Rip-Roaring Russell* (Morrow, 1983); *Russell Rides Again* (Morrow, 1985); and *Russell Sprouts* (Morrow, 1987). Accelerated primary students and intermediate students will enjoy Hurwitz's Aldo Applesauce series: *Much Ado About Aldo* (Morrow, 1978); *Aldo Applesauce* (Morrow, 1979); and *Aldo Ice Cream* (Morrow, 1981). Hurwitz has written many other books that introduce other zany characters that readers will enjoy.

56 Hurwitz, Johanna
School's Out

Hurwitz, Johanna. *School's Out*. Illustrated by Sheila Hamanaka. Morrow, 1991. 107 pp. ISBN 0-688-09938-6.
Listening Level: Primary (ages 6-7; grades 1-2)
Read-Alone Level: Primary Accelerated (ages 7-8; grades 2-3)

Lucas Cott has survived his third-grade year (*Class Clown*) and now school is out. His improvement during the school year pleases both his teacher and his parents. On the final day of school he arrives home to find that his mother has two presents for him—a bicycle helmet that he has been wanting and the news that a French "au pair" is coming for the summer to help care for the children: Lucas and his three-year-old twin brothers, Marcus and Marius. Lucas knows that the best presents are gift wrapped, so he is not looking forward to the arrival of Genevieve, the au pair. From the time she arrives, Genevieve is the subject of Lucas's efforts to take advantage of her—ice cream for dinner and a popcorn blizzard are the results of just two of his escapades. He tries her patience when he climbs on the painter's ladder and sits on the roof. He does find out that the best presents do not necessarily come in gift-wrapped boxes.

School Vacations

Readers first meet Lucas Cott in *Class Clown* (Morrow, 1987). *School's Out* focuses on his activities during the summer following his third-grade year. Intermediate readers will enjoy Keith Robertson's books about Henry Reed and his summertime escapades: *Henry Reed, Inc.* (Viking, 1958); *Henry Reed's Journey* (Viking, 1963); *Henry Reed's Baby-Sitting Service* (Viking, 1966); *Henry Reed's Think Tank* (Viking, 1986); and *Henry Reed's Big Show* (Viking, 1970). Primary readers or intermediate readers who read at a lower level will enjoy Patricia Reilly Giff's 12 stories in the Kids of the Polk Street School series. Each book focuses on the same group of children during a different month of the school year. *The Beast in Ms. Rooney's Room* (Dell, 1984) begins the series with a story about the class during the month of September. The following books in the series follow the months through June and summer vacation. *Say "Cheese"* (Dell, 1985);

Sunny-Side Up (Dell, 1986); and *Pickle Puss* (Dell, 1986) take place during June, July, and August. Giff has also written several books in the New Kids at the Polk Street School series. That series includes the titles *Watch Out! Man-Eating Snake* (Dell, 1988) and *Spectacular Stone Soup* (Dell, 1989). A recent series by Giff, The Lincoln Lions Band, features children nearing fifth grade, but the books read at a primary level. The first two titles in The Lincoln Lions Band series are *Meet the Lincoln Lions Band* (Dell, 1992) and *Yankee Doodle Drumsticks* (Dell, 1992). After reading several Polk Street School titles by Giff, a group of readers may wish to read *Show Time at the Polk Street School: Plays You Can Do Yourself* by Patricia Reilly Giff (Delacorte, 1992). The plays are based on books by Giff: *The Candy Corn Contest* (Dell, 1984); *The Secret at the Polk Street School* (Dell, 1987); and *Fancy Feet* (Dell, 1988).

57 Irwin, Hadley
The Original Freddie Ackerman

Irwin, Hadley. *The Original Freddie Ackerman*. McElderry, 1992. 183 pp. ISBN 0-689-50562-0.
Listening Level: Intermediate (ages 9-10; grades 4-5)
Read-Alone Level: Intermediate Accelerated+ (ages 10-11+; grades 5-6+)

Trevor Frederick Ackerman has an original mother and an "other dad Charlie"; before that he had an "other dad Norman." He also has an original father and an "other mother Daphne." At his dad's house he is bothered by his stepsiblings and half-siblings—the thems and its. So when his mother and other dad Charlie plan a summer trip to Bermuda, Trevor must go to his original dad's house unless he wants to visit his great-aunt Calla and great-aunt Louise on Blue Isle, Maine. He chooses Blue Isle and the two eccentric aunts he has never met. From the minute Trevor arrives he realizes that he will have to become very ingenious to make the summer the least bit interesting. There is no television and very few kids his age. He survives at first by listening to his portable headset and becoming "Freddie" Ackerman in his imagination. The days promise to be incredibly boring until he discovers the ads in the back of his aunt's magazines—and begins to respond to some of them. Soon he is receiving the most mail of anyone on the island, and finds himself in the middle of a stakeout for smugglers, a search to verify information in a valuable book, and friendship with Ariel. He learns that there are plenty of family secrets to keep, and the days get more and more exciting—almost too exciting.

More Books by Hadley Irwin

Hadley Irwin is the pseudonym of Lee Hadley and Ann Irwin. They met while both were professors of English at Iowa State University in Ames, Iowa. They began writing together in the late 1970s. Their books often reflect actual situations of people with whom they have become acquainted. More mature readers will enjoy some of their other books: *The Lilith Summer* (Feminist, 1979)—a story of Ellen, who is being paid to be a summer companion to elderly Lilith Adams, who is being paid to babysit Ellen, who thinks that she is too old to have a babysitter while her mother works; *Moon and Me* (Atheneum, 1981)—a story in which 14-year-old E. J., who has traveled all over the world, now finds herself living, for six months, with her grandparents on their Iowa farm; and *Kim/Kimi* (Viking, 1987)—a story about 16-year-old Kim, who is searching for answers about her Japanese-American father, who died before she was born. Her search leads to discovering information about the "resettlement" camps endured by her father's family during World War II.

---

58 Kehret, Peg
Nightmare Mountain

Kehret, Peg. *Nightmare Mountain.* Cobblehill/Dutton, 1989. 164 pp.
ISBN 0-525-65008-3.
Listening Level: Early Intermediate (ages 8-9; grades 3-4)
Read-Alone Level: Intermediate (ages 9-10; grades 4-5)

Molly Newman is looking forward to visiting her Aunt Karen's and Uncle Phil's llama ranch at the foot of Mount Baker in Washington State. She will be able to meet her new cousin, Uncle Phil's son, Glendon. Molly is sure that they will become friends and have some fun times. But Glendon is not at all friendly. In fact, he acts hostile and tells her, in disgust, that she is just like Gladys; the identity of Gladys is a mystery. A few days after Molly arrives, her Aunt Karen becomes gravely ill and is taken to the hospital by ambulance. Uncle Phil accompanies his wife to the hospital, leaving Molly and Glendon in charge of the house and the llamas. But strange things have been occurring at the ranch, and the events get scarier and more dangerous. Years ago, Uncle Phil's brother, Craine, was in partnership with Phil, but he stole part of the money from the partnership and later was imprisoned for some other thefts. Now he is out of prison and plotting to steal some of the llamas. It is while Craine is attempting to steal the llamas that Glendon and Molly's lives are put in danger. Only through Molly's ingenuity does she convince Craine to go back for the two llamas that remain. His greediness gives her time to escape and later to rescue Glendon off the mountaintop, where he was left with a broken limb. It seems that Craine made two mistakes: He sold the first llamas for a low price and used an old business card from earlier days when he had been a legitimate partner in the business. The buyer notified the sheriff, and as Craine was making his getaway, the sheriff was approaching the ranch. Craine retreats to the ranch even though the road dead ends. The sheriff is in hot pursuit and, after a confrontation, corners Craine on the back porch. Craine breaks out a window and opens the door to the kitchen, injuring Glendon in the process. Craine demands that the sheriff and his deputies put down their guns. Just at that moment Molly throws a cup and startles Craine long enough to give the sheriff and his deputies a chance to disarm him and take him into custody.

In the Face of Danger

Gloria Skurzynski's *Trapped in Slickrock Canyon* (Lothrop, 1984) is another story that has cousins facing danger. Justin thinks his rich, spoiled-brat cousin, Gina, will get in his way during the summer Gina and her father visit Justin's family in the mesa country of Arizona. But on the day the two cousins decide to go into a canyon, they come across thieves attempting to remove a valuable petroglyph from the canyon wall. They find themselves being pursued through the dangerous canyon, trapped by a flash flood coming down the canyon.

Another tale of danger on a ranch is told in Bill Wallace's *Shadow on the Snow* (Holiday House, 1985). Tom Burke is staying on his grandfather's ranch and is finding it rather boring until he makes friends with Justin. A panther is terrorizing the ranchers' livestock. When Tom's sister becomes ill, his parents rush her to the hospital and leave Tom with his grandfather. Grandfather falls and breaks his hip, and because the phone lines are out, Tom just ride to Justin's to get help. But on the way his pregnant horse decides to give birth and leaves Tom vulnerable to the danger of the panther. When *Shadow on the Snow* was published in paperback by Simon & Schuster in 1987, it was published as *Danger on Panther Peak*.

Another tale of danger involves Rachel, a young girl whose family escapes from Russia. The story of that harrowing escape is told in alternating chapters in *The Night Journey* by Kathryn Lasky, illustrated by Trina Schart Hyman (Warne, 1981). A classic tale of survival is *Call It Courage* by Armstrong Sperry (Macmillan, 1940). In *Call It Courage*, Mafatu sets out to conquer his dread of the water by sailing off into the ocean with only his pet albatross and his dog.

59 Keller, Beverly

Desdemona Moves On

Keller, Beverly. *Desdemona Moves On*. Bradbury, 1992. 164 pp. ISBN
0-02-749751-8.
Listening Level: Early Intermediate (ages 8-9; grades 3-4)
Read-Alone Level: Intermediate (ages 9-10; grades 4-5)

Desdemona "Dez" Blanks lives in a household with her father and
five-year-old twin brother and sister, Anthony and Aida. They and their
housekeeper are being evicted to make way for a large shopping mall. Very
few people want to show a house to a single father with three children and
three dogs. But the rich playboy, Bramwell Grove, needs someone to care for
his dog while he's away, and he just can't bear to leave him in some kennel
where he would be alone and hardly given food and water, let alone be talked
to and pampered. Mr. Blanks won't even consider keeping another dog while
he and his family are searching for a place to live. Before long Grove is
offering to rent them one of his many houses if they will agree to keep his dog
when he is out of town. The house is beyond Dez's expectations. She finally
gets a room by herself, and this one has glass windows along one side and a
terrific view. There is a swimming pool and a badminton court. Before long
Dez's father is courting Mrs. Carlson, her best friend's mother. The adults are
planning a ski trip together and arrange to leave the children in their new home
for the weekend. The most popular guy in school is rumored to be coming to
Dez's house. And a grand surprise housewarming party is being planned for
the Sunday Dez's father and Mrs. Carlson arrive home. Mix in a Chinese
swimming team who show up to train in the swimming pool, some eccentric
shop owners who come to the party, and an unexpected visit from two police
officers who find themselves responding to reports of "They're ripping all
their insides out!" It turns out that Aida and Anthony are only attempting to
mummify their dolls, but by then the police officers have drawn their guns
and several guests (and the Chinese swim team) end up in the swimming pool.
The end to her father's relationship may have come when Mr. Blank helps his
daughter out of the pool while leaving the fully clothed but wet Mrs. Carlson
to her own devices.

More Desdemona

The fact that Desdemona and her friend, Sherman, campaign
for animal rights in this story reflects the author's tireless fight
on behalf of animals. Like Desdemona Blanks's family, Beverly
Keller shares her home with a pack of large rescued dogs. It is
easy to believe that perhaps Desdemona's unleashed spirit

reflects other facets of the author's personality. Desdemona is intelligent, creative, and certainly not one to let life grow dull. Other books about Desdemona include *No Beasts! No Children!* (Harper, 1983); *Desdemona—Twelve Going on Desperate* (Lothrop, 1986); and *Fowl Play, Desdemona* (Lothrop, 1989). Those intermediate readers who enjoy Desdemona's smart and quirky personality will find books by Lois Lowry about Anastasia (including *Anastasia at This Address* [Houghton, 1991] and several others) and Constance Green's books about Al (including *Al(exandra) the Great* [Viking, 1982] and *Just Plain Al* [Viking, 1986]) equally interesting.

60 King-Smith, Dick
The Cuckoo Child

King-Smith, Dick. *The Cuckoo Child.* Illustrated by Leslie W. Bowman. Hyperion, 1993. 127 pp. ISBN 1-56282-350-7.
Listening Level: Primary Accelerated (ages 7-8; grades 2-3)
Read-Alone Level: Early Intermediate (ages 8-9; grades 3-4)

From the time Jack Daw is a toddler he loves birds. As a four-year-old he tucked three brown hen's eggs under his bed covers in an effort to keep them warm and to hatch chicks. That ended in a disaster, but by the time he was five he knew more about how chicks are hatched and his father promised him some birds of his own. On his fifth birthday he was given a pair of colorful budgerigars, on his sixth birthday he received bantams, and on his seventh birthday he received ducks. On his eighth birthday he received a beautiful pair of geese—a handsome young white gander and a beautiful young white goose arrived at his family's farm. Jack's adventure begins when his school class takes a trip to the zoo and they observe ostriches. The zookeeper shows them the large eggs and explains that the ostrich lays more eggs than she can hatch so the keepers remove some of them and feed them to the snakes. Jack manages to put one of the ostrich eggs in his bag and successfully takes it home, where he fools the goose into brooding the egg until it hatches. And hatch it does—a beautiful but awkward-looking young bird. As the ostrich grows, Jack's parents investigate the origins of the bird and insist that the zoo director be contacted. From that point Jack's relationship with the ostrich, Oliver, is in doubt. But all ends well as both Jack and Oliver grow to adulthood and find a way to maintain their friendship.

Being an Ornithologist

An ornithologist is a person who studies birds. Ornithology is a branch of zoology that concerns itself with the life and habits of birds. Jack Daw was very interested in birds, and when he reached adulthood he became a zookeeper at the zoo where the ostrich he raised was kept. Jack might have also gone to school to study birds in a formal way and become an ornithologist. Youngsters who are interested in birds may wish to read *Bird* by David Burnie (Knopf, 1988), a volume in the series of Eyewitness Books, which are known for their informative photographs and fact-filled captions. *Bird* includes information ranging from the structure of feathers to the nests and eggs of various birds. Information about specific birds can be found in Paul Fleischman's *Townsend's Warbler* (Zolotow/HarperCollins, 1992) and Brenda Z. Guiberson's *Spoonbill Swamp* (Holt, 1992).

Those wishing to learn more about zoos will enjoy *Zoos* by Daniel Cohen and Susan Cohen (Doubleday, 1992) and *Dear Bronx Zoo* by Joyce Altman and Sue Goldberg (Macmillan, 1991). Georgeanne Irvine's book *Protecting Endangered Species at the San Diego Zoo* (Simon & Schuster, 1990) emphasizes the role of zoos in ensuring a future for endangered species. And while Irvine's book does not deal specifically with birds, it does contain information about many animals and the zookeepers who care for them.

---

61 Kline, Suzy
Herbie Jones and the Dark Attic

Kline, Suzy. *Herbie Jones and the Dark Attic*. Illustrated by Richard Williams. Putnam, 1992. 101 pp. ISBN 0-399-21838-6.
Listening Level: Primary Accelerated (ages 7-8; grades 2-3)
Read-Alone Level: Early Intermediate (ages 8-9; grades 3-4)

Herbie Jones has finished third grade and is ready to begin fourth grade. His third-grade teacher, Miss Pinkham, has switched to fourth grade, and most of last year's class will be in Miss Pinkham's class again this year. Nothing too exciting. Miss Pinkham decides to change the way the reading groups are organized and Annabelle, the smartest girl in the class, and Herbie and his friend, Raymond, are put in the same group. They are to select a book and read it, then do projects about the book. In the meantime, the Jones family receives word that Grandpa is coming to visit for two weeks. Herbie has always wanted to sleep in the attic, so he volunteers to give his room to Grandpa and to sleep upstairs during the time Grandpa is visiting. Once he has volunteered he begins to think about all the things that could happen once he gets in the dark attic. The first night he sleeps in the attic he convinces his friend, Raymond, to stay overnight. Raymond loves spooky stuff and spying in the dark. But neither of them is prepared for the raccoon that comes to visit. Many of Herbie's friends end up visiting the Jones's house and gather in the attic. It isn't long before the friends decide to form a club and to meet in the attic at least once a week. And because they are "fans of the attic" they name their group "Fanattics." After playing hide-and-seek in the attic and having friends there, Herbie knows that he will not be afraid to sleep in the attic again.

Club Membership

Intermediate readers will enjoy the story of another group of friends who form a club in *Me, My Goat, and My Sister's Wedding* by Stella Pevsner (Clarion, 1985). In Pevsner's book, Doug and his friends keep the goat in their clubhouse a secret from their families until the day an unexpected guest (the goat) turns up at Doug's sister's wedding. Early primary readers will enjoy the activities of the Pee Wee Scouts in books written by Judy Delton. Titles include *Pee Wee Jubilee* (Dell, 1989) and *Pee Wees on Parade* (Dell, 1992). A little more mature reader will enjoy the friendship groups in Patricia Reilly Giff's The Kids of Polk Street School series. The first title in Giff's series is *The Beast in Ms. Rooney's Room* (Dell, 1984). Early intermediate students will enjoy reading titles in Stephen Roos's Pet Lovers Club series. The first of Roos's titles is *Love Me, Love My Werewolf* (Delacorte, 1991). Other titles include *Crocodile Christmas* (Delacorte, 1992) and *The Cottontail Caper* (Delacorte, 1992).

---

62 Kovacs, Deborah
Brewster's Courage

Kovacs, Deborah. *Brewster's Courage*. Illustrated by Joe Mathieu. Simon & Schuster, 1992. 104 pp. ISBN 0-671-74016-4.
Listening Level: Primary Accelerated (ages 7-8; grades 2-3)
Read-Alone Level: Early Intermediate (ages 8-9; grades 3-4)

Brewster is a shy, black-footed ferret from South Dakota. He loves to ride his bicycle more than anything. One day he heard the music of Wild Turkey and the Loblollies from the Moustafaya Swamp in Louisiana's bayou country. Brewster wants to hear that music again, so he sets off on his bicycle to travel the long miles to Cajun country—the Moustafaya Swamp. The swamp seems wonderful to Brewster, but the other animals in the swamp do not make him feel welcome. Swamp Sallie befriends Brewster, introduces him to special places in the swamp, and takes him to the famous Jolie Blonde Café where Wild Turkey and the Loblollies perform their music. But Swamp Sallie's friendship does little to change the attitude of the other animals. On the day that the popular Moustafaya Mix-up is scheduled in the swamp, Wild Turkey's accordion is accidentally broken. Without music the Mix-up would have to be cancelled. Brewster offers to ride his bicycle through the swamp and take the accordion to be repaired at Happy Jack's. Because the bloodhounds are sure to chase him, the journey will be very dangerous. Brewster's courage brings him acceptance and encourages him to start a successful messenger business—the Moustafaya Messenger Service—and to settle in the Moustafaya Swamp permanently.

Animals in Charge

Kovacs uses personified animals to create a compelling and interesting story. George Selden Thompson is another writer who has featured personified animals in his books. Thompson wrote his books using George Selden as his pseudonym because by the time he started writing there already was a writer named George Thompson. Selden's most popular books feature Chester Cricket and his friends in an urban setting. Selden says that the idea for *A Cricket in Times Square* (Farrar, 1960) was born late one night when Selden heard a cricket chirp in the Times Square subway station: "The idea for the story formed immediately." Soon Selden had developed the cast of characters: Mario Bellini and his parents, who operate an unsuccessful newsstand in Times Square; Chester, a liverwurst-loving cricket who had been carried there in a picnic basket from his Connecticut home; Tucker, a mouse; and Harry the lovable cat. *A Cricket in Times Square* brought many honors to Selden, and many readers wrote to ask him to write a sequel. Eventually Selden did write a sequel, *Tucker's Countryside* (Farrar, 1969). It turned out to be a favorite story of both Selden and his readers. Other books that feature Chester Cricket and his friends include *Chester Cricket's Pigeon Ride* (Farrar, 1981) and *Harry Kitten and Tucker Mouse* (Farrar, 1986). The readability of Selden's books will make them most appropriate for intermediate readers.

63 Lawlor, Laurie
George on His Own

Lawlor, Laurie. *George on His Own*. Illustrated by Toby Gowing. Whitman, 1993. 192 pp. ISBN 0-8075-2823-4.
Listening Level: Intermediate (ages 9-10; grades 4-5)
Read-Alone Level: Intermediate Accelerated (ages 10-11; grades 5-6)

George, a 12-year-old, is part of the Mills family living on the Dakota prairie. Addie is the oldest child, a gifted student who has earned a scholarship to high school. George has two younger brothers, Burt and Lew, and a younger sister, Nellie May. *George on His Own* tells the story of a Dakota pioneer family from the point of view of a young boy. George is not a very good student but does enjoy playing a trombone. His father thinks that playing is a waste of time and wants George to concentrate on becoming a farmer. But George hates farming and does not want to contemplate a lifetime on the prairie. Early scenes describe the birthing of a calf and the death of both the cow and calf; the arrival home of Addie; and the family's tragic encounter with measles. When Nellie May dies as a result of the measles and George's father threatens to sell the trombone, it becomes too much for George. He leaves a note and sets out to find the Barrett's traveling troupe. Little does he realize that he is about to join up with unsavory characters who not only steal provisions from the government, but soon make plans to get rid of him and sell his trombone. George manages to survive on his own, but when he realizes what has been going on, he decides to return home.

Stories of the Prairie

George on His Own is the fourth book Laurie Lawlor has written about life on the Dakota prairie. The first three titles, *Addie Across the Prairie* (Whitman, 1988), *Addie's Dakota Winter* (Whitman, 1989), and *Addie's Long Summer* (Whitman, 1992), tell about life as a Dakota pioneer from the point of view of George's older sister. Other books that tell about pioneer life include books for the younger reader: *Wagon Wheels* by Barbara Brenner (Harper, 1978); *Pioneer Cat* by William H. Hooks (Random, 1988); *The Long Way Westward* by Joan Sandin (Harper, 1989); and *Next Spring an Oriole* by Gloria Whelan (Random, 1987). Other titles that may interest readers include *Caddie Woodlawn* by Carol Ryrie Brink (Macmillan, 1935; 1973); *Children of the Wild West* by Russell Freedman (Clarion, 1983); and *Log Cabin in the Woods: A True Story About a Pioneer Boy* by Joanne Landers Henry (Four Winds, 1988). Middle school readers will enjoy Kathryn Lasky's *Beyond the Divide* (Macmillan, 1983). Lasky's 1850s tale is about young Meribah Simon, who accompanies her father to the West after he is shunned by their Amish community. Along the way they encounter cruel emigrants, death, selfishness, and much misery. When her father dies, Meribah must find a way to survive and eventually makes her home in the Northwest.

64 Leroe, Ellen
Ghost Dog

Leroe, Ellen. *Ghost Dog*. Illustrated by Bill Basso. Hyperion, 1993. 63 pp. ISBN 1-56282-268-3.
Listening Level: Primary Accelerated (ages 7-8; grades 2-3)
Read-Alone Level: Early Intermediate (ages 8-9; grades 3-4)

Artie Jensen is a nine-year-old who longs to have a dog. He wishes and wishes for one until he gets a *ghost* dog. In addition to being invisible, Artie's dog is also a troublemaker. All the havoc that takes place in the house is blamed on Artie. Artie begins to think that the dog is anything but "man's best friend." However, when a valuable baseball card (given to Artie by his grandfather) is stolen, Artie looks to his Ghost Dog for help. Will they be able to find the card before the thief has a chance to sell it? Will they be able to solve the crime?

Solving Mysteries with a Little Help from Ghosts

Lila McGinnis has written a novel, *The Ghost Upstairs* (Hastings House, 1982), that focuses on Otis White, a ghost that has, for 70 years, inhabited the house next door to Albert Snook's family home. When the house is demolished to make way for a new city library, Otis takes up residence in Albert's upstairs bedroom. Otis creates havoc in Albert's house in much the same way that the Ghost Dog created havoc in Artie's home. And when the library next door is vandalized, Otis helps Albert apprehend the vandals. Other ghost stories that are good reading include those in the series by Richard Peck, featuring Blossom Culp. The titles in that series include *The Ghost Belonged to Me* (Viking, 1975); *The Dreadful Future of Blossom Culp* (Delacorte, 1983); and *Blossom Culp and the Sleep of Death* (Delacorte, 1986). Other authors who write compelling ghost stories are Betty Ren Wright, C. S. Adler, and Mary Downing Hahn.

65 Levoy, Myron
The Magic Hat of Mortimer Wintergreen

Levoy, Myron. *The Magic Hat of Mortimer Wintergreen.* Zolotow/Harper, 1988. 211 pp. ISBN 0-06-023841-0.
Listening Level: Early Intermediate (ages 8-9; grades 3-4)
Read-Alone Level: Intermediate (ages 9-10; grades 4-5)

Thirteen-year-old Joshua and his eleven-year-old sister, Amy, are left in the care of their abusive Aunt Vooch after the untimely death of their parents in the wilds of South Dakota in 1893. After suffering the ultimate humiliation from their aunt, who handcuffs the children in the pigpen to sleep with the pigs, the two run away and meet up with the mysterious Mortimer Wintergreen. Wintergreen has a magic hat and travels about the countryside in his wagon, putting on magic shows and hawking his wares, including an astonishing tonic that cures ailments too numerous to mention. When the two children find Wintergreen they sneak aboard his wagon, and when he finds them he agrees to take them East to their grandparents in New York. A fantasy journey follows as the three concoct a

plan to earn money from spectators by lifting the wagon and horse off the ground with hot-air balloons. Instead, the balloons fly them over the midwestern states and on to New York City, where their quest to find just where their grandparents live brings several more adventures.

Medicine Shows in the Wild West

Mortimer Wintergreen was a huckster who sold his goods from the back of his wagon. He did magic tricks under tents and sold his "famous Wintergreen's All-Season Health Tonic." Primary-aged readers may want to read about another traveling road show in the Wild West. Betsy Byars tells of the antics of May-May and Rose in *The Golly Sisters Go West* (HarperCollins, 1985) and *Hooray for the Golly Sisters!* (HarperCollins, 1990); both titles are I Can Read Books. May-May and Rose entertain readers onstage and off with magic pig tricks and a high-wire dance to the tune of "The High-Wire Waltz," and hilarious antics that make their audiences laugh. Although Levoy took a story about the mistreatment of two orphans and created humor, the treatment of orphans in the late 1800s and early 1900s was not usually funny. Joan Lowery Nixon has written several stories for older intermediate and middle school readers about orphans who were sent West from New York City on trains known as orphan trains. Children were sent to families in the Midwest—sometimes the families wanted to help the children and sometimes the children were wanted for the help they could give to the families on the farms. Nixon's orphan train series includes *In the Face of Danger* (Bantam, 1988) and *A Place to Belong* (Bantam, 1989).

66 Lindbergh, Anne
Three Lives to Live

Lindbergh, Anne. *Three Lives to Live*. Little, Brown, 1992. 183 pp. ISBN 0-316-52628-2.
Listening Level: Intermediate (ages 9-10; grades 4-5)
Read-Alone Level: Intermediate Accelerated+ (ages 10-11+; grades 5-6+)

Garet had no memories of being anywhere but with her Gratkins (Grandmother Atkins). Gratkins always said that Garet had come to live with her when she was two; Garet had arrived with a little ceramic piglet in her dress pocket. Her life from age 2 to 13 was rather uneventful until a girl just her age fell out of the laundry chute. Dressed in a party dress, this girl, Daisy, seemed right at home in Garet and Gratkins's house. Who is Daisy? Where did she come from? Why does Gratkins treat Daisy like a special guest and tell people Daisy and Garet are sisters—twins at that? Slowly Garet begins to put the pieces of the puzzle together. Daisy has somehow come through a time tunnel (the laundry chute) into the future. And who is Daisy? Garet suspects that Daisy is actually Gratkins when she was a 13-year-old girl. She has traveled forward 50 years in time, from 1943 to 1993. Garet feels that if she can get Daisy to go back in time all their problems will be over—but when Daisy does leave, new questions and problems arise. How had Garet come to live with Gratkins? Could Garet also be Gratkins as a child? Had she come forward 11 years before? There is plenty of foreshadowing to help the reader discover the secret Gratkins has held since the day Garet arrived.

Face to Face in Time

Gratkins actually meets herself when Daisy arrives via the laundry chute in the house in which they both grow up. The same is true when Cynthia Voigt writes about Brann Connell, who crawls into a fortress built of his father's childhood building blocks and awakens 37 years in the past, in his father's room. In Lindbergh's book, Daisy (and later we find out Garet) are actually created from Gratkins's existence and the two girls become individual entities, while in Voigt's time travel book, Brann returns to his father's era but remains an observer of his father's youth. Both Voigt and Lindbergh's books are intriguing time-slip stories for a slightly younger audience than most books in this genre.

67 Lowry, Lois
Anastasia at This Address

Lowry, Lois. *Anastasia at This Address*. Houghton, 1991. 130 pp. ISBN 0-395-56263-5.
Listening Level: Intermediate (ages 9-10; grades 4-5)
Read-Alone Level: Intermediate Accelerated (ages 10-11; grades 5-6)

Anastasia was only 13, but age difference is just a small obstacle when two people have all the same interests. Both Anastasia and her new pen pal are movie buffs who hate smoking. The only problem is that Anastasia got acquainted with her new pen pal through a personals ad that read "SWM, 28, boyish charm, inherited wealth, looking for a tall young woman, nonsmoker, to share Caribbean vacations, reruns of *Casablanca*, and romance." In response to a request to send a photograph, Anastasia sends a photo of her mother at the age of 22. Meanwhile, Anastasia, who will be a junior bridesmaid in her friend's older sister's wedding, is shopping with her friends for dresses, shoes, etc. All goes well until Sep*tim*us Smith shows up at the wedding—Uncle Tim is an usher at the wedding and he plans on stopping by Anastasia's house after the wedding. She must think of a way out of her predicament of sending her mother's photo—or confess all to her parents.

Anastasia Again and Again

Lois Lowry first wrote about Anastasia Krupnik in a short story for a magazine. Lowry liked Anastasia so much that she decided Anastasia needed to be given a full-length book. *Anastasia Krupnik* (Houghton, 1979) became the first book in a series about Anastasia. Anastasia is based on the antics of Lowry's two daughters, Kristin and Alix, both of whom are active, outgoing, and *very* independent. Read all about Anastasia's escapades in all of the books about her: *Anastasia Again!* (Dell, 1981); *Anastasia at Your Service* (Dell, 1982); *Anastasia, Ask Your Analyst* (Dell, 1984); *Anastasia on Her Own* (Dell, 1985); *Anastasia Has the Answers* (Dell, 1986); and *Anastasia's Chosen Career* (Dell, 1987).

Lowry's son, Grey, who loves airplanes, gave Lowry the idea of having Anastasia's younger brother, Sam, interested in airplanes. Sam finally got a book of his own when Lowry wrote *All About Sam* (Houghton, 1988). Readers who want to know more about Lois Lowry and where she gets her ideas for writing may be interested in viewing the videotape *A Visit with Lois Lowry* from Houghton's video author/illustrator series.

68 Lowry, Lois
Number the Stars

Lowry, Lois. *Number the Stars*. Houghton, 1989. 132 pp. ISBN 0-395-51060-0.
Listening Level: Intermediate (ages 9-10; grades 4-5)
Read-Alone Level: Intermediate Accelerated (ages 10-11; grades 5-6)

Annemarie Johansen finds herself in the middle of the Danish Resistance and the Nazis' occupation of Denmark during the early 1940s. The Germans are planning to "relocate" all the Jews in Denmark, so in order to protect Annemarie's best friend, Ellen Rosen, the Johansens take her in and pretend that she is their sister. The girls must think quickly when Nazi officers show up and question why Ellen is not blonde like the rest of the family. This historical fiction tale is based on the experiences of families who lived in Copenhagen during the 1940s when the Danish Resistance managed to smuggle almost the entire Jewish population (almost 7,000 people) across the sea to Sweden.

More Tales from World War II

Another story detailing the actions of the Danish Resistance and the movement of Jews into Sweden is Carol Matas's *Lisa's War* (Scribner's, 1987). Lisa is just 12 years old when the Nazis invade Denmark, forcing her and other teenage Jews to become involved in the underground resistance movement. Eventually their actions force them to flee to Sweden. Another moving tale of World War II and the courage shown by children in an occupied country is Marie McSwigan's *Snow Treasure* (Dutton, 1942; 1970; Scholastic, 1958). During the occupation of Norway, children on sleds succeed in getting 13 tons, nearly $9 million worth, of Norwegian gold bullion past Nazi sentries and shipped to Baltimore. The children slip the bullion past the troops and get it to a boat hidden in a fiord. When the bullion is safe on board, the boats set sail for America. Two picture books that could introduce a focus on World War II are Christobel Mattingley's *The Angel with a Mouth-Organ* (Holiday House, 1984), in which Mattingley artfully retells a story told by Peter and Ingrid's mother of her own family's separation, flight from their war-torn homeland, and eventual reunion; and *Rose Blanche* by Christopher Galloz and Roberto Innocenti (Creative Education, 1985), the story of a little German girl and a group of young German citizens who died protesting the war—both sharing the name Rose Blanche. Wise beyond her years, Rose Blanche suffers from the effects of the war but shows her own compassion when she establishes her own war effort and helps to ease the hunger of some of the relocated Jewish children outside her village. But war is not king, and when the Allied soldiers arrive, Rose Blanche meets an untimely death. A gripping tale.

69 Mahy, Margaret

The Girl with the Green Ear: Stories About Magic in Nature

Mahy, Margaret. *The Girl with the Green Ear: Stories About Magic in Nature*. Illustrated by Shirley Hughes. Knopf, 1992. 100 pp. ISBN 0-679-82231-3.
Listening Level: Early Intermediate (ages 8-9; grades 3-4)
Read-Alone Level: Intermediate (ages 9-10; grades 4-5)

Mahy's nine stories include tales about a man who collects thunderstorms, a girl whose dyed-green ear allows her to listen to the plants, a man-eating plant that gets loose, and an ancient tree and a tree that has a craving for chocolate porridge. Each of the stories displays a reverence for nature and brings us closer to the green world. In the first story, "The Good Wizard of the Forest," a wizard loves to make chocolate cakes. He invites all the children of the town to come and eat cake with him, but they think he must be a wicked wizard and will not come. Because the wizard is lonely, he brings a tree home and cares for it until it grows big and shades his house. But he suspects that trees get lonely too, so he brings another one home and plants it. Each day he makes himself a chocolate cake and the tree a plant food cake, and then he sits by the tree and has cake and tea and talks. Time goes on and the wizard plants more and more trees. The other wizards forget him and the witches do not invite him to their midnight parties. One day after many years, the wizard is sitting by his tree when he looks up and sees a group of children who have come to visit the good wizard of the woods. They are the grandchildren and grandnieces and grandnephews of the children he had once asked to come eat chocolate cake with him. The children had found the long-ago invitations and thought that the cards had been so pretty that certainly the wizard could not be wicked. And besides, only a good wizard would bother to plant a forest. So the wizard and the children enjoy chocolate cake together, and nobody is lonely. In "The Girl with the Green Ear," Millie finds that her father's insistence that she learn to play the French horn overbearing so she leaves and, in an effort to disguise herself, has her hair dyed green. But the hairdresser is careless and dyes one ear green too—inside and out. Once the ear is dyed, Millie can hear plants talk. She begins a new career, taking care of plants. One of the plants she encounters is a carnivorous-eating plant that runs wild. Eventually Millie saves the community from the plant, learns how to play the harp (as therapy for her plants), and falls in love with a French horn player.

Stories with Nature in Mind

In an age when concern for the fate of the earth and the animals that inhabit it is at its height, stories that focus on ecology and endangered animals will be well received. Picture books that are thematically related to the ecology/endangered animals theme include *Brother Eagle, Sister Sky: A Message from Chief Seattle* by Susan Jeffers (Dial, 1991); *Forgotten Forest* by Laurence Anholt (Sierra/Little, Brown, 1992); *Who Is the Beast?* by Keith Baker (Harcourt, 1990); *The Great Kapok Tree: A Tale of the Amazon Rain Forest* by Lynne Cherry (Gulliver/Harcourt, 1990); and *Hey! Get Off Our Train* by John Burningham (Crown, 1989). Intermediate readers will get much information from *Bringing Back the Animals* by Teresa Kennedy (Amethyst, 1991); *My First Green Book* by Angela Wilkes (Knopf, 1991); and *An Adventure in the Amazon* by the Cousteau Society (Simon & Schuster, 1992). Many other titles focus specifically on ecosystems in a specific location. Among the best titles are those by Barbara Taylor: *Coral Reef*; *Desert Life*; *Pond Life*; and *Rain Forest* (all published by Dorling, 1992). Each of Taylor's volumes is illustrated with sparkling photographs that will interest the reader and give more information. Other titles that will be of interest for reading aloud or reading alone include *Journey of the Red-Eyed Tree Frog* by Tanis Jordan (Simon & Schuster/Green Tiger Press, 1992) and *Rain Forest Secrets* by Arthur Dorros (Scholastic, 1990).

70 McHargue, Georgess
Beastie

McHargue, Georgess. *Beastie*. Delacorte, 1992. 179 pp. ISBN 0-385-30589-3.
Listening Level: Intermediate (ages 9-10; grades 4-5)
Read-Alone Level: Intermediate Accelerated (ages 10-11; grades 5-6)

Does the Loch Ness Monster really exist? Professor Hanford is convinced that his expedition will yield absolute proof of the monster's existence. He has raised more than one million dollars for the summer's research and has gathered a team of professionals and volunteers to work on the project. He has even brought in a team with a special infrared camera to record, once and for all, the monster's existence. All the expedition team has to do is to locate the monster with sonar and then photograph it. Meanwhile, three youngsters brought together because their parents are part of the expedition, think up their own method of finding the monster in the Loch. Mary Wendell, the daughter of the expedition's secretary; Scott Hanford, the director's son; and Theo Chun, the son of important government scientists, join together to form an expedition of their own. They explore an abandoned castle, become "moles" to find out information from the adults, and set out on the Loch themselves. Eventually the three find out that Tayzie, a six-and-a-half-year-old local girl, holds the key to more information than their parents' expedition has uncovered all summer. Now the question seems to be: Do they reveal what they know or do they help keep Tayzie's secret?

Monsters—Do They Exist?

The existence of the Loch Ness Monster has been the subject of many books, including *The Mystery of the Loch Ness Monster* by Harriett Abels (Crestwood, 1987)—a book intermediate readers may wish to read to learn more about the monster—and a more difficult title, *Loch Ness Monster: Opposing Viewpoints* by Robert San Souci (Greenhaven, 1989). Books about the Abominable Snowman, the Loch Ness Monster, and the mysteries of the Bermuda Triangle can be located by using your library or media center's catalog. An easier-to-read fiction story that focuses on a strange monster lurking nearby is Mary Calhoun's *The Night the Monster Came* (Morrow, 1982). At the end of *Beastie*, Scott Hanford reveals that plans for the next summer include his dad's expedition to Australia to investigate the Bunyip—"some sort of water monster they're supposed to have." A picture story about this monster is *The Bunyip of Berkeley's Creek* by Jenny Wagner (Macmillan, 1978). Those who would rather make up their own stories about monsters closer to home might be encouraged to write their own accounts after reading or hearing Patricia Polacco's picture book *Some Birthday!* (Simon & Schuster, 1991).

---

71 McKissack, Patricia C.
The Dark-Thirty: Southern Tales of the Supernatural

McKissack, Patricia C. *The Dark-Thirty: Southern Tales of the Supernatural.* Illustrated by Brian Pinkney. Knopf, 1992. 122 pp. ISBN 0-679-81863-4.
Listening Level: Intermediate (ages 9-10; grades 4-5)
Read-Alone Level: Intermediate Accelerated (ages 10-11; grades 5-6)

This collection contains 10 original tales based on memories of stories told by the author's grandmother. The storytelling sessions often took place on the family's front porch at dusk when it was neither day nor night—during the dark-thirty, a special half hour of twilight. The 10 stories include one about a retired Pullman porter who hears a ghostly whistle and knows it's the last train he'll ever ride; a white bus driver who refuses a ride to a penniless black woman and then encounters her ghost; etchings that appear on a man's windowpanes—etchings that show him to be guilty of a lynching; and the story of a straw doll that helps a slave gain his freedom.

Tales of African-Americans

Other tales that should not be missed are included in two collections by Virginia Hamilton: *The People Could Fly: American Black Folktales* (Knopf, 1985) and *Many Thousands Gone: African-Americans from Slavery to Freedom* (Knopf, 1993). Both volumes are illustrated by Caldecott artists Leo Dillon and Diane Dillon. A novel that deals with the slavery issue is James Berry's *Ajeemah and His Son* (Willa Perlman/HarperCollins, 1991). Several picture books focus on flights to freedom: *Aunt Harriet's Underground Railroad in the Sky* by Faith Ringgold (Crown, 1992); *Follow the Drinking Gourd* by Jeanette Winter (Knopf, 1988); and Deborah Hopkinson's *Sweet Clara and the Freedom Quilt* (Knopf, 1993).

72 *Michael Bond's Book of Bears*

Michael Bond's Book of Bears. Aladdin, 1992. 143 pp. ISBN 0-689-71649-4.
Listening Level: Early Primary (ages 5-6; grades K-1)
Read-Alone Level: Primary (ages 6-7; grades 1-2)

This book contains 14 stories about bears and teddy bears. Listeners/readers will meet Jane Hissey's Old Bear ("There Were Four in Bed") and bears that have a strong sense of right and wrong ("The Half-Price Bear"). Included is a traditional version of "The Three Bears" and stories about a bear who realizes that being first isn't always the most important thing in life. Graham J. Brooks's story "Bozzy Finds a Friend" will have a message for anyone who has ever been the last one in a crowd to be chosen for someone's team. Michael Bond and Karen Bond's story "Paddington Takes Over" will draw listeners/readers to the many books by Bond featuring Paddington, and Else Holmelund Minarik's "Little Bear's Wish" will introduce Little Bear to the same audience.

Bears • Bears • Bears

This collection of reading stories to share can stimulate much more reading about bears. Jane Hissey's story will lead readers to her picture books about Old Bear—*Old Bear* (Philomel, 1986); *Old Bear Tales* (Philomel, 1988); *Jolly Tall* (Philomel, 1990); *Jolly Snow* (Philomel, 1991); *Little Bear's Trousers* (Philomel,

1987); *Little Bear Lost* (Philomel, 1989); and *Best Friends: Old Bear Tales* (Philomel, 1989). Else Holmelund Minarik's early reading books about Little Bear include *A Kiss for Little Bear* (Harper, 1959); *Little Bear* (Harper, 1957); *Little Bear's Friend* (Harper, 1960); and *Little Bear's Visit* (Harper, 1961). Maurice Sendak illustrated the Little Bear books, and those reading *A Kiss for Little Bear* will most likely recognize Little Bear's drawing as one resembling one of Sendak's Wild Things from his own book *Where the Wild Things Are* (Harper, 1963). In 1992, Caedmon released a 60-minute audiocassette tape celebrating the thirty-fifth birthday of Little Bear. The tape includes readings of the four titles listed above. Early intermediate readers will enjoy the subtle humor in Bond's series about Paddington Bear—the first in the series is *A Bear Called Paddington* (Houghton, 1960). Other famous bears will extend the bear focus, including A. A. Milne's books about Pooh Bear. Most delightful are the Dutton editions of Milne's titles that feature the quaint illustrations rendered by E. H. Shepard. Four titles are *Winnie-the-Pooh* (Dutton, 1926), *The House at Pooh Corner* (Dutton, 1928), *Now We Are Six* (Dutton, 1927), and *When We Were Very Young* (Dutton, 1924). And not to be missed is the story of the first teddy bear, *The First Teddy Bear* by Helen Kay (Stemmer House, 1985). Kay's book will attract early- and middle-grade readers with its easy-to-understand text and abundance of pictures. Older students will find the book a concise, informative account of one incident in President Theodore Roosevelt's life.

73 Myers, Walter Dean
The Righteous Revenge of Artemis Bonner

Myers, Walter Dean. *The Righteous Revenge of Artemis Bonner*. HarperCollins, 1992. 140 pp. ISBN 0-06-020844-9.
Listening Level: Intermediate Accelerated (ages 10-11; grades 5-6)
Read-Alone Level: Intermediate Accelerated+ (ages 10-11+; grades 5-6+)

In a rollicking parody on adult westerns, this tale has 15-year-old Artemis Bonner being summoned by his aunt to Tombstone, Arizona. The year is 1882 and Artemis is being asked to avenge the death of his Uncle Ugly. Artemis's aunt promises him half of the money that his uncle has left and tells him of the possibility of more treasure if he is able to follow the treasure map and find the buried treasure that Uncle Ugly supposedly hid during his travels. Artemis follows the dastardly Catfish Grimes and his woman, Lucy Featherdip,

from Arizona to Alaska and back. On the way, Artemis teams up with a 13-year-old Cherokee Indian boy with the unlikely name of Frolic. Together they face danger and death as they catch Catfish Grimes and Miss Featherdip and then find that the outlaws have managed to outwit them once again. In a final shoot-out, Artemis fells Catfish and Lucy Featherdip is wounded by Catfish's own gun. Satisfied that he has avenged his uncle's death, Artemis (and his friend, Frolic) return to New York City only to receive a letter from Lucy Featherdip informing Artemis that Catfish had already found Uncle Ugly's buried treasure and only pretended to be killed. In reality, he had tricked Artemis one more time and had run off with another woman, Annie Hartnett. Lucy Featherdip suggests that Artemis return to the Wild West to get Catfish Grimes and Annie Hartnett—for good.

The Wild West

Myers's tale is for more mature readers, but it is an interesting play on a literary form made popular by adult western writers. Those who wish to read mainstream fiction about adventures in the western states might read Gloria Skurzynski's *Trapped in Slickrock Canyon* (Lothrop, 1984) or Gery Greer and Bob Ruddick's *Max and Me and the Wild West* (Harper, 1988). Picture books that give a flavor of the West include Eric A. Kimmel's *Four Dollars and Fifty Cents* (Holiday House, 1990) and *Charlie Drives the Stage* (Holiday House, 1989). Joan Lowery Nixon's picture books *Beats Me, Claude* (Viking, 1986); *Fat Chance, Claude!* (Viking, 1987); and *You Bet Your Britches, Claude* (Viking, 1989) are also about the frontier and pioneer life in the West.

74 Namioka, Lensey
Yang the Youngest and His Terrible Ear

Namioka, Lensey. *Yang the Youngest and His Terrible Ear.* Illustrated by Kees de Kiefte. Joy Street/Little, Brown, 1992. 128 pp. ISBN 0-316-59701-5.
Listening Level: Early Intermediate (ages 8-9; grades 3-4)
Read-Alone Level: Intermediate (ages 9-10; grades 4-5)

Nine-year-old Yingtao Yang is the youngest in a family that has arrived in Seattle, Washington, from China. Everyone in the Yang family is a talented musician except for Yingtao. Yingtao must struggle to learn English and now he is feeling the pressure to play the violin at an important recital. The recital is important because it may attract more music students for his father and that will mean that he can support the family. How can Yingtao tell his family that he does not enjoy music and that he likes baseball a whole lot better? And no matter how much he practices his violin, Yingtao does not feel that he can represent his family admirably. Then Yingtao concocts a plan: Perhaps his new best friend would be a better choice to play in the quartet at the recital. But how can he convince his friend to take his place, and where does his future in baseball fit into all of this?

For the Love of Baseball

Johanna Hurwitz wrote about Ezra Feldman, a nine-year-old boy who loved baseball, in *Baseball Fever* (Morrow, 1981). His European-born father did not understand the game (much like Mr. Yang) and did not see the merits of learning anything about it. Just as Mr. Yang thought his son should learn how to play the violin better, Mr. Feldman wanted his son to learn to play chess better. Through an interesting turn of events, Ezra gets his chance just as Yingtao manages to get his chance at playing ball. Two other books feature a child's own apprehension with the game of baseball. *My Horrible Secret* by Stephen Roos (Delacorte, 1983) and *Skinnybones* by Barbara Park (Knopf, 1982) both deal with youngsters who are not able to compete successfully at baseball. Roos describes the turmoil felt by 11-year-old Warren Fingler, who cannot throw or catch a ball, but is expected to go to a summer camp where the emphasis is on playing baseball, and worse yet, the camp is his brother's alma mater. His brother is known as the best and most popular athlete in town. Park describes Alex Frankovitch's dilemma when he is challenged to a pitching duel by T. J. Stoner, a new kid in town who is about to pitch his 125th straight win.

75 Naylor, Phyllis Reynolds
Josie's Troubles

Naylor, Phyllis Reynolds. *Josie's Troubles*. Illustrated by Shelley Matheis. Atheneum, 1992. 99 pp. ISBN 0-689-31659-3.
Listening Level: Primary (ages 6-7; grades 1-2)
Read-Alone Level: Primary Accelerated (ages 7-8; grades 2-3)

Josephine has a new friend, Sarah, and they seem to be destined to be best friends forever. That is, until Josie and Sarah have a stand-up piano race, in which both girls race to play every key, reach the middle of the keyboard, and sit on the piano bench before the other, and break the leg on an expensive rosewood piano bench. Sarah's parents suggest that the two fourth-graders pay the cost of the repair. Josie writes a letter to a famous quarterback asking if he might send them the money, but she only gets a telephone call inquiring about how she is doing. In order to earn the necessary $60, Josie and Sarah advertise their pet- and plant-sitting service. From the very beginning their business is filled with troubles. Their exclusivity threatens their relationship with their classmates (and onetime friends) Kimberley and Ellen Ann, and at every turn their business ventures bring missing cats, dead fish, and dogs that insist on walking the girls (instead of the girls walking the dogs).

Being in Business

Another tale of business enterprise is told in Richard Boughton's *Rent-a-Puppy, Inc.* (Atheneum, 1992). Nikki Savier tries to devise a way to keep all six of her beagle's puppies; when her friend, Tyler G. Hubbs, helps her start a rental business, there are plenty of puppy antics to keep pet lovers interested in reading.

Intermediate readers may enjoy reading about Henry Reed's escapades in a series of books by Keith Robertson that begins with *Henry Reed, Inc.* (Dell, 1958; Viking, 1986). Henry and his friend, Midge, always seem to have some type of scheme to make money, and the schemes often get the two friends into predicaments that they must struggle to get out of. Willo Davis Roberts's

> *Baby-Sitting Is a Dangerous Job* (Atheneum, 1985) and *Pet-Sitting Peril* (Atheneum, 1985) combine being in business with a large measure of mystery and excitement.

76 Naylor, Phyllis Reynolds
Shiloh

Naylor, Phyllis Reynolds. *Shiloh*. Atheneum, 1991. 144pp. ISBN 0-689-31614-3.
Listening Level: Early Intermediate (ages 8-9; grades 3-4)
Read-Alone Level: Intermediate (ages 9-10; grades 4-5)

Marty Preston enjoys his solitude in the hills behind his home in Friendly, West Virginia. But this day is different. Marty encounters a young beagle on the road just past the old Shiloh schoolhouse. From the way the animal is acting, Marty is sure that the dog is being abused. But Marty knows that he should not keep the dog; the dog must be returned to its owner, Judd Travers. But when the dog runs away and comes to Marty's house again, Marty decides that he must keep the dog anyway—a choice that brings near tragedy. Marty does not let his parents know that he is going to keep the dog, and so he hides him in the woods. He builds a fenced enclosure for the dog, but it isn't high enough and a German shepherd gets in and fights Shiloh. Shiloh is badly hurt, so Marty has to tell his dad about him. Together they take the dog to the veterinarian, who fixes up the dog's wounds. But when Travers finds out that his dog has been to Doc Murphy's, he shows up at the Preston door asking for his dog. When the Prestons ask to buy the dog, Travers refuses, saying that the dog isn't for sale. On the day the dog is to go back to Travers, Marty makes an early morning trip to Travers's cabin, and along the way sees him illegally kill a doe. Using that as a bargaining chip, Marty negotiates for the right to buy the dog he calls Shiloh. They finally agree on 20 hours of work in exchange for the dog. The work is back-breaking, but every day at three o'clock Marty shows up at Travers's cabin. At the end of the two weeks, Marty has learned a lot about Travers and perhaps Travers has learned some things from Marty. But the best part is that Marty has Shiloh.

A Boy (or a Girl) and a Dog

Phyllis Reynolds Naylor got the idea for her story when she came across "the saddest dog I ever saw" in West Virginia. When she returned to her home in Maryland, she couldn't get the dog out of her head. Later she found out that her friends in West Virginia located the dog and took her in. They renamed the dog Clover. Other stories of a youngster finding and loving an abused animal are told in Helen V. Griffith's *Foxy* (Greenwillow, 1984). Foxy, the dog in the story, was based on a dog the author found near her barn. The car crash, the thunderstorm, and the camping in the Florida Keys in *Foxy* all came from Griffith's experiences, but it was an item in a newspaper that suggested the plot for the book. Two other books that deal with a relationship involving a lost or stray dog are *Scruffy* by Jack Stonely (Random, 1979) and *Comeback Dog* by Jane Resh Thomas (Houghton, 1981).

Naylor's books are humorous and often contain incidents from her own life. Included in the list of books by Naylor are *The Agony of Alice* (Atheneum, 1985); *Alice in Rapture, Sort of* (Atheneum, 1989); *Beetles, Lightly Toasted* (Atheneum, 1987); *Bernie and the Bessledorf Ghost* (Atheneum, 1990); *The Bodies in the Bessledorf Hotel* (Atheneum, 1986); *Eddie, Incorporated* (Atheneum, 1980); *How I Came to Be a Writer* (Atheneum, 1987); *The Keeper* (Atheneum, 1986); *Night Cry* (Atheneum, 1984); *One of the Third-Grade Thonkers* (Atheneum, 1988); *Reluctantly Alice* (Atheneum, 1991); *The Solomon System* (Atheneum, 1983); and a book she wrote with her mother, Lura Schield Reynolds, *Maudie in the Middle* (Atheneum, 1988).

77 Nixon, Joan Lowery
Land of Hope

Nixon, Joan Lowery. *Land of Hope*. Bantam, 1992. 169 pp. ISBN 0-553-08110-1.
Listening Level: Intermediate (ages 9-10; grades 4-5)
Read-Alone Level: Intermediate Accelerated (ages 10-11; grades 5-6)

In the early 1900s, the Levinsky family, including 15-year-old Rebekah, made the decision to emigrate to America. Even though Mr. Levinsky has a successful business in Russia, as Jews they feel that they are in danger of being caught in a pogrom. They sell all that they can and travel across Austria and Germany by train. Once the family reaches Hamburg, Germany, there are long lines, questions, and inspections as the steamship company attempts to ensure that all of those who board will be accepted at New York's Ellis Island. One by one the Levinskys—Elias (father); Leah (mother); Nessin (Rebekah's older brother); Jacob (Rebekah's younger brother); Sofia (Rebekah's younger sister); and Mordecai (grandfather)—pass through the inspection lines and soon they are all crowded onto the steamer. Many of the passengers travel first or second class—and eventually will avoid the strict scrutiny that the Levinskys will undergo when they reach Ellis Island. The Levinskys travel third class and are, for the most part, confined to the main deck or below in steerage. From Germany the steamship reaches England, where it takes on additional passengers and then heads to the United States. Jacob gets seasick, and the family feels a sense of sadness in leaving their homeland. Leah grieves for her children and her parents that she left buried in Russia. Rebekah knows she will never see her best friend again. But the decision has been made and life in the United States will be much better. On board the steamship, Rebekah finds new friends, Kristin Swensen, a Swedish girl, and Rose Carney, who is Irish. It is Kristin who tells Rebekah of the freedoms that women have in the United States. Women go to school in the United States, and in several of the states the women can even vote for the president. Rebekah's grandfather has always encouraged her and now she realizes that she can have a chance at a real future. She sets her goal on attending school in the United States. But once the family arrives at Ellis Island, things do not go as Rebekah had envisioned. First, Mordecai's limp causes the inspectors at Ellis Island to examine his credentials more closely. Because he is old and not likely to get a job, he is denied entrance. He is turned away and must go back. Although returning to Russia is not a viable option, he does return to England where the family has cousins. Meanwhile, Elias and the rest of the Levinsky family leave Ellis Island to meet his brother, Avir, and his wife, Anna. Avir has written that he has a good life in America. But Elias and his family come to realize that the good life means working seven days a week, twelve hours a day, and abandoning the keeping of the Jewish Sabbath. Conflicts between old-world values and what must be done in the new world to succeed upset Rebekah. It does not help when the family receives word that Mordecai has died in England; he never made his way back to his family and the United States. Rebekah is crushed, but in many ways her grandfather's death strengthens her determination. Although Rebekah's anger and the family's situation is not completely resolved at the end of the book, one can surmise that Elias and Leah will eventually move from their sweatshop operation and begin to create the finely tailored clothing that Elias had made in his homeland. And there is really no doubt that Rebekah will succeed. She has already enrolled in night school—she wants to take all the courses she'll need in order to enter Columbia University. Rebekah knows that the United States is the land of opportunity. She will not give up her dream "no matter how hard it is to reach it."

Immigrating to America

Patricia Polacco's family were also Russian Jews who immigrated to the United States. Her family came to New York City and later moved to Michigan, where the family farmed as they had in the old country. The traditions and customs of Polacco's family are the subject of a picture book, *The Keeping Quilt* (Simon & Schuster, 1988). Other picture books that focus on emigration include *They Were Strong and Good* by Robert Lawson (Viking, 1940) and *Gooseberries to Oranges* by Barbara Cohen, illustrated by Beverly Brodsky (Lothrop, 1982). Among the heavily illustrated information books about emigrants are *Immigrant Kids* by Russell Freedman (Dutton, 1980) and *Hector Lives in the United States Now* by Joan Hewett (Lippincott, 1990). Longer books about travels to America include Beatrice Siegel's *Sam Ellis's Island* (Four Winds, 1985); Anne Pellowski's *First Farm in the Valley: Anna's Story* (Philomel, 1982); Jamie Gilson's *Hello, My Name Is Scrambled Eggs* (Lothrop, 1985); Yoshiko Uchida's *The Happiest Ending* (McElderry, 1985); and Sonia Levitin's *Journey to America* (Aladdin, 1970).

78 Nye, Naomi Shihab, selector
This Same Sky: A Collection of Poems from Around the World

Nye, Naomi Shihab, selector. *This Same Sky: A Collection of Poems from Around the World.* Illustrated by Deborah Maverick Kelley. Four Winds, 1992. 184 pp. ISBN 0-02-768440-7.
Listening Level: Intermediate (ages 9-10; grades 4-5)
Read-Alone Level: Intermediate Accelerated (ages 10-11; grades 5-6)

This collection of 155 poems reaches from 68 points on the globe and represents 129 poets. The poems speak of parakeets in mango trees, of silent beaches, towns blanketed with snow, beautiful orange trees, and of horses on green hills waiting for the moon to rise. They speak of orphans, and peace, and spring.

Poetry

Poetry speaks of the essence of life. There is a poem for every day and every occasion. Select poems from among these titles:

Bauer, Caroline Feller. *Halloween: Stories and Poems.* Illustrated by Peter Sis. Lippincott, 1989.

————. *Rainy Day: Stories and Poems.* Illustrated by Michele Chessare. Lippincott, 1986.

————. *Snowy Day: Stories and Poems.* Illustrated by Margot Tomes. Lippincott, 1986.

————. *Windy Day: Stories and Poems.* Illustrated by Dirk Zimmer. Lippincott, 1986.

de Regniers, Beatrice Schenk, et al., editors. *Sing a Song of Popcorn: Every Child's Book of Poems.* Illustrated by Marcia Brown, et al. Scholastic, 1988.

Elledge, Scott, collector and editor. *Wider Than the Sky: Poems to Grow Up With.* Harper, 1990.

Kennedy, X. J., and Dorothy M. Kennedy. *Talking Like the Rain: A First Book of Poems.* Illustrated by Jane Dyer. Little, Brown, 1992.

Larrick, Nancy, and Wendy Lamb, editors. *To Ride a Butterfly.* Bantam/Doubleday/Dell, 1991.

Prelutsky, Jack, selector. *For Laughing Out Loud: Poems to Tickle Your Funnybone.* Illustrated by Marjorie Priceman. Knopf, 1991.

————. *The Random House Book of Poetry for Children.* Illustrated by Arnold Lobel. Random, 1983.

————. *Read-Aloud Rhymes for the Very Young.* Illustrated by Marc Brown. Knopf, 1986.

79 Park, Barbara
My Mother Got Married (and Other Disasters)

Park, Barbara. *My Mother Got Married (and Other Disasters)*. Knopf, 1989. 138 pp. ISBN 0-394-82149-1.
Listening Level: Early Intermediate (ages 8-9; grades 3-4)
Read-Alone Level: Intermediate (ages 9-10; grades 4-5)

There was no way 11-year-old Charles Hickle was going to like this new arrangement. He did not like the idea that his parents had gotten divorced and he did not like the fact that his mother had gotten remarried—but most of all, he did not like his new stepfather, Ben Russo, moving into his house and bringing his teenage daughter, Lydia, and his obnoxious five-year-old son, Thomas, with him. And when Charles's mother tells him that he must share his bedroom with Thomas, it seems like the last straw, but it isn't. Worse than that, Thomas insists on hanging around every time one of Charles's friends comes over. Whenever Charles turns he hears "Charrulls." Thomas follows Charles everywhere. The worst episode begins when Lydia and Thomas's grandmother drops in unexpectedly and ends with Thomas falling off the roof and breaking his collarbone. But times do change and with Ben's help, Charles's memories of a happy family are not forgotten.

Dealing with Divorce

Barbara Abercrombie's book, *Charlie Anderson*, illustrated by Mark Graham (McElderry, 1990), tells the story of a cat who manages to have two homes and two families to love him. His story is not unlike those of children who have two homes because their parents have established separate homes. The picture book could anchor a theme-related reading focus on books dealing with relationships that must change when families separate. Two titles that might further that focus for the fans of Park's books are Betsy Byars's *The Animal, the Vegetable, and John D. Jones* (Delacorte, 1982), which tells the tale of three children's painful adjustments when Clara and Deanie's father asks a widow, John D.'s mother, to marry him; and Carol Lea Benjamin's *The Wicked Stepdog* (Crowell, 1982), in which 12-year-old Lou tells her painful and humorous reactions to her father's new wife and her new "stepdog." More mature readers will enjoy Norma Klein's *Mom, the Wolf Man, and Me* (Pantheon, 1971), the story of a professional photographer who enters the life of a teenage girl and her mother. An especially humorous tale dealing with a"step" is *My Stepfather Shrank!* by Barbara Dillon (HarperCollins,

1992). When nine-year-old Mallory's mother goes away for the weekend, Mallory finds that she inadvertently causes her stepfather to shrink. While the four books cited above deal with adjustments within stepfamilies, Beverly Cleary's *Dear Mr. Henshaw* (Morrow, 1983) is the story of a sixth-grader who attempts to deal with his loneliness and emotional conflict caused by his parents' separation and divorce.

80 Paulsen, Gary
A Christmas Sonata

Paulsen, Gary. *A Christmas Sonata.* Illustrated by Leslie Bowman. Delacorte, 1992. 76 pp. ISBN 0-385-30441-2.
Listening Level: Intermediate (ages 9-10; grades 4-5)
Read-Alone Level: Intermediate Accelerated (ages 10-11; grades 5-6)

While his father is in Europe fighting in World War II, a young boy and his mother travel by train to spend Christmas 1943 with his Uncle Ben, Aunt Marilyn, and cousin, Matthew, in northern Minnesota. Not only has the boy's faith in Santa Claus been shaken—he saw Mr. Henderson, who drank red wine and did not like the boy, dressed as Santa Claus—but the boy knows that this is the last time he will be with his cousin, who is dying. Even though Matthew is confined to his bed, the cousins play. They make faces, the boy reports back to Matthew what is going on in the family's store, and they discuss dying and Santa Claus. When Uncle Ben overhears the boys say that there is no Santa Claus, he takes steps to make a Christmas miracle happen—a miracle that restores the boys' faith in the spirit of Christmas and the fact that Santa really *does* exist.

More in the Spirit of Christmas

The holiday season is a time of reflection and for examining our own goals in life. Paulsen's *A Christmas Sonata* is a perfect read-aloud to use as a discussion starter to focus on the real meaning of our existence. Picture book titles on this same theme include Chris Van Allsburg's *Polar Express* (Houghton, 1985); *Tree of Cranes* by Allen Say (Houghton, 1991); and *Uncle Vova's Tree* by Patricia Polacco (Philomel, 1989). Other holiday stories that will have readers reflecting on what they can do to contribute to making the lives of others better include *Angels & Other Strangers: Family Christmas Stories* by Katherine Paterson (Harper,

1988); *The Bells of Christmas* by Virginia Hamilton (Harcourt, 1989); and *The Best Christmas Pageant Ever* by Barbara Robinson (Harper, 1972).

81 Paulsen, Gary
Dunc and the Flaming Ghost

Paulsen, Gary. *Dunc and the Flaming Ghost.* Dell Yearling, 1992. 80 pp. ISBN 0-440-40686-2 (paperback).
Listening Level: Early Intermediate (ages 8-9; grades 3-4)
Read-Alone Level: Intermediate (ages 9-10; grades 4-5)

Duncan "Dunc" Culpepper and his accident-prone friend, Amos, find themselves in the old Rambridge mansion searching for Amos's dog, Scruff. The mansion is said to be haunted by ghosts, and during Dunc and Amos's first visit they are scared away by a white ghost holding a lantern with matches flaming from under the brim of his hat. Subsequent visits bring them to find Eddie, who used to be a teacher but was fired for passing notes. He has been dressing up to look like Blackbeard the ghost so he could scare away the two men who use the basement of the house. Who are these men? No one knows, but they show up regularly with boxes and disappear into the basement. When they come out, they don't have the boxes. Together, Dunc and Amos and their new friend, Eddie, decide to figure out what is going on. They slip down the stairs and hide behind the wine shelves and wait for the men. Soon they hear them arrive, and in a short time they discover that the men are hiding Russian sables—an animal that is illegal to take out of Russia. The men have been hiding the sables in a room accessed through a door that can be opened only by a secret, water-activated lock. Dunc knows about this type of lock, used frequently before the days of electricity, and the Russian sables, because he has read books about them. After Dunc and Amos's discovery, they are caught in the room by the two men when they return. It is then that the boys learn the real identity of their friend. "Ghostly" Eddie calls in other ghosts, who successfully scare the men. The boys are able to tie the smugglers up and notify the police. Only then do they realize that perhaps Eddie the teacher might just *be* the real Blackbeard—the pirate whose real name was Edward Teach.

The Culpepper Adventures

Gary Paulsen is a three-time Newbery Honor award winner. His books for young adolescents are popular among intermediate or older readers. His Culpepper Adventure series (published by Dell Yearling, 1992) will appeal to those who read at a lower level. *The Case of the Dirty Bird* has Dunc and Amos in search of a buried treasure mentioned by a parrot in a pet store. *Dunc's Doll* has the two friends sleuthing for a band of doll thieves. Dunc and Amos are researching the Civil War cannon that stands in the town square in *Culpepper's Cannon*. Before the two boys know it, they find themselves in downtown Chatham on March 8, 1862—the day before the historic clash between the *Monitor* and the *Merrimac*. *Dunc Gets Tweaked* teams the friends with a new buddy named Lash—together they are off on a search of Lash's stolen skateboard. In *Dunc's Halloween*, Amos is bitten by a werewolf and becomes a werepuppy. *Amos Gets Famous* has the friends stumbling onto a burglary ring. Involved is a code that they find in a library book and Dunc's girlfriend (although she doesn't know he's alive), Melissa. One of Paulsen's Culpepper Adventure books is *Dunc Breaks the Record*, which alludes to one of Paulsen's Newbery Honor books, *Hatchet* (Bradbury, 1987). In *Dunc Breaks the Record*, the boys crash into the wilderness while hang gliding. Luckily Amos has read a book, *Hatchet*, about a boy who survived in the wilderness for 54 days. However, Amos does not have a hatchet, and things go from bad to worse when a wild man captures the boys and holds them captive.

---

82 Peters, Julie Anne
The Stinky Sneakers Contest

Peters, Julie Anne. *The Stinky Sneakers Contest.* Illustrated by Cat Bowman Smith. Little, Brown, 1992. 59 pp. ISBN 0-316-14079-1.
Listening Level: Primary (ages 6-7; grades 1-2)
Read-Alone Level: Primary Accelerated (ages 7-8; grades 2-3)

Damian always cheats at everything. He cheats and wins when he and Earl play Nintendo or when they race their bikes. Earl and Damian are best friends, but Earl wishes he could just once win at something. Then comes the contest of contests. The winner of the Feetfirst Factory's Stinky Sneakers contest will receive a 10-year supply of Jaguars—the coolest sneakers made. Each pair of Jaguars Jetstreams cost $200. But the stakes are higher than just a 10-year supply of sneakers. If Damian wins, his often-absent father promised to take him on a fishing trip. Damian buys old sneakers at the Goodwill store and sets out to stink them up with liverwurst and Limburger cheese. That, says Earl, is cheating. But Damian doesn't care. The day of the contest arrives, and all 37 Stinky Sneakers contestants line up. Family members wave and cheer on their favorite contestants—except for Damian's family. His father isn't there and neither is his mother. The contest comes down to a tie, so a final "smell-off" is held. Damian cheats one more time, inserting an odor repellent under the innersole of his shoe during the intermission. Earl wins the contest, but later realizes what happened and the disappointment he knows Damian is feeling. Disappointment, not because he lost, but because his father was still so uninterested in him. In the end the boys' friendship remains intact, the Earl invites Damian to accompany his family on their next camping trip.

Fathers and Sons

The Stinky Sneakers Contest has as a major theme that of Damian's relationship with his father. Damian seldom saw his father even though he sent him wonderfully expensive birthday presents and would buy him the newest and best sneakers without a thought. It was the lack of thought that disturbed Damian. His father paid little or no attention to him. Divorce often brings about fractured relationships and necessitates the building of new bridges between parent and child. Other titles that deal with family relationships, specifically father-and-son relationships, include a picture book, *The Lost Lake*, by Allen Say (Houghton, 1989), about an early morning camping trip taken by Luke and his father to discover a very special and secret place. Another picture book that exemplifies the father-son relationship is *The Gold Watch* by Bernice Myers (Lothrop, 1991). In Myers's tale, Joey's father loses his job, and to get money, pawns his beloved gold watch. In a show of unselfishness, Joey trades his bicycle to retrieve the watch. Intermediate and older readers will enjoy *Finn's Island* by Eileen Dunlop (Holiday House, 1992); *The Haymeadow* by Gary Paulsen (Delacorte, 1992); *Bobby Baseball* by Robert Kimmel Smith (Delacorte, 1989); *Breaking Out* by Barthe DeClements (Delacorte, 1991); and *Face to Face* by Marion Dane Bauer (Clarion, 1991).

83 Pettit, Jayne
My Name Is San Ho

Pettit, Jayne. *My Name Is San Ho.* Scholastic, 1992. 149 pp. ISBN
0-590-44172-8.
Listening Level: Early Intermediate (ages 8-9; grades 3-4)
Read-Alone Level: Intermediate (ages 9-10; grades 4-5)

This story begins in a small village in Vietnam where a horrifying war
forces San Ho and his family to dig trenches in which to hide. San Ho's story
continues in the city of Saigon, where he is taken by his mother to live with a
friend. While San Ho is in Saigon, his mother meets a United States service-
man, marries him, and travels to the United States. A few years later she is
able to arrange for San Ho to join her. Once in the United States, San Ho must
struggle to adjust to many new things: food, language, school, and his stepfather. Although there are various ups and downs in San Ho's adjustment, none
weighs to heavily as the racism he and his mother endure while his stepfather
is away. In some ways the struggles the family has in adjusting to one another
bring them closer together. Although the racism does not evaporate, San Ho
and his family feel the kindness and compassion of many people around them.
San Ho eventually is able to think of the United States as his home.

We All Came

Many of the stories of immigrants arriving in the United
States focus on the Europeans who settled the United States or
the African-Americans who were brought forcibly to become
slaves in the New World. Many of the stories reflect the same
bias that was present in the immigration policy that was used until
World War II. For many years the majority of European immigrants arrived from Ireland, Germany, Great Britain, and France.
During the second wave of immigration that began in 1880, three
out of every four immigrants came from northern or western
Europe. Immigration controls began in 1882 and were designed
to keep out immigrants from the Asian countries—primarily
China and Japan—and when quotas were made part of the law in
1921, they were based on the population already living in the
United States, thus favoring European settlers. During World
War II the quota system was made more equitable. The United
States involvement in the Vietnam War brought many immigrants to its shores, but few books have been written about the
experience of the Vietnamese young people who found themselves in the United States. Jamie Gilson's *Hello, My Name Is*

Scrambled Eggs (Lothrop, 1985) tells the story of Tuan Nguyen, who comes to America with his family when a church group sponsors them. Diane Hoyt-Goldsmith writes about another refugee in her book about a Vietnamese boy who now lives in the United States, *Hoang Anh: A Vietnamese-American Boy* (Holiday House, 1992).

84 Pollack, Pamela, selector
The Random House Book of Humor for Children

Pollack, Pamela, selector. *The Random House Book of Humor for Children.* Illustrated by Paul O. Zelinsky. Random, 1988. 304 pp. ISBN 0-394-88049-8.
Listening Level: Early Intermediate (ages 8-9; grades 3-4)
Read-Alone Level: Intermediate (ages 9-10; grades 4-5)

These 34 selections are aimed at interesting middle-grade students in books that are humorous, and whetting their appetites for further reading. The selections vary from portions taken from Judy Blume's *Tales of a Fourth Grade Nothing* to Frank B. Gilbreth and Ernestine G. Carey's *Cheaper by the Dozen* to Thomas Rockwell's *How to Eat Fried Worms* to Garrison Keillor's *Lake Wobegon Days.* Some are short stories, but many are selections from longer novels. All will bring chuckles to listeners and inspire many of them to seek out other, similar titles.

Reading Chuckles

The longer pieces from which the selections in *The Random House Book of Humor for Children* were taken will provide many students with more reading. The reading level of the selections will vary, but all will appeal to students in the intermediate grades. The books from which the selections were chosen include the following:

Babbitt, Natalie. *The Devil's Storybook.* Farrar, 1974.

Blume, Judy. *Tales of a Fourth Grade Nothing.* Dutton, 1972.

Byars, Betsy. *The Midnight Fox.* Viking, 1968.

Callen, Larry. *Who Kidnapped the Sheriff?* Little, Brown, 1985.

Cameron, Ann. *The Stories Julian Tells.* Random, 1981.

Cleary, Beverly. *Beezus and Ramona.* Morrow, 1955.

Dahl, Roald. *The Witches.* Farrar, 1983.

Eager, Edward. *Half Magic.* Harcourt, 1954.

Elliott, Bob, and Ray Goulding. *Write If You Get Work: The Best of Bob and Ray.* Random, 1975.

Ephron, Delia. *How to Eat Like a Child.* Viking, 1977; 1978.

Fisher, Dorothy Canfield. *Understood Betsy.* Holt, 1945.

Fitzhugh, Louise. *Harriet the Spy.* Harper, 1964.

Fleischman, Sid. *McBroom's Almanac.* Little, Brown, 1984.

Gilbreth, Frank B., Jr., and Ernestine Gilbreth Carey. *Cheaper by the Dozen.* Harper, 1963.

Jackson, Shirley. *Life Among the Savages.* Farrar, 1981.

Juster, Norton. *The Phantom Tollbooth.* Random, 1961.

Keillor, Garrison. *Lake Wobegon Days.* Viking, 1985.

Keller, Beverly. *No Beasts! No Children!* Morrow, 1983.

Kipling, Rudyard. *Just So Stories.* Doubleday, 1972. (Many versions are available.)

Levenson, Sam. *In One Era and Out the Door.* Simon & Schuster, 1973.

MacDonald, Betty. *Mrs. Piggle-Wiggle's Magic.* Harper, 1949.

McCloskey, Robert. *Homer Price.* Viking, 1943.

McManus, Patrick F. *The Grasshopper Trap.* Holt, 1985.

Munro, H. H. *The Complete Short Stories of Saki.* Viking, 1930; 1958.

Nesbit, E. *The Story of the Treasure Seekers.* British Book Center, 1974.

Peck, Richard. *Ghosts I Have Been.* Viking, 1977.

Peck, Robert Newton. *Soup.* Knopf, 1974.

Robinson, Barbara. *The Best Christmas Pageant Ever.* Harper, 1972.

Rockwell, Thomas. *How to Eat Fried Worms.* Watts, 1973.

Rodgers, Mary. *Freaky Friday.* Harper, 1972.

Singer, Isaac Bashevis. *Naftali the Storyteller and His Horse.* Farrar, 1973; 1976.

Thurber, James. *Fables of Our Time.* Harper, 1940; 1968.

Twain, Mark. *The Adventures of Tom Sawyer.* Macmillan, 1962. (Many versions are available.)

White, T. H. *The Sword in the Stone.* Putnam, 1939.

85 Radin, Ruth Yaffe
Carver

Radin, Ruth Yaffe. *Carver.* Illustrated by Karl Swanson. Macmillan, 1990. 70 pp. ISBN 0-02-775651-3.
Listening Level: Early Intermediate (ages 8-9; grades 3-4)
Read-Alone Level: Intermediate (ages 9-10; grades 4-5)

This is a short but poignant story of a 10-year-old boy, Jon, who is blinded at age two in a car accident—the same accident that kills his father. Shortly after the accident Jon and his mother move to Washington state where they live for eight years. Now they have moved back to Kellam's Landing, where Jon will have to attend public school. Jon is apprehensive because his teacher doesn't want a blind student in her classroom. Jon does make a friend, Matt, who sets out to help Jon accomplish a goal. Jon does not remember his father but has felt the many wood carvings his father had created. Jon would do anything to be able to carve like his father did, but he knows his mother would think he could not do it. Through Matt, Jon meets a local sculptor, Carver. Carver has kept to himself since his wife died and is known for his unpleasant disposition. But Matt and Jon make their way through his grouchy exterior and find the help Jon needs to create a carved bird for his mother. His next carving will be a plover, carved for his friend, Matt. And by the time the carving is finished, Jon and his teacher have begun to get used to one another and Carver's personality becomes somewhat more pleasant.

Blindness in Fiction

The challenge of being blind is incorporated into several stories for children. Patricia MacLachlan tells the story of a boy who attempts to learn to "see" like his blind grandfather in *Through Grandpa's Eyes* (Harper, 1980). Other titles include Leon Garfield's *Follow My Leader* (Viking, 1957; 1985) and Laura Ingalls Wilder's *On the Banks of Plum Creek* (Harper, 1937; 1953) and *By the Shores of Silver Lake* (Harper, 1939; 1953). In Wilder's *On the Banks of Plum Creek*, she tells of her sister, Mary, becoming blind as a result of contracting scarlet fever. *By the Shores of Silver Lake* includes information about Mary being sent from their home in Dakota Territory back to the Iowa Braille and Sight Saving School in Vinton, Iowa. The school still exists today. A well-known person who met the challenge of her disability is Helen Keller. Keller's tale of courage is often told; she was challenged both by her lack of sight and her deafness. In addition to many biographies written for intermediate students, David A. Adler tells Keller's story in *A Picture Book of Helen Keller* (Holiday House, 1990). The story of Keller's teacher, Annie Sullivan, is told in the biography *The Silent Storm* by Marion Brown and Ruth Crone, illustrated by Fritz Kredel (Abingdon, 1963). Before Helen Keller was taught by Annie Sullivan, Laura Bridgman pioneered the technique used to teach Keller. Bridgman's story is told in *A Child of the Silent Night* by Edith Fisher Hunter (Houghton, 1963).

---

86 Radley, Gail
The Golden Days

Radley, Gail. *The Golden Days*. Macmillan, 1991. 137 pp. ISBN 0-02-775652-1.
Listening Level: Early Intermediate (ages 8-9; grades 3-4)
Read-Alone Level: Intermediate (ages 9-10; grades 4-5)

Cory is living in his third foster home and now his foster parents, Michele and Dan, are going to have their own baby. Ms. Hanks, the social worker, is of little help. She is the one who keeps moving him in and out of homes, and she insists that the "Foster Friends" entertain at the local nursing home. But it is at that home that Cory meets Carlotta, a 75-year-old woman. Carlotta does not like living at Miss Sybil's nursing home any more than Cory likes living in foster homes. In the middle of one night Cory and Carlotta run away. They board a bus for Lanton, where they find a one-room sleeping room with kitchen privileges and a bathroom to share. They have little money but then come up with the idea to make some of Carlotta's Turkish candy to sell in local restaurants and grocery stores. Their business is just taking off when a police officer begins to inquire about Cory's presence around town during the day—boys his age should be in school. The two of them decide that they must set out once again. They board the bus and make their way to a town two hours away. Carlotta spent most of her life with the circus, and by coincidence they arrive in Hurley just as a circus is opening. The jobs they get with the circus prove to be too taxing for Carlotta; she faints and is taken to the hospital. The story ends happily when Michele and Dan use the postmark on a card Cory sends to trace him to the hospital where Carlotta is resting for a few days. Cory is hesitant to return to Michele and Dan's, but when they suggest that Carlotta come to live with them too, Cory realizes that they really do want him. Dan suggests that Carlotta can be the foster mother to the foster mother. They all agree to give it a try. And the reader is left with the idea that it will work out.

Intergenerational Friendships

Readers who enjoyed *The Golden Days* will want to read some of the following titles. Lillian Eige's *The Kidnapping of Mister Huey* (Harper, 1983) deals with a similar friendship between Willy, who doesn't want to go to the macho summer camp his father has chosen, and Mister Huey, who is being threatened with placement in "a home for old folks." Willy and Mister Huey make plans to run away to the old man's boyhood hometown. They settle into an abandoned store and are quite comfortable until their home is threatened by a gang of teenagers. In *This Is Your Captain Speaking* by Ivy Ruckman (Walker, 1987), a somewhat more conventional friendship between generations takes place. At Sunnyside, a home for the elderly, Tom meets the "Captain," Roger. Tom learns a lot about himself and about life through his friendship with Roger. In *Dangerous Ground* by Gloria Skurzynski (Bradbury, 1989), Angela's relationship with her great-aunt Hil helps her face her greatest fears and a very real danger. Readers will also enjoy the relationships in Diane Johnston Hamm's *Second Family* (Scribner's, 1992). Slightly easier to read is Kristi Holl's *Just Like a Real Family* (Atheneum, 1983) and its sequel, *No Strings Attached* (Atheneum, 1988).

87 Roberts, Willo Davis
Jo and the Bandit

Roberts, Willo Davis. *Jo and the Bandit*. Karl/Atheneum, 1992. 185
pp. ISBN 0-689-31745-X.
Listening Level: Early Intermediate (ages 8-9; grades 3-4)
Read-Alone Level: Intermediate (ages 9-10; grades 4-5)

Josephine Eleanor Elizabeth Whitman and her brother, Andrew, have lost
their father, mother, and grandmother, and are on their way to stay for a time
with their bachelor uncle, Judge Macklin, when their stagecoach is stopped
by five bandits. Later in the summer the two children's aunt will come for
them, but meanwhile, they must adjust to being in Muddy Wells. Judge
Macklin is surprised to find that "Jo" is a *girl*. But Jo helps to change her
uncle's attitude about girls when she helps him in his store and is artistic
enough to draw pictures of two of the bandits. Jo finds out that one of the
bandits is a young boy, Rufus. Once she finds out the circumstances of his
involvement, she decides to help him turn over a new leaf. This story is set in
Texas shortly after the Civil War.

The Wild West

Other writers have set their stories in the West when lawless
individuals roamed the frontier. In Gery Greer and Bob Ruddick's *Max and Me and the Wild West* (Harper, 1988), Steve and
his friend, Max, use their time machine to travel into the past.
Two picture books by Eric A. Kimmel and illustrated by Glen
Rounds present a humorous view of the wild West. *Four Dollars
and Fifty Cents* (Holiday House, 1990) has Widow Macrae turning the tables on a deadbeat cowboy, Shorty Long. She gives him
the choice of paying her the money he owes or being buried alive.
The outcome is a funny story just right for sharing aloud. Kimmel
and Rounds have produced an early title set in the West, *Charlie
Drives the Stage* (Holiday House, 1989). In this latter title, just
as Joe does in *Jo and the Bandit*, Charlie is a female who teaches
some males about the ability and determination of the opposite
sex.

88 Roberts, Willo Davis
What Could Go Wrong?

Roberts, Willo Davis. *What Could Go Wrong?* Karl/Atheneum, 1989.
169 pp. ISBN 0-689-31438-8.
Listening Level: Intermediate (ages 9-10; grades 4-5)
Read-Alone Level: Intermediate Accelerated (ages 10-11; grades 5-6)

When Aunt Molly cannot make a family get-together in Seattle, Washington, she instead invites her niece, Gracie, and her nephews, Charlie and Eddie, to fly to San Francisco to visit her. Charlie's parents are agreeable because Charlie is 13 years old and has traveled alone several times, but Gracie's parents are reluctant to agree because they view Charlie as someone who always manages to be in the midst of trouble or controversy. But finally all of the parents agree and the three cousins board the plane for San Francisco. Even before the three are off the ground, they inadvertently foil a plan to pass a coded message giving the location of a million dollars (money from illegal activities) and find themselves in the midst of the criminals' efforts to retrieve the message that Gracie has. A bomb threat to their airplane forces it to land in Portland, Oregon, and when they deplane, the three youngsters realize that they must have something that one of the two strange men at the airport wants. Their plane eventually continues on to San Francisco but not before both men manage to get on board. After landing in San Francisco, the three cousins realize that they have found the key to a locker that holds all the secrets—but the men are close behind them. When FBI agents show up, Charlie, Eddie, and Gracie feel they are safe, but the unsavory-looking men the three know as "Hawaiian Shirt" and "Mr. Upton" aren't out of the picture yet, and neither are Aunt Molly or Agent Santori.

Mysteries and Espionage

Charlie, Gracie, and Eddie manage to uncover the clues that lead the FBI to a money-laundering ring dealing in millions of dollars. The money stakes are not quite so high in some of Willo Davis Roberts's other mystery novels, but they are nonetheless exciting. Read *Pet-Sitting Peril* (Atheneum, 1985);

Baby-Sitting Is a Dangerous Job (Atheneum, 1985); *The View from the Cherry Tree* (Atheneum, 1975); and *Scared Stiff* (Atheneum, 1991). Other youngsters take a detective role in novels that early intermediate readers will enjoy, such as titles in the Fourth Floor Twins series by David A. Adler (Viking) and Adler's Cam Jansen series (Viking). Those students who read at a primary level will enjoy the Polka Dot mystery series by Patricia Reilly Giff. Titles in that series include *The Mystery of the Blue Ring* (Dell, 1987); *The Case of the Cool-Itch Kid* (Dell, 1989); *The Riddle of the Red Purse* (Dell, 1987); *Garbage Juice for Breakfast* (Dell, 1989); *The Secret at Polk Street School* (Dell, 1987); *The Trail of the Screaming Teenager* (Dell, 1990); *The Powder Puff Puzzle* (Dell, 1987); and *The Clue at the Zoo* (Dell, 1990).

89 Roos, Stephen
The Pet Lovers Club: Crocodile Christmas

Roos, Stephen. *The Pet Lovers Club: Crocodile Christmas.* Illustrated by Jacqueline Rogers. Delacorte, 1992. 126 pp. ISBN 0-385-30681-4.
Listening Level: Primary Accelerated (ages 7-8; grades 2-3)
Read-Alone Level: Early Intermediate (ages 8-9; grades 3-4)

Lem is the new boy in town and the new member of the Pet Lovers Club. Lem, his four-year-old brother, Stuart, and his mother had to move because Lem's father died. His mother is only working two or three days a week and they can't afford the same things they once had even though Grandfather is selling his farm and coming to live with them. Grandfather's help may make things easier, but they still won't be able to afford a pet—and certainly not the crocodile that Lem wants. Lem's friends in the Pet Lovers Club all have pets—rabbits, hamsters, and even a parrot—the pet Marsha will be receiving for Christmas. To keep the others from feeling sorry for him because he doesn't have a pet, he makes up a story about his mother's new job, his grandfather selling his farm for a lot of money, and his "crocodile Christmas." When Lem's mother finds out that Lem is a Pet Lovers Club member, she thinks Lem is setting himself up for a lot of disappointment because they will not be able to afford a pet. She forbids him from being a member of the group. Lem does not understand that his mother is worried about him, and in retaliation he runs away from home. The journey ends in a protest on the top of Marsha's flat roof—the Pet Lovers Club members all join with Lem in protesting his mother's edict about the club membership and in supporting Lem's wish to have a crocodile Christmas. The protest does not solve any of Lem's problems, but it does result in his mother getting a job offer at the local police station and Grandfather finding a way to give Lem (and all his friends in the Pet Lovers Club) a crocodile Christmas—at the zoo.

Pet Lovers Club Books

Although a step up in reading level, Stephen Roos's Pet Lovers Club series have been cited by *School Library Journal* as being "similar to Patricia Reilly Giff's Polk Street School series." *Crocodile Christmas* is the third in Roos's Pet Lovers Club series. The first two titles in the series are *Love Me, Love My Werewolf* (Delacorte, 1991) and *The Cottontail Caper* (Delacorte, 1992). Those who read independently at a lower level will enjoy reading Giff's the Kids of the Polk Street School series. *The Beast in Ms. Rooney's Room* (Dell, 1984) begins the series with a story about the pupils in one classroom during the month of September. Each of the following books in the series follows the same classroom of children through each month of the year. Giff has also written the New Kids at the Polk Street School series, including the titles *Watch Out! Man-Eating Snake* (Dell, 1988) and *Spectacular Stone Soup* (Dell, 1989). A recent series by Giff, The Lincoln Lions Band, features children nearing fifth grade, but the books read at a primary level. The first two titles in The Lincoln Lions Band series are *Meet the Lincoln Lions Band* (Dell, 1992) and *Yankee Doodle Drumsticks* (Dell, 1992). Other titles by Giff can be located by using your school media center or public library catalogs.

At the end of *Crocodile Christmas*, Stephen Roos gives some information about crocodiles and alligators, both of which are members of a family of animals called crocodilians. Learn more about crocodiles by reading *Alligators and Crocodiles* by John Bonnett Wexo (Wildlife, 1984); *Alligator* by Jack Denton Scott (Putnam, 1984); *The Crocodiles Still Wait* by Carol Carrick (Houghton, 1980); *Crocodiles and Alligators* by Norman Barrett (Watts, 1989); *Alligators and Crocodiles* by Michael Bright (Gloucester, 1990); and *Alligators and Crocodiles* by Lesley Dow (Facts on File, 1990).

90 Sachar, Louis
Dogs Don't Tell Jokes

Sachar, Louis. *Dogs Don't Tell Jokes.* Knopf, 1991. 209 pp. ISBN 0-679-82017-5.
Listening Level: Early Intermediate (ages 8-9; grades 3-4)
Read-Alone Level: Intermediate (ages 9-10; grades 4-5)

Gary Boone is known by his classmates as Goon—Gary + Boone. He is constantly telling jokes, some funny and some not so funny. In fifth grade he was voted class clown. No one seems to take him seriously. He has no friends at school. His classmates just make fun of him; although Gary sometimes thinks they are laughing with him, they are often laughing at him. When his sixth-grade class decides to hold a talent show, Gary thinks that this might be the opportunity to earn the respect of his classmates. His parents are apprehensive about the talent show, and while they don't tell him that he should not enter, they do convince him to spend the next three weeks *not* telling jokes to anyone, anywhere. For the $100 they have promised him, he agrees. But he also has his eye on the $100 talent show prize. Each day he restrains himself from telling his jokes, and each night he thinks of jokes and practices the way he will tell them. His days of not telling jokes just seem to highlight the way the others treat him at school. He begins to believe that maybe he wasn't as funny as he once thought he was. He quits the talent show and decides to collect baseball cards. Nothing seems to be going quite right, so despite his original thoughts he decides to be in the talent show after all. Two of his classmates decide that it will be hilarious to sabotage Gary's performance, but their efforts only heighten the laughter surrounding Gary's well-planned performance—a performance readers will not want to miss.

Louis Sachar—Funny Books

Louis Sachar studied to become a lawyer and for a time did practice law, but during law school he tried writing books and found that he liked doing that better than going into courtrooms. His first book, *Sideways Stories from Wayside School* (Follett, 1978; Avon, 1985) was not an immediate success, but eventually young readers started to take notice, and before long the humor in the book captured readers who begged for more. Sachar followed with *Wayside School Is Falling Down* (Lothrop, 1989) and *Sideways Arithmetic from Wayside School* (Scholastic, 1989). Each of the stories from Wayside School takes place in a classroom in a school that was mistakenly built 30 stories high (with one room on each floor) instead of one floor with 30 rooms.

Louis is a "yard-teacher" who sometimes helps (or hinders) the children in their learning quest. Most often the children and Louis are involved in some humorous goings-on that will make readers laugh. *Sideways Arithmetic from Wayside School* is mentioned in *Dogs Don't Tell Jokes* as one of the few books that sit alongside of Gary's many joke books. Other books by Louis Sachar include *Johnny's in the Basement* (Avon, 1981); *Someday Angeline* (Avon, 1983); *There's a Boy in the Girls' Bathroom* (Knopf, 1987); *Sixth-Grade Secrets* (Scholastic, 1987); and *The Boy Who Lost His Face* (Knopf, 1989).

91 Sachs, Marilyn
What My Sister Remembered

Sachs, Marilyn. *What My Sister Remembered.* Dutton, 1992. 122 pp. ISBN 0-525-44953-1.
Listening Level: Early Intermediate (ages 8-9; grades 3-4)
Read-Alone Level: Intermediate (ages 9-10; grades 4-5)

Molly and Beth are sisters, but each has a different set of parents. Molly's mother is Beth's aunt, but Beth's mother is not even related to Molly. If this is confusing, so is the whole situation. When Molly and Beth were very young their birth parents were killed in a car accident. Molly went to live with her "mother," who was really her dead mother's older sister. Beth, however, was injured and had to spend a lot of time in the hospital. One of the nurses there came to like Beth a lot and wanted to adopt her. So rather than go home with Molly and her aunt, Beth was taken home by Mr. and Mrs. Lattimore. The girls have not seen each other for eight years. The Lattimores live in California in a big house. Beth has a lot of the material things in life. Molly lives with her mother/aunt and father/uncle in a small apartment on the East Coast, and while they are not destitute, they are certainly not financially well-off. When the sisters finally do meet, Beth seems hostile and resentful. At times she is pleasant but at other times she seems to resent everything her aunt (Molly's mother) is doing for them. Molly thinks that Beth should be grateful that she has all the comforts of life rather than be so self-centered. What is not known until the end of the story is that Molly's father/uncle was an alcoholic and, at the time of the death of the girls' parents, was not really helping to raise his own two children (sons, Jeff and Alex, now grown) either emotionally or financially. Molly's mother/aunt simply felt that she could not cope with the additional pressure of an injured child who required a lot of care. So she kept Molly but put Beth in a foster home. The foster home was not one of the best situations. Beth was often shut in her room and told to "just get used to the situation." Although her aunt had promised that she and Molly would visit often, the visits were rare. Eventually Mrs. Lattimore, a nurse, became acquainted with the situation and, along with her husband, persuaded everyone involved that they should be allowed to adopt Beth. So Beth was adopted by the Lattimores and Molly stayed with her aunt and uncle, who adopted her. All of these years Molly was unaware of her uncle's alcoholism while Beth had been hurt emotionally by her memories of rejection. On the last day of Mrs. Lattimore and Beth's visit, a huge blowup causes all of the facts to come out. Molly begins to realize why Beth is resentful toward her aunt (Molly's mother). But Beth also begins to realize that at the time of her birth parents' deaths, her aunt was under much pressure and close to having a nervous breakdown herself. Nothing can undo the harm done by Beth's years of feeling rejected in favor of her younger sister, but she does come to understand the circumstances. Meanwhile, there are signs that perhaps there will be new bonds formed between the two families and that maybe the scars will someday heal.

Keeping Secrets

Sometimes secrets being kept are those of a dysfunctional family; sometimes the secrets involve simple fears and other times devastating events that take place behind closed doors. Hadley Irwin authored a book for older intermediate readers, *Kim/Kimi* (Viking, 1987). Kim is a 16-year-old who has been raised by her mother and stepfather; her Japanese-American father died before she was born. Kim knows little about her father and sets out to learn the *secrets* of her father's Japanese heritage. In the process she has to deal with the knowledge that her country (the United States) confined Japanese-Americans in "resettlement" camps during World War II. Irwin has also written a story, *Abby, My Love* (Atheneum, 1985), that includes a sensitive secret that Abby has been keeping since she was five years old: Her father has been sexually abusing her. Only with her friend Chip's support and encouragement is Abby able to confront her respected dentist father and get the help that the whole family needs. Other books that involve some type of secret being discovered include *Find a Stranger, Say Goodbye* by Lois Lowry (Houghton, 1978); *The Secret Life of Dagmar Schultz* by Lynn Hall (Scribner's, 1988); and *On My Honor* by Marion Dane Bauer (Clarion, 1986). Somewhat younger intermediate readers will enjoy reading about the secrets in *Anastasia at This Address* by Lois Lowry (Houghton, 1991); *Family Secrets* by Barbara Corcoran (Atheneum, 1992); and *Bear's House* by Marilyn Sachs (Avon, 1971).

92 Say, Allen
El Chino

Say, Allen. *El Chino*. Houghton, 1990. 32 pp. ISBN 0-395-52023-1.
Listening Level: Primary (ages 6-7; grades 1-2)
Read-Alone Level: Primary Accelerated (ages 7-8; grades 2-3)

A superb picture biography of Bong Way "Billy" Wong, the first Chinese matador to realize his dream of fighting to a sold-out crowd in a Spanish bullring. Billy Wong's parents emigrated from Canton, China, and settled in Nogales, Arizona. Billy's father always told his six children that in America they could be anything they wanted to be. Billy always wanted to be an athlete and was a spectacular basketball player, but he was too short to become involved professionally in the sport. He studied and became an engineer like his brother. On his first vacation he traveled to Europe and discovered Spain and bullfighting. He decided to stay in Spain and learn how to become a bullfighter. He did not get the same opportunities to show that he could fight bulls because no one thought a Chinese man could be a Spanish bullfighter. Then he realized that he needed to become a Chinese bullfighter. So instead of dressing in a Spanish costume, he dressed in Chinese attire and soon was given an opportunity to show what he could do. He became the famed *El Chino*, a master bullfighter.

Dreamers and Doers

From the time Billy Wong was young, he knew that he wanted to be an athlete. In Pat Cummings's *Talking with Artists* (Bradbury, 1992), David Wiesner, a Caldecott Award picture book artist, is quoted as saying, "I think that I always knew I wanted to become an artist." Some have dreams of their goals as very young people; others must find their dream. Stories of others who envision a dream and challenge themselves to turn the dream into reality include *Native American Doctor: The Story of Susan LaFlesche Picotte* by Jeri Ferris (Carolrhoda, 1991); *Living Dangerously: American Women Who Risked Their Lives for Adventure* by Doreen Rappaport (HarperCollins, 1991); *Follow the Dream* by Peter Sis (Knopf, 1991); *Chingis Khan* by Demi (Holt, 1991); *Mr. Blue Jeans: A Story About Levi Strauss* by Maryann N. Weidt (Carolrhoda, 1990); *Prairie Visions: The Life and Times of Solomon Butcher* by Pam Conrad (HarperCollins, 1991); *The Last Princess: The Story of Princess Káiulani of Hawaii* by Fay Stanley, illustrated by Diane Stanley (Four Winds, 1991);

> *Black Inventors and Their Inventions* by Jim Haskins (Walker, 1991); and *From Rags to Riches: People Who Started Businesses from Scratch* by Nathan Aaseng (Lerner, 1990).

93 Schulman, L. M., selector
The Random House Book of Sports Stories

Schulman, L. M., selector. *The Random House Book of Sports Stories.* Illustrated by Thomas B. Allen. Random, 1990. 246 pp. ISBN 0-394-82874-7.
Listening Level: Intermediate (ages 9-10; grades 4-5)
Read-Alone Level: Intermediate Accelerated (ages 10-11; grades 5-6)

The theme in this collection is struggle for success in physical and psychological conflicts. This collection contains 16 stories from many well-known writers: James Thurber, Ernest Hemingway, Roger Angell, Bruce Brooks, William Faulkner, and others. Included in the collection is Jack London's "The Mexican," a story about a boxer who fights for much more than personal gain, and James Thurber's hilarious account of the shortest baseball legend in history, "You Could Look It Up." William Faulkner has written "The Bear," a story about a hunter who must confront not only the animal he stalks but his own fear as well. Ernest Hemingway's story, "My Old Man," is a tale about the pleasures and perils of horse racing. The issue of racism is confronted in a selection from Bruce Brooks's *The Move Makes the Man.*

Sports Stories

The longer pieces from which the selections in *The Random House Book of Sports Stories* were taken will provide many students with more reading. The reading level of the selections will vary, but all will appeal to students in the intermediate grades. The books from which the selections were chosen include the following:

Bambara, Toni Cade. *Gorilla My Love.* Random, 1970.

Brooks, Bruce. *The Move Makes the Man.* Harper, 1984.

Faulkner, William. *Uncollected Stories of William Faulkner.* Random, 1942; 1970.

Hemingway, Ernest. *In Our Time*. Scribner's, 1925; 1953.

Kersh, Gerald. *Night and the City: Short Stories from the World of Sport*. Sterling, 1958.

Lardner, Ring. *The Best Short Stories of Ring Lardner*. Scribner's, 1957.

McInerney, Jay. *Ransom*. Random, 1985.

Saroyan, William. *My Name Is Aram*. Harcourt, 1938; 1966.

Thurber, James. *My World—And Welcome to It*. Harcourt, 1942.

Updike, John. *Museums and Women and Other Stories*. Knopf, 1968.

94 Sharpe, Susan
Chicken Bucks

Sharpe, Susan. *Chicken Bucks*. Bradbury, 1992. 132 pp. ISBN 0-02-782353-9.
Listening Level: Early Intermediate (ages 8-9; grades 3-4)
Read-Alone Level: Intermediate (ages 9-10; grades 4-5)

Twelve-year-old Mark Swenson has his heart set on having a calf to raise for this year's 4-H project, but his parents' farming operation is in trouble and there is no money for planting seeds and fertilizer, let alone a $500 calf to raise. Disappointed, Mark resigns himself to not having a calf but almost quits 4-H too. Then, in a turn of events, he decides that he could choose a more affordable project and soon is the owner of 50 laying hens. Soon he is in the egg-selling business and his friend, Emma Halvorsen, is in the vegetable and flower gardening business. Together they form the Cob Town Co-op. The new 4-H leader values money made, not just the showiest project, and offers a special $100 prize to the 4-H member who makes the most net income on his or her project during the year. Emma and Mark are determined to win the prize, even though Mark's cousins are sure they will be winning with their championship calves. Meanwhile, Mark's parents are contemplating the farming operation of their neighbors, the Fogelmans. The Fogelmans farm with no tilling and very little herbicide or chemicals to kill weeds. Their method helps to keep the topsoil from eroding and prevents poisonous chemicals from entering into a place where rain could wash them into water supplies and harm other living things. Even though the Fogelmans always make money, the neighbors think they are a little odd because of the patchwork look of their fields. However, the money Mark's parents could save on herbicides and other chemicals would go a long way toward helping pay the mortgage, so they decide to try some of the same techniques used by the Fogelmans. Mark and Emma must work hard to make their project pay off, and Mark must also suffer the insults about the farming techniques his father is using and about his nonconventional 4-H project as well. In the end the value of diversity and making your own decisions with an eye toward the final objective is shown.

More Books by Susan Sharpe

Chicken Bucks is Susan Sharpe's third novel that has featured environmental concerns. Her first book, *Waterman's Boy* (Bradbury, 1990), is the story of Ben, who wants to be a Chesapeake Bay waterman like his father, but pollution threatens to make that a difficult way of life. One of the guests in his mom's bed-and-breakfast is looking for an oil leak in the bay. Ben decides to help locate where the oil is being dumped and discover who the polluters are. *Waterman's Boy* has been described by *Booklist* as a "well-paced ecological mystery-adventure." A second book by Sharpe, *Spirit Quest* (Bradbury, 1991), deals with fifth-grader Aaron's reluctance to spend a summer at LaPush, a Quileute Indian reservation, while his mother studies the sea life along the coast of Washington State. But during the summer Aaron meets a Quileute Indian boy, Robert—a boy his own age—and learns to respect, appreciate, and in some ways, envy Robert's rich heritage.

---

95 Slote, Alfred
The Trading Game

Slote, Alfred. *The Trading Game*. Lippincott, 1990. 200 pp. ISBN 0-397-32397-2.
Listening Level: Early Intermediate (ages 8-9; grades 3-4)
Read-Alone Level: Intermediate (ages 9-10; grades 4-5)

Tubby Watson knows his baseball cards, and he has the one that Andy Harris really wants. The card, an Ace 459 Jim Harris 1b, is only worth 25 cents but it features Andy's hero—his grandfather. Tubby has it and he isn't selling, but he will trade. Soon Andy will have baseball cards to trade—he is inheriting his dad's collection and one of them is the 1952 Mickey Mantle card that Tubby wants. The problem is that the Mantle card is worth $2,500. But trading it to Tubby seems to be the only way that Andy is going to get the card that features his "grampa." The only way, that is, until Alice Cartwright enters the "trading game." Alice is the third baseman on the Watson Chevrolet Little League team—the same team that Tubby and Andy play on. Alice is a card collector herself and she knows the value of the cards as well as anyone. She also knows the value of friendship and manages to teach both Andy and Tubby a thing or two. Meanwhile, Andy manages to get to know his grampa a little bit better and comes to understand the relationship his grandfather and father had—the love and the turmoil.

Baseball and Those Who Love It

Johanna Hurwitz's book, *Baseball Fever* (Morrow, 1981), tells of Ezra Feldman and his love of baseball and baseball history. His European-born father doesn't understand the game and thinks Ezra should be learning to play chess instead. Neither one can see the virtue in the other's interest.

Intermediate readers who enjoy learning about baseball and about those who played the game will enjoy browsing through the facts and statistics in *The Baseball Book* by Zander Hollander (Random, 1991). Younger readers will enjoy *Baseball's Best: Five True Stories* by Andrew Gutelle (Random, 1990). Hall of Famers Babe Ruth, Joe DiMaggio, Jackie Robinson, Roberto Clemente, and Hank Aaron are profiled.

---

96 Smith, Janice Lee
The Show-and-Tell War
and Other Stories About Adam Joshua

Smith, Janice Lee. *The Show-and-Tell War and Other Stories About Adam Joshua.* Illustrated by Dick Gackenbach. Harper, 1988. 162 pp. ISBN 0-06-025814-4.
Listening Level: Primary (ages 6-7; grades 1-2)
Read-Alone Level: Primary Accelerated (ages 7-8; grades 2-3)

Adam Joshua had planned on doing a lot of things during the summer, but school would start soon and he had many things that he still hadn't done. He makes a list of things he needs to do *next* summer and then goes back to his tree house. The one thing he hasn't started doing yet is worrying about going to school. He hopes that the bully, Elliot Banks, will not be in his class again, and that he will be better at math. He'll certainly miss his fish and his dog, George, when school starts. Adam Joshua has his problems. He has trouble returning the book he has stolen from the library. His dog, George, pays a lot of attention to his younger sister. But his worst problem is show-and-tell. Every time Adam Joshua brings something, Elliot brings something to top it. But when Adam Joshua brings his best friend, Nelson, for show-and-tell, he manages to do something that Elliot could not do. Elliot tries to buy a friend to bring to show-and-tell but to no avail. That marks a turning point. At the end of the story, Elliot brings his fossil collection to school, something that interests many of the students in the class. And Elliot and Adam Joshua look over at one another and smile.

Adam Joshua and His Friends

Janice Lee Smith and illustrator Dick Gackenbach have written other books about Adam Joshua: *The Kid Next Door and Other Headaches* (Harper, 1984); *The Monster in the Third Dresser Drawer and Other Stories About Adam Joshua* (Harper, 1981); and *There's a Ghost in the Coatroom: Adam Joshua's Christmas* (Harper, 1991). These books will challenge the primary reader, but the interest level will be on target.

---

97 Spinelli, Jerry
The Bathwater Gang Gets Down to Business

Spinelli, Jerry. *The Bathwater Gang Gets Down to Business.* Illustrated by Meredith Johnson. Little, Brown, 1992. 59 pp. ISBN 0-316-80808-3.
Listening Level: Primary (ages 6-7; grades 1-2)
Read-Alone Level: Primary Accelerated (ages 7-8; grades 2-3)

Bertie Kidd and her friends have formed Bathwater Inc., a pet cleaning business, and Bertie is its president. On the first day the group is equipped with a metal tub, scrub brushes, pet shampoo, and Granny's business advice. The group's objective is to make enough money to buy tickets to the circus. They make posters to advertise their service. But no one seems to want to hire them, and they earn only 5 cents on the first day. On the second day they take a wagon load of mud up and down the street. They encourage all the neighbors' pets to wallow in the mud. Shortly after they return to their own yard, pet washing business animals begin showing up. At the end of the day they have earned more than $15—enough to buy tickets to the circus. But Granny finds out that they had really flimflammed their customers and makes them give all the money back. Bertie knows that she is to blame—and the flimflam was her fault. She stays in her room and refuses to eat or go to the circus parade. But then Granny tells Bertie that she must try one more time to follow directions. Granny tells her to call all of the Bathwater Inc. members and to have them report to the circus gate. Together the gang gets a job to wash an elephant; in return they will each receive a pass to the circus and a certificate for $5 in refreshments. Bertie even makes friends with Robert, the boy who had sabotaged their business on the first day.

In the Business

Stories about real-life business people are included in Nathan Aaseng's *From Rags to Riches: People Who Started Businesses from Scratch* (Lerner, 1990). Included in the stories are those of the entrepreneurs who started Folger's, Heinz, DuPont, and Dow Chemical. Aaseng has also written *Midstream Changes: People Who Started Over and Made It Work* (Lerner, 1990). This collective biography features anecdotes about Levi Strauss, Milton Bradley, Colonel Sanders, and Mary Kay Ash.

A fictionalized account of a business venture is included in a picture book, *Arthur's Pet Business* by Marc Brown (Joy Street/Little, Brown, 1990). A fictionalized account of a pet business written for older intermediate readers is Willo Davis Roberts's *Pet-Sitting Peril* (Atheneum, 1985).

---

98 Spinelli, Jerry
Maniac Magee

Spinelli, Jerry. *Maniac Magee*. Little, Brown, 1990. 184 pp. ISBN 0-316-80722-2.
Listening Level: Intermediate (ages 9-10; grades 4-5)
Read-Alone Level: Intermediate Accelerated (ages 10-11; grades 5-6)

No one seems to know how Jeffrey Lionel Magee ended up in Two Mills, but almost everyone had a theory or two. Jeffrey's parents died and he was sent to live with an aunt and uncle. He was barely tolerated in their home and the situation was not to his liking either, so he left Holidaysburg. He shows up in Two Mills looking like the scraggly little kid he is with his feet hanging out of sneakers with soles flapping against the pavement. His first acquaintance turns out to be Amanda Beale. Amanda befriends Jeffrey and her family takes him in, but his white face does not fit on the East Side. But his reputation is building and his running and daring feats earn him the nickname Maniac. But the more visible he becomes, the more difficult his life gets. He is run out of the East Side, and for a while Maniac sleeps in the buffalo pen in the zoo. Later, after making friends with the zookeeper, Maniac sets up a "house" of sorts under the stadium in the baseball room. During his encounters with the McNabs he fares little better than he did on the East Side. But little by little, through his contacts with people from all parts of the town, Maniac begins to help the East Siders understand the West Siders and vice versa. His gentle efforts begin to build bridges between those from the East Side and those from the West Side, yet for all of Maniac's success he still doesn't have a family or a real home. When he returns to the buffalo pen it is time for Amanda to get back into the action.

Dealing with Differences

In *Maniac Magee*, Grayson was somewhat surprised that the blacks on the East Side ate mashed potatoes and used tooth-brushes—misconceptions that were easily cleared up. But Maniac was not sure where he fit into the town's population. Which side should he embrace or should there be sides? Walter Dean Myers is another author who writes stories of young people who must face challenges and make decisions that will affect the rest of their lives. Intermediate readers will enjoy Myers's *Crystal* (Viking, 1987); *Won't Know Till I Get There* (Viking, 1982); *Fast Sam, Cool Clyde, and Stuff* (Viking, 1975), and *The Young Landlords* (Viking, 1979). Accelerated readers will enjoy reading Myers's *It Ain't All for Nothin'* (Viking, 1978) and *Motown and Didi: A Love Story* (Viking, 1984).

---

99 St. George, Judith
Dear Dr. Bell ... Your Friend, Helen Keller

St. George, Judith. *Dear Dr. Bell ... Your Friend, Helen Keller*. Putnam, 1992. 95pp. ISBN 0-399-22337-1.
Listening Level: Intermediate Accelerated (ages 10-11; grades 5-6)
Read-Alone Level: Intermediate Accelerated+ (ages 10-11+; grades 5-6+)

Helen Keller was born in 1880 and by the age of six months was speaking a couple of words. At the age of 19 months she was stricken with an illness that left her deaf and blind. For the next five-and-a-half years she grew up doing whatever she wanted with little guidance. One day she locked her mother in the pantry and sat for three hours enjoying the vibrations of her mother pounding on the door. A household worker happened by and unlocked the pantry door. That is the day that Helen Keller's parents knew they must get help for Helen. Soon Helen and her father travel to see a world famous eye doctor in hope that he might be able to restore some of Helen's sight. Although he does not hold out any hope for the restoration of any sight, he does recommend that she be taken to see Alexander Graham Bell. Bell had long been interested in helping the deaf to learn, so the Kellers sought advice on educating Helen. Bell's suggestions eventually bring about the arrival of teacher Annie Sullivan to the Keller household on March 3, 1887—coincidentally it was also Alexander Graham Bell's fortieth birthday. Over the years Helen Keller would often seek Bell's advice. He was her advisor and helped her financially as well. He encouraged her to speak out on political issues and supported her through good times and bad. This account of Helen Keller's life focuses on the relationship and remarkable friendship between two extraordinary people.

People Who Achieve

Much of the work done with Helen Keller was based on the education of Laura Bridgman, the first deaf-blind child who was educated to communicate with the outside world. The work with Bridgman, 50 years before Helen Keller, helped to pave the way for Helen Keller's education. Laura Bridgman's story is told in Edith Fisher Hunter's *Child of the Silent Night* (Houghton, 1963). Others who challenged the limits of established norms include writer Emily Dickinson. Her story is told in *I'm Nobody! Who Are You? The Story of Emily Dickinson* by Edna Barth (Clarion, 1971). Other biographies that are interesting reading include *Lincoln: A Photobiography* by Russell Freedman (Clarion, 1987); *Franklin Delano Roosevelt* by Russell Freedman (Clarion, 1991); and *Founding Mothers: Women in America in the Revolutionary Era* by Linda Grant DePauw (Houghton, 1975).

---

100 Talbert, Marc
Double or Nothing

Talbert, Marc. *Double or Nothing.* Illustrated by Toby Gowing. Dial, 1990. 129 pp. ISBN 0-8037-0832-7.
Listening Level: Early Intermediate (ages 8-9; grades 3-4)
Read-Alone Level: Intermediate (ages 9-10; grades 4-5)

Sam has a loving relationship with his Uncle Frank, a magician—"Phantasmagoric Frank." But now Uncle Frank has died and all of his magic boxes have been sent to Sam, an aspiring magician. Through a series of flashbacks, Sam remembers magic tricks his uncle taught him; special memories of the times the two of them had together. Each year on his own birthday, Uncle Frank sent Sam a "birthday" present; Frank said it was his birthday and he could do anything he wanted to—and he wanted to give Sam a present. So he did. The presents were always unusual and often brought about a new tradition, or motivated Sam to learn a new magic trick. The magician's name he choose for himself was "Excyclamazing Sam." After Frank's death, Sam could not rest until he too visited Cathedral Park and performed magic tricks for those visiting the park. Sam's parents would not approve, but Sam has to do it—for Uncle Frank.

Boxes of Magic

In *Double or Nothing*, Sam receives many boxes from his Uncle Frank—and presumably many of them contain magic tricks for Sam to learn. A box of magic is also a major element in Brian Selznick's illustrated junior novel *The Houdini Box* (Knopf, 1991). Selznick's book is loosely based on the life of the great magician Harry Houdini. An author's note at the end of the book explains the facts that are included in the book, as well as the liberties Selznick took with the facts. Interestingly, one of the facts Selznick thought he was making up for the story—the existence of Houdini's box of magic—was, according to a newspaper report he found later, reportedly true. Those who wish to learn a few magic tricks for themselves will find 23 magic tricks in Robert Friedhoffer's *Magic Tricks, Science Facts* (Watts, 1990) and more than 30 visual tricks and optical illusions in David Thomson's *Visual Magic* (Dial, 1991).

---

101 Thomas, Jane Resh
The Princess in the Pigpen

Thomas, Jane Resh. *The Princess in the Pigpen*. Clarion, 1989. 130 pp. ISBN 0-395-51587-4.
Listening Level: Early Intermediate (ages 8-9; grades 3-4)
Read-Alone Level: Intermediate (ages 9-10; grades 4-5)

Standing in the middle of a pigpen in Iowa is not somewhere most princesses find themselves, but that is exactly where Elizabeth, daughter of the Duke of Umberland, finds herself. The last thing Elizabeth remembers is being on a sickbed (in the seventeenth century). Now she finds herself in the middle of oinking pigs (in the twentieth century). Ann, a girl about Elizabeth's age, finds her on the farm and at first cannot believe her story. And Elizabeth is having a hard time believing that women doctors exist, especially one who can cure her of the sickness that is plaguing all of England—including her desperately ill mother. When Ann finds Elizabeth's picture in a history book, she realizes that Elizabeth really has traveled through time. She agrees to help Elizabeth return to England and the seventeenth century. The only question that faces the girls is whether or not Elizabeth should risk changing the course of history by taking with her the only thing that might cure her desperately ill mother—penicillin.

Traveling in Time

It was a flash of light that brought Elizabeth into the twentieth century, but time machines also enable travel through time. Blossom Culp, a character created by Richard Peck, is transported from the early 1900s into the 1980s. Blossom encounters Alexander, a high school freshman, who tells the story *The Ghost Belonged to Me* (Delacorte, 1975). Later Blossom tells some of her own tales in *Ghosts I Have Been* (Delacorte, 1977) and *The Dreadful Future of Blossom Culp* (Delacorte, 1983). In Carol Gorman's *T. J. and the Pirate Who Wouldn't Go Home* (Scholastic, 1990), Uncle Ainsley's time machine brings a pirate from the nineteenth century into the present. Being a pirate, Captain Billy gets into a lot of trouble in the nineteenth century. Characters who travel forward in time present one type of problem for those around them, while characters who travel back in time find themselves with other problems. Gery Greer and Bob Ruddick send Max and Steve back to the Middle Ages in *Max and Me and the Time Machine* (Harcourt, 1983), and out to the wild West in *Max and Me and the Wild West* (Harcourt, 1988). Fifth- and sixth-grade students will enjoy one of the most intriguing time travel stories written—Cynthia Voigt's *Building Blocks* (Atheneum, 1984). In Voigt's story, a young boy goes back in time to his father's youth and actually meets his own father as a child. While the stories of Peck, Greer and Ruddick, and Voigt use the time travel element, they are basically realistic tales of life during the time period in which the story is set. However, many writers of modern science fantasy also use the dimension of the time warp in their fanciful tales—among those writers are Madeleine L'Engle, Margaret J. Anderson, Andre Norton, and David Wiseman. Able intermediate readers and beyond will enjoy reading stories told by these master storytellers.

102 Wallace, Bill

Danger in Quicksand Swamp

Wallace, Bill. *Danger in Quicksand Swamp.* Holiday House, 1989. 181
pp. ISBN 0-8234-0786-1.
Listening Level: Intermediate (ages 9-10; grades 4-5)
Read-Alone Level: Intermediate Accelerated (ages 10-11; grades 5-6)

It is just a quirk of circumstances that lead Ben and Jake to find the boat
filled with rocks and sunk in the sandy river bottom behind their house. When
they find a treasure map in an old jar under the seat of the bow their excitement
grows. If they can just find the money they'll be able to buy a new boat. Going
to the island to find the spot marked on the map is going to take some
maneuvering. Their parents do not want them to go and for good reasons—the
island has quicksand, and unbeknownst to the boys, there are alligators. Once
the boys arrive at the island they find that their boat has been stolen—and they
are being pursued by a man who seems to prefer the two boys dead. Alligators,
quicksand, and a desperate man who wants to cover up a murder provide
plenty of action.

A Run for the Money

Ben and Jake find themselves in great danger and all because
of their attempt to locate a treasure. Readers who enjoy this book
will also enjoy Avi's *Windcatcher* (Bradbury, 1991) and Thomas
J. Dygard's *Wilderness Peril* (Morrow, 1985). In Dygard's book,
two teenage canoeists find themselves in the Boundary Waters
Canoe Area with a hijacker's stashed $75,000 in ransom money,
and unknowingly they encounter the hijacker. Once the hijacker
realizes that the boys have his money, he pursues them to the edge
of the wilderness—and pushes them past the point of adventure
and excitement.

103 Walter, Mildred Pitts
Have a Happy ...

Walter, Mildred Pitts. *Have a Happy ....* Illustrated by Carde Byard.
Lothrop, 1989. 106 pp. ISBN 0-688-06923-1.
Listening Level: Primary Accelerated (ages 7-8; grades 2-3)
Read-Alone Level: Early Intermediate (ages 8-9; grades 3-4)

Christopher Noel Dodd's birthday is on Christmas Day. He has always
felt his birthday got lost in the shuffle of the holiday. But this year his father
is out of work and there is not much money. The family probably will not have
much of a Christmas and Chris's birthday will likely go unnoticed. On
December 26 the family will begin the seven-day celebration of their African-
American heritage, Kwanzaa. More than anything Chris wants his father to
find a job so that the family doesn't have to move; next to that he wants a
bicycle of his own. Walter tells a story of how holiday wishes come true when
one has *imani* (faith), *kujichagulia* (self-determination), *kuumba* (creativity),
nia (purpose), *ujamaa* (cooperative economics), *ujima* (collective work and
responsibility), and *umoja* (unity)—the seven principles of Kwanzaa.

Kwanzaa

Kwanzaa is an African-American holiday celebration that
begins on December 26 and ends on January 1. The holiday was
founded in 1966 by Dr. Maulana Karenga as a time of ingathering
of African-Americans to celebrate their history. An explanation
of how this ethnic holiday got its start and how it is celebrated is
available for the beginning reader in *Kwanzaa* by A. P. Porter,
illustrated by Janice Lee Porter (Carolrhoda, 1991); *Kwanzaa*
by Deborah M. Newton Chocolate, illustrated by Melodye
Rosales (Children's, 1990); and Diane Hoyt-Goldsmith's *Celebrating Kwanzaa*, illustrated by Lawrence Migdale (Holiday,
1993).

104 Warner, Gertrude Chandler
The Disappearing Friend Mystery

Warner, Gertrude Chandler. *The Disappearing Friend Mystery.* Illustrated by Charles Tang. Whitman, 1992. 121 pp. ISBN 0-8075-1627-9.
Listening Level: Early Intermediate (ages 7-8; grades 3-4)
Read-Alone Level: Intermediate (ages 8-9; grades 4-5)

The Alden children, Henry, Jessie, Violet, and Benny, lived in a boxcar before they had come to Greenfield to live with their grandfather Alden. The children had been orphaned and had run away when they were told that they would have to live with their grandfather, a man that they had heard was mean. Eventually Grandfather Alden finds the children living in the boxcar and convinces them to come to live with him. The children do and soon realize that he is not mean. In fact, he has their boxcar moved behind his house so the children can visit it whenever they want. During a grocery shopping trip, the children read about a fund drive a local hospital is having to raise money for a new hospital wing, and meet a new friend, Beth Simon. Before long, the children and Beth agree that they could earn money to contribute to the fund-raiser. They plan to meet and make posters to advertise their new helper service. But from the beginning their activities seem to be sabotaged. Their art supplies disappear and they must buy new supplies before they can make the posters. When they leave to go home, Benny's bike tires are flat. Strange things continue to occur—posters are torn, gardens they plant are ruined, and keys to houses are missing. Their new friend, Beth, seems to like them one moment, and then the next time they meet she doesn't seem to know what is going on. In the end, the mysterious happenings, including the strange behavior of Beth, are solved. It turns out that Beth has a twin, Heather, who has been trying to sabotage the efforts being made by Beth and her friends. Once the Boxcar children realize that there is a twin, they decide to include her in their activities—and all ends well.

The Boxcar Children

As a child Gertrude Chandler Warner watched trains go by on the tracks opposite her family home. She often wondered what it might be like to set up housekeeping in a caboose or freight car. When she grew up, Warner became a teacher and soon after was searching for books that were both easy and fun to read. She decided to write some of her own and wrote *The Boxcar Children*. It became a very successful title, and soon she was asked to write more adventures of Henry, Jessie, Violet, and Benny Alden. In each story she tried to include a special setting and introduced unusual or eccentric characters. Often those characters did the unpredictable. Warner liked to stress the resourcefulness and independence of the Alden children. Originally the four children lived alone in the boxcar. Eventually Dr. Moore, who had given Henry some work, figured out the mystery of Grandfather Alden's missing grandchildren; it was Dr. Moore who had helped bring Grandfather Alden and the Alden children together. Now the four children live with their grandfather and their house-keeper, Mrs. McGregor. Their boxcar sits in their backyard and they use it for all kinds of activities. Introduce the four children and read some of their other stories in Boxcar Children Mysteries. Newer titles include *The Animal Shelter Mystery* (Whitman, 1991); *The Deserted Library Mystery* (Whitman, 1991); *The Mystery of the Hidden Painting* (Whitman, 1992); *The Old Motel Mystery* (Whitman, 1992); *The Amusement Park Mystery* (Whitman, 1992); and *The Haunted Cabin Mystery* (Whitman, 1991). Gertrude Chandler Warner died in 1979. At the time of her death she was living in Putnam, Connecticut. Titles issued since her death have been written by ghostwriters hired by the publisher. Each title has been written in a style and format similar to those of the original titles written by Warner herself.

105 Warren, Cathy
Roxanne Bookman: Live at Five!

Warren, Cathy. *Roxanne Bookman: Live at Five!* Bradbury, 1988. 100 pp. ISBN 0-02-792492-0.
Listening Level: Primary Accelerated (ages 7-8; grades 2-3)
Read-Alone Level: Early Intermediate (ages 8-9; grades 3-4)

First Roxanne Bookman contributes to the sorry performance of the Lazy Hills Hornets and to their loss against the Edgebrook Eagles in the baseball battle of the season. Then Roxanne nominates her favorite teacher (and summer baseball coach), Mr. Diggins, as the best teacher for the competition on Channel Six's "Live at Five" program. During the interview, Mr. Diggins makes a poor showing and Miss Hills, a teacher at Edgebrook, wins handily. Roxanne finds out about a Brain Teaser Contest to be held on an expanded Saturday version of "Live at Five." Mr. Diggins allows Roxanne to get a team together to represent Lazy Hills, but after his experience with coaching he has decided not to coach any team again. Roxanne's parents come to the rescue and the team begins to practice. However, they

are too anxious and too competitive—and are setting themselves up for another defeat. But when Mr. Diggins steps back into the picture, the team is ready to move forward and they do—to muster one final attack against the Edgebrook Eagles.

Underdogs Win

The Lazy Hills School seemed to be taking second place in baseball, school facilities, teachers, and were generally regarded as second class. That is until the team representing Lazy Hills challenged the Edgebrook Eagles, in their matching polo shirts, to a Brain Teaser Contest. Alex Frankovitch faces a similar situation in *Skinnybones* by Barbara Park (Knopf, 1982). In *Skinnybones*, Alex is not only the skinniest kid on his losing team, but one of the least talented players. And then there is T. J. Stoner, who can't seem to lose and doesn't let "Skinnybones" forget it. However, Alex does not stay in second place forever. In a sequel written by Park, *Almost Starring Skinnybones* (Knopf, 1988), Alex once again faces some embarrassing situations even though he is now a media celebrity. Other titles by Park feature characters who face adversity caused by the approval or disapproval of their peers: *The Kid in the Red Jacket* (Knopf, 1987); *Maxie, Rosie, and Earl—Partners in Grime* (Knopf, 1990); and *Operation: Dump the Chump* (Knopf, 1982).

---

106 Weiss, Ellen, and Mel Friedman
The Poof Point

Weiss, Ellen, and Mel Friedman. *The Poof Point*. Knopf, 1992. 166 pp. ISBN 0-679-83257-2.
Listening Level: Early Intermediate (ages 8-9; grades 3-4)
Read-Alone Level: Intermediate (ages 9-10; grades 4-5)

Mr. and Mrs. Bickers are inventors. And they often invent things that go haywire. This time the Bickers are working on a time machine. With the help of their mysterious friend, Ozzie Regenbogen, the two of them figure out how to make the time machine function. Only instead of taking the two to another time in the universe, the time machine takes them to another time in their own lives. While the Bickers's children, Marie and Eddie, watch, their parents regress to teenage science nerds and later to being a seven- and nine-year-old. Ozzie Regenbogen promises to help the children undo the time machine's effect. However, if Ozzie does not succeed before the Bickers reach "the poof point" (age zero), no one knows what will happen. The children and Ozzie must discover a way to reverse the time machine's function or Marie and Eddie might never see their parents again.

Traveling in Time

Readers who are more able and who are interested in science fiction will enjoy reading Ruth Park's *Playing Beatie Bow* (Atheneum, 1982) and books by William Sleator. In *Playing Beatie Bow*, Abigail Kirk, a 14-year-old Australian, finds that she has been sent to Sydney during 1870 to preserve "the gift" to foretell the future. William Sleator's *The Duplicate* (Dutton, 1988) is described by the author as being about "a boy who makes a duplicate copy of himself, thinking it will solve all his problems. Of course, it only creates a lot more problems." In Sleator's *Singularity* (Dutton, 1985), 16-year-old identical twins, Harry and Barry Krasner, travel to their mother's newly inherited Illinois farm and discover a playhouse that has the ability to speed up time. The playhouse is built around one side of a singularity—a black hole—which is the egress from another universe. The results of Harry's overnight stay in the playhouse bring to the reader the mystique of twins, external forces, science fiction elements, and some hints of scientific theory. Jane Resh Thomas's *The Princess in the Pigpen* (Clarion, 1989; described in this book) is a time travel novel.

---

107 Whayne, Susanne Santoro
Watch the House

Whayne, Susanne Santoro. *Watch the House.* Illustrated by Leslie Morrill. Simon & Schuster, 1992. 70 pp. ISBN 0-671-75886-1.
Listening Level: Primary Accelerated (ages 7-8; grades 2-3)
Read-Alone Level: Early Intermediate (ages 8-9; grades 3-4)

Those who enjoy tales of animals and their antics will be enthralled with the story of family pets—Phillo, a golden Labrador retriever; Beverly, the canary; Harriet, a calico cat; Butch, a guinea pig; two guppies named Bonnie and Clyde; and Jules, a kitten. Shortly after Katey and Neal go off to their fifth-grade class and Mom and Dad drop the baby off at the sitter's house before going to work, the pets (all except Bonnie and Clyde) are convinced, by Jules, that they should see what they are missing in the great outdoors. Even though they have been admonished to "watch the house," the five friends set off to see what the day will bring—outside. They survive attacks from hornets, a hawk, and an encounter with a porcupine. For a time Beverly is feared lost and her friends frantically search for her. Eventually the five return home—just in time.

Animal Hijinks

Those who enjoyed this tale of animal escapades will enjoy James Howe's junior novel *Hot Fudge* (Morrow, 1990). This tale introduces Harold and Chester, animal characters popular in Howe's novels for a slightly older reader. Harold relates a day's events and reveals his love of chocolate and his sense of duty and responsibility. Other junior novels about these characters include Howe's *Creepy-Crawly Birthday* (Morrow, 1991); *The Fright Before Christmas* (Morrow, 1988); and *Scared Silly: A Halloween Treat* (Morrow, 1989). *Howliday Inn*, coauthored with Deborah Howe (Atheneum, 1982; Avon, 1987) and *The Celery Stalks at Midnight* (Atheneum, 1983; Avon, 1984) will be popular with intermediate students. Leslie Morrill, the illustrator of the Whayne title, has also illustrated several of the Howe titles.

---

108 Whelan, Gloria
Hannah

Whelan, Gloria. *Hannah*. Illustrated by Leslie Bowman. Knopf, 1991. 63 pp. ISBN 0-679-81397-7.
Listening Level: Primary Accelerated (ages 7-8; grades 2-3)
Read-Alone Level: Early Intermediate (ages 8-9; grades 3-4)

The year is 1897 and the Braille method of reading and writing has just recently reached America. However, nine-year-old Hannah, who is blind, doesn't know anything about reading and writing; she isn't even allowed to go to school. This year the new teacher, Miss Robbins, will live with Hannah's family. Hannah knows that she won't get to go to school but hopes that just knowing Miss Robbins will give her something to look forward to. Her world is the farmhouse where the family lives and the church that the family attends each Sunday. Miss Robbins has more of an impact than Hannah had hoped for. Hannah's first experience is a walk around her own family's farm—she has never been around the animals. Miss Robbins is determined to help Hannah become independent. Eventually Hannah's mother agrees to let Hannah go to school. The first day is a disaster and both Hannah and her mother are reluctant to consider a second day. But Hannah does go back and finds support and encouragement among her classmates. In a touching climax, Carl, the school's oldest (and naughtiest) student, finds a way to help Hannah earn the money for the $5 device Hannah needs to help her learn how to write in Braille.

Overcoming Challenges

Hannah will find her way in the world with the love and support of her family and many friends. A picture book that portrays the triumph of a young blind boy is *Cakes and Miracles: A Purim Tale* by Barbara Diamond Goldin (Viking, 1991). An angel reminds the boy that he does see things, in his mind. The next morning the boy arises and makes cookies that match the images dancing in his head. All the townspeople flock to buy the pretty cookies shaped like flowers and animals. The book includes a recipe for *hamantashen*. Intermediate readers will enjoy reading about Mary, Laura Ingalls Wilder's sister in her Little House Books, in *On the Banks of Plum Creek* (Harper, 1937; 1953) and *By the Shores of Silver Lake* (Harper, 1939; 1953). Laura Ingalls Wilder wrote about her sister's blindness and the challenges Mary faced. Another story—a short but powerful one—has a young person (in a contemporary setting) facing the challenges of blindness in Ruth Yaffe Radin's *Carver* (Macmillan, 1990; see the entry in this book). Jean Little, an author who writes for more mature readers, is legally blind. Her writing often speaks of challenges brought about because of physical disabilities. In 1991, HarperCollins released a new edition of a book for Little, *Listen for the Singing*, first published by Dutton in 1977. Introduced in *From Anna* (Harper, 1972), Anna flourishes in high school despite her poor vision. The stories about Anna are set in Canada in the late 1930s. Sally Hobart Alexander tells her own story of blindness and living a fulfilling, independent life through the viewpoint of her daughter in a 48-page book, *Mom Can't See Me* (Macmillan, 1990). This book is filled with photographs and inspiration.

109 Wood, June Rae
The Man Who Loved Clowns

Wood, June Rae. *The Man Who Loved Clowns*. Putnam, 1992. 224 pp.
ISBN 0-399-21888-2.
Listening Level: Intermediate (ages 9-10; grades 4-5)
Read-Alone Level: Intermediate Accelerated (ages 10-11; grades 5-6)

A poignant story of 13-year-old Delrita, who leads a mostly solitary life because her parents also care for her uncle—an uncle challenged with Down's syndrome. Delrita loves her uncle, Punky, but hates situations where his behavior causes strangers to stop and stare and sometimes even make offensive comments. Each time a situation occurs, Delrita draws further into her shell. She has not made any friends in her new school and considers herself "invisible." Other students don't usually talk to her and teachers rarely call on her. At home the family has to deal with the disapproval of Aunt Esther (or Aunt Queenie, as she is known). Aunt Queenie disapproves of the way Delrita's mother takes care of Punky. Aunt Queenie thinks he is coddled too much and doesn't mind saying so. Then tragedy strikes the family in Silver Dollar City, Missouri, where Delrita was going to meet her idol, a master wood-carver. (She had already carved several clowns for Punky and now wanted to know more about the beautiful carved swan she had seen on their last trip.) While she and Punky are waiting for her parents to return to the town square, they are notified that they have been killed in a car accident. Uncle Bert and Aunt Queenie become the guardians of Punky and Delrita. Delrita's friendship with Avanelle Shackleford and Avanelle's older brother, "Tree," helps Delrita deal with her parents' death, but now she is faced with Aunt Queenie and her prissy ways. Over Delrita's objections, Aunt Queenie enrolls Punky in a sheltered workshop. Punky loves the workshop from the first moment, and soon Delrita realizes that Aunt Queenie does love both her and Punky—that Aunt Queenie is just trying to let each of them "get their wings and fly free." Then the unthinkable happens—Punky's heart gives out and he dies. Delrita's talent as a wood carver had given Punky a lot of pleasure and now this talent and her friends will give her the courage to emerge, spread her wings, and fly free.

Challenges in Life

Wood's character "Punky" was patterned after her own brother, who was born with Down's syndrome and was cared for by her parents for 36 years. Although the characters are, according to Wood, from her imagination, they almost certainly were reflections of many of her own emotions. Other books that focus on emotions involved with physical or mental disabilities can help readers identify with the efforts that have to be made by others. Blind protagonists are the focus of the novel *Carver* by Ruth Yaffe Radin (Macmillan, 1990). A young boy, blinded since the age of two, yearns to be a wood-carver like his father had been. A picture book, *Cakes and Miracles: A Purim Tale* by Barbara Diamond Godin (Viking, 1991), describes the images that come into a blind boy's head that help him contribute to his hardworking mother's efforts to support the family. In a junior novel set in Michigan during the 1887s, Patricia MacLachlan tells the story of a boy who attempts to learn to "see" like his blind grandfather in *Through Grandpa's Eyes* (Harper, 1980). Perhaps the most moving stories about being blind or visually disabled are two biographies written for intermediate readers by noted Canadian author Jean Little. Her first volume of memoirs, *Little by Little* (Viking, 1988) and its sequel, *Stars Come Out Within* (Viking, 1991), describe her depression and sense of imprisonment that her very limited vision brings. Other titles deal with characters who are challenged mentally. Karen Hesse's novel, *Wish on a Unicorn* (Holt, 1991), features Mags, a sixth-grader, who comes to understand just how important her family is when her brain-damaged younger sister finds a dirty stuffed unicorn—a unicorn that she believes can grant each of them a wish. A nonfiction photo essay by Kathleen M. Dwyer, *What Do You Mean I Have a Learning Disability?* (Walker, 1991), focuses on Jimmy's poor self-image and his struggle to cope with his disability. Dwyer's book also lists some famous people who have been learning disabled. Deafness is an element in a picture book, *Mandy*, by Barbara D. Booth (Lothrop, 1991) and in *Special Parents, Special Children* by Joanne E. Bernstein and Bryna J. Fireside (Whitman, 1991). *Special Parents* features photo essays about four families—one father is blind, and one is wheelchair-bound; one set of parents is deaf; and another pair are dwarfs.

TITLES FROM THE BOOKSHELF

Listening Level Categorizations

Entries from the preceding list of 109 read-alouds are arranged within the six suggested listening level categories. Within each of the categories the entries are listed by author, title, and sequential entry number used in the main listing.

Early Primary. The following books are recommended for reading aloud in the early primary years (ages 5-6; grades K-1). Picture books are often the most successful read-alouds at this age. *Michael Bond's Book of Bears* is a new collection of classic stories that, in their individual book edition, will also make great read-alouds.
> Gormley, Beatrice. *Ellie's Birthstone Ring*, #39
> Howard, Ellen. *The Cellar*, #50
> Hurwitz, Johanna. *"E" Is for Elisa*, #54
> *Michael Bond's Book of Bears*, #72

In addition to the junior novels and collections suggested in the entries cited above, Chapter 1 lists the *latest and greatest* picture books that can be read aloud to early primary listeners and enjoyed by older students as well.

Primary. During the primary years (ages 6-7; grades 1-2), children tend to move away from their egocentric nature and are better able to focus on a story that continues from one day to the next. Their increasing ability to conserve and their increasing attention span also enhance their ability to listen to a story and keep that story in their memory to build on during a subsequent read-aloud session. Even within this level there is a variety of content and length of selections. Many of the titles listed in this category will also be appropriate for the upper primary child, as well as some intermediate children.
> Blume, Judy. *Fudge-a-mania*, #7
> Brown, Margaret Wise. *Under the Sun and the Moon and Other Poems*, #10
> Carris, Joan. *Howling for Home*, #15
> Christopher, Matt. *Centerfield Ballhawk*, #17
> Cleary, Beverly. *Muggie Maggie*, #20
> Duffey, Betsy. *A Boy in the Doghouse*, #29
> ———. *Wild Things*, #30
> Greenwald, Sheila. *Here's Hermione: A Rosy Cole Production*, #40
> Hurwitz, Johanna. *Hurray for Ali Baba Bernstein*, #55
> ———. *School's Out*, #56
> Naylor, Phyllis Reynolds. *Josie's Troubles*, #75
> Peters, Julie Anne. *The Stinky Sneakers Contest*, #82
> Say, Allen. *El Chino*, #92
> Smith, Janice Lee. *The Show-and-Tell War and Other Stories About Adam Joshua*, #96
> Spinelli, Jerry. *The Bathwater Gang Gets Down to Business*, #97

Primary Accelerated. These books are listed for the most mature of the primary age readers, primary accelerated readers (ages 7-8; grades 2-3). These stories include animal tales, mysteries, fantasy tales involving toys that come to life, time travel stories, and stories about slavery in the South. Also included is a story of the Kwanzaa holiday celebrated by African-Americans from December 26 to January 1 and a story of a blind child who wishes only to attend school.

Cleary, Beverly. *Strider*, #21

Clifford, Eth. *Harvey's Wacky Parrot Adventure*, #22

Conford, Ellen. *Can Do, Jenny Archer*, #24

Dicks, Terrance. *Sally Ann on Her Own*, #28

Eisenberg, Lisa. *Leave It to Lexie*, #31

Fox, Paula. *Amzat and His Brothers: Three Italian Tales Remembered by Floriano Vecchi*, #33

Greer, Gery, and Bob Ruddick. *Jason and the Aliens Down the Street*, #41

Hooks, William H. *The Ballad of Belle Dorcus*, #48

———. *Moss Gown*, #49

King-Smith, Dick. *The Cuckoo Child*, #60

Kline, Suzy. *Herbie Jones and the Dark Attic*, #61

Kovacs, Deborah. *Brewster's Courage*, #62

Leroe, Ellen. *Ghost Dog*, #64

Roos, Stephen. *The Pet Lovers Club: Crocodile Christmas*, #89

Walter, Mildred Pitts. *Have a Happy ...*, #103

Warren, Cathy. *Roxanne Bookman: Live at Five!*, #105

Whayne, Susanne Santoro. *Watch the House*, #107

Whelan, Gloria. *Hannah*, #108

Early Intermediate. The stories listed for the early intermediate age group (ages 8-9; grades 3-4) extend and build on those listed for the primary accelerated level. Many of the entries will include collaborative reading titles for thematic and curriculum units. The subject index at the end of this book will assist in locating titles that integrate into specific areas of study.

Angell, Judie. *Don't Rent My Room!*, #1

Avi. *Windcatcher*, #3

Christian, Mary Blount. *Sebastian (Super Sleuth) and the Impossible Crime*, #16

Christopher, Matt. *Takedown*, #18

———. *Undercover Tailback*, #19

Danziger, Paula. *Not for a Billion Gazillion Dollars*, #27

Fairman, Tony. *Bury My Bones but Keep My Words: African Tales for Retelling*, #32

Geras, Adèle. *My Grandmother's Stories: A Collection of Jewish Folk Tales*, #36

Getz, David. *Almost Famous*, #37

Hall, Lynn. *Here Comes Zelda Claus and Other Holiday Disasters*, #43

Howe, James. *Return to Howliday Inn*, #51

Hoyt-Goldsmith, Diane. *Hoang Anh: A Vietnamese-American Boy*, #52

Hurwitz, Johanna. *Class President*, #53
Kehret, Peg. *Nightmare Mountain*, #58
Keller, Beverly. *Desdemona Moves On*, #59
Levoy, Myron. *The Magic Hat of Mortimer Wintergreen*, #65
Mahy, Margaret. *The Girl with the Green Ear: Stories About Magic in Nature*, #69
Namioka, Lensey. *Yang the Youngest and His Terrible Ear*, #74
Naylor, Phyllis Reynolds. *Shiloh*, #76
Park, Barbara. *My Mother Got Married (and Other Disasters)*, #79
Paulsen, Gary. *Dunc and the Flaming Ghost*, #81
Pettit, Jayne. *My Name Is San Ho*, #83
Pollack, Pamela, selector. *The Random House Book of Humor for Children*, #84
Radin, Ruth Yaffe. *Carver*, #85
Radley, Gail. *The Golden Days*, #86
Roberts, Willo Davis. *Jo and the Bandit*, #87
Sachar, Louis. *Dogs Don't Tell Jokes*, #90
Sachs, Marilyn. *What My Sister Remembered*, #91
Sharpe, Susan. *Chicken Bucks*, #94
Slote, Alfred. *The Trading Game*, #95
Talbert, Marc. *Double or Nothing*, #100
Thomas, Jane Resh. *The Princess in the Pigpen*, #101
Warner, Gertrude Chandler. *The Disappearing Friend Mystery*, #104
Weiss, Ellen, and Mel Friedman. *The Poof Point*, #106

Intermediate. The stories listed for the intermediate age group (ages 9-10; grades 4-5) extend and build on those listed for the early intermediate level. Many of the entries will provide collaborative reading titles for thematic and curriculum units. The subject index at the end of this book will assist in locating titles that integrate into specific areas of study.

Avi. *"Who Was That Masked Man, Anyway?"*, #2
Beatty, Patricia. *Who Comes with Cannons?*, #4
Berry, James. *Ajeemah and His Son*, #6
Brittain, Bill. *The Ghost from Beneath the Sea*, #8
Brooke, William J. *Untold Tales*, #9
Bulla, Clyde Robert. *Charlie's House*, #11
Bunting, Eve. *Coffin on a Case*, #12
Byars, Betsy. *Bingo Brown's Guide to Romance*, #13
———. *Coast to Coast*, #14
Clifford, Eth. *Will Somebody* Please *Marry My Sister?*, #23
Conrad, Pam. *Stonewords: A Ghost Story*, #25
Coville, Bruce. *Jeremy Thatcher, Dragon Hatcher*, #26
Fox, Paula. *Monkey Island*, #34
George, Jean Craighead. *On the Far Side of the Mountain*, #35
Gorman, Carol. *Die for Me*, #38
Hahn, Mary Downing. *The Dead Man in Indian Creek*, #42
Hamilton, Virginia. *Cousins*, #44
Hamm, Diane Johnston. *Second Family*, #45

Helfman, Elizabeth. *On Being Sarah*, #46
Hildick, E. W. *The Case of the Weeping Witch*, #47
Irwin, Hadley. *The Original Freddie Ackerman*, #57
Lawlor, Laurie. *George on His Own*, #63
Lindbergh, Anne. *Three Lives to Live*, #66
Lowry, Lois. *Anastasia at This Address*, #67
———. *Number the Stars*, #68
McHargue, Georgess. *Beastie*, #70
McKissack, Patricia C. *The Dark-Thirty: Southern Tales of the Supernatural*, #71
Nixon, Joan Lowery. *Land of Hope*, #77
Nye, Naomi Shihab, selector. *This Same Sky: A Collection of Poems from Around the World*, #78
Paulsen, Gary. *A Christmas Sonata*, #80
Roberts, Willo Davis. *What Could Go Wrong?*, #88
Schulman, L. M., selector. *The Random House Book of Sports Stories*, #93
Spinelli, Jerry. *Maniac Magee*, #98
Wallace, Bill. *Danger in Quicksand Swamp*, #102
Wood, June Rae. *The Man Who Loved Clowns*, #109

Intermediate Accelerated. The stories listed for the intermediate accelerated age group (ages 10-11; grades 5-6) extend and build on those listed for the intermediate level. There is little distinction between the intermediate level and the intermediate accelerated level. The variety of titles in the early intermediate and intermediate levels is as varied as the levels of children's backgrounds. Myers's book is reserved for this accelerated level because of its level of parody, and the St. George title is listed here because of its lengthy sections giving background information within the narrative.

Bellairs, John. *The Mansions in the Mist*, #5
Myers, Walter Dean. *The Righteous Revenge of Artemis Bonner*, #73
St. George, Judith. *Dear Dr. Bell ... Your Friend, Helen Keller*, #99

Titles Arranged Alphabetically by Title

Entries from the preceding list of 109 read-alouds are arranged alphabetically by title. Titles are followed by the entry number used in the main listing and by the code (in parentheses) for the suggested listening level given in the main listing. The codes for the listening levels are as follows: EP–Early Primary; P–Primary; PAc–Primary Accelerated; EI–Early Intermediate; I–Intermediate; and IAc–Intermediate Accelerated.

Ajeemah and His Son, #6 (I)
Almost Famous, #37 (EI)
Amzat and His Brothers: Three Italian Tales Remembered by Floriano Vecchi, #33 (PAc)
Anastasia at This Address, #67 (I)
The Ballad of Belle Dorcus, #48 (PAc)
The Bathwater Gang Gets Down to Business, #97 (P)

Jeremy Thatcher, Dragon Hatcher, #26 (I)
Jo and the Bandit, #87 (EI)
Josie's Troubles, #75 (P)
Land of Hope, #77 (I)
Leave It to Lexie, #31 (PAc)
The Magic Hat of Mortimer Wintergreen, #65 (EI)
The Man Who Loved Clowns, #109 (I)
Maniac Magee, #98 (I)
The Mansion in the Mist, #5 (IAc)
Michael Bond's Book of Bears, #72 (EP)
Monkey Island, #34 (I)
Moss Gown, #49 (PAc)
Muggie Maggie, #20 (P)
My Grandmother's Stories: A Collection of Jewish Folk Tales, #36 (EI)
My Mother Got Married (and Other Disasters), #79 (EI)
My Name Is San Ho, #83 (EI)
Nightmare Mountain, #58 (EI)
Not for a Billion Gazillion Dollars, #27 (EI)
Number the Stars, #68 (I)
On Being Sara, #46 (I)
On the Far Side of the Mountain, #35 (I)
The Original Freddie Ackerman, #57 (I)
The Pet Lovers Club: Crocodile Christmas, #89 (PAc)
The Poof Point, #106 (EI)
The Princess in the Pigpen, #101 (EI)
The Random House Book of Humor for Children, #84 (EI)
The Random House Book of Sports Stories, #93 (I)
Return to Howliday Inn, #51 (EI)
The Righteous Revenge of Artemis Bonner, #73 (IAc)
Roxanne Bookman: Live at Five!, #105 (PAc)
Sally Ann on Her Own, #28 (PAc)
School's Out, #56 (P)
Sebastian (Super Sleuth) and the Impossible Crime, #16 (EI)
Second Family, #45 (I)
Shiloh, #76 (EI)
The Show-and-Tell War and Other Stories About Adam Joshua, #96 (P)
The Stinky Sneakers Contest, #82 (P)
Stonewords: A Ghost Story, #25 (I)
Strider, #21 (PAc)
Takedown, #18 (EI)
This Same Sky: A Collection of Poems from Around the World, #78 (I)
Three Lives to Live, #66 (I)
The Trading Game, #95 (EI)
Under the Sun and the Moon and Other Poems, #10 (P)
Undercover Tailback, #19 (EI)
Untold Tales, #9 (I)
Watch the House, #107 (PAc)
What Could Go Wrong?, #88 (I)

What My Sister Remembered, #91 (EI)
Who Comes with Cannons?, #4 (I)
"Who Was That Masked Man, Anyway?", #2 (I)
Wild Things, #30 (P)
Will Somebody Please *Marry My Sister?*, #23 (I)
Windcatcher, #3 (EI)
Yang the Youngest and His Terrible Ear, #74 (EI)

Chapter
3

Going Beyond Reading Aloud

Robert Frost once said the best way to get kids to read is to surround them with so many books they stumble over them. Few people would argue that to become a great basketball player one would have to practice and practice. The same is true for those golfers who make the pro golf tour or those musicians who earn a seat in the municipal orchestra or who hope to play in Carnegie

Hall. The adage "practice makes perfect" is heard often. Whether we are parents or teachers, if we want our children to read we must read to them and give them time to read. Mark Twain said, "The man who does not read good books has not advantage over the man who can't read them." The same thing can be said of children: "The child who does not read good books has not advantage over the child who can't read."

Those who created the blueprint for a literate society, *Becoming a Nation of Readers*,[1] concluded that reading aloud is "the single most important activity for building the knowledge required for eventual success." Choosing quality read-alouds and constructing opportunities to expand on the selection and discussions that help listeners to make connections with other pieces of writing help maximize the benefits of the read-aloud experiences. When the piece of literature read aloud is carefully chosen, children will have the opportunity to explore the patterns and connections within and among different pieces of fiction or information literature. The children may also be given the opportunity to compare thematic material through discussions based on their own personal responses to the piece of literature. Through the shared literature experience inherent in a read-aloud, the children in the listening group are given an opportunity to explore and share their own connections and responses.

What is the status of reading in the United States? Elys McLean-Ibraham created a graphic depiction for *USA Today* (March 21, 1989; page 10). That graph, titled "USA Snapshots: A Look at Statistics That Shape Our Lives," presented information from a Martiz AmeriPoll national survey of 1,000 adults. According to that survey, almost half the adults in the U.S.A. read 10 or more books per year; conversely, a little more than half do not read even 10 books a year. How can we put our children in the half that does read, or better yet, how can we increase the population that reads? The answer, I believe, lies in our attempts to "Build a Nation of Readers." The first step to building a nation that reads is to build families that read, classrooms that read, schools that read, cities that read, states that read—and finally we *will have* a nation of readers. But the first step is to build families that read—parents can help here—and classrooms that read—teachers can help here. The common thread that will help both the parents and the teachers who work with children is the element of reading aloud. A young friend of mine was babysitting for a 23-month-old little girl. The babysitter's only complaint was that the little girl had begged her to read book after book that evening. In all, the sitter had read 35 picture books, ranging from Leo Lionni's *Frederick* (Knopf, 1967) to Ruth Sawyer's *Journey Cake, Ho!* (Viking, 1953). Not the usual baby read-aloud by any means. That child had been read to often. She knew that *Journey Cake, Ho!* had lots of animals in it. She also knew that *Frederick* was about mice. Her favorite book, though, was probably *The Pop-Up Mice of Mr. Brice* by Theo LeSieg (Random, 1989). LeSieg's[2] book has many doors to open and several moving parts to manipulate. Together the two of them read and enjoyed the stories. Often it is the parents who do not feel that they have the time to read aloud, and teachers are often in the same position. There is so much to teach, so much curriculum to "get through," that reading aloud and silent reading time fall by the wayside. The bottom line is this: If we want children to be readers we must make it our priority and we must help children make it their priority. Reading aloud novels, picture books, and other books at home and in the classroom is the first step toward making reading a priority. In the list that follows are 21 additional steps that will help us all go beyond reading aloud to infuse reading-related activities throughout our day—helping to keep the focus on reading and its benefits.

TWENTY-ONE STEPS TO BUILDING A FAMILY/CLASSROOM OF READERS

1.   *Read books/articles aloud to one another.*

At home: Reading aloud should include spontaneous reading. In our family we often read aloud an announcement of a marriage that interests others in the family. We might read an interesting article about college students and the elements that help them succeed, or we might read an article highlighting the high school basketball game. It seems eerily strange that sometimes we will have just been talking about something and there will be an article in the newspaper about it. One day we had mentioned Kwanzaa—an African-American holiday; we did not know much about it. But the very next day we came across a short article about the holiday, which begins December 26, in the newspaper. The article highlighted its origins and told about a local observance of the celebra-

tion. Later that week one of the children was at the public library doing some research on another topic and noticed a couple of books about Kwanzaa (*Kwanzaa* by A. P. Porter, illustrated by Janice Lee Porter [Carolrhoda, 1991] and *Kwanzaa* by Deborah M. Newton Chocolate, illustrated by Melodye Rosales [Children's, 1990]). He checked out the titles, and we shared highlights of the books that night. Another time we had discussed the impact of the relaxed income rules for federal aid for college students. That week an article appeared in the newspaper explaining the changes and the lack of additional funding. Those articles provided material to read aloud and discuss.

At school: Reading activities at school should include spontaneous opportunities for the reading and sharing of many types of reading selections from a variety of sources. Information included in magazines and newspapers often ties into discussions or simply includes something of interest. For example, one day the children in a classroom were discussing the humanitarian efforts being undertaken by the United States military forces in Somalia. Some of the children were reading about the events in the newspaper, and judging from the comments they were making, their families had also been discussing the events in Somalia. One of the students questioned why we were so worried about Somalia when the Sudanese were in a similar plight and nothing was being done to help them. That question led to some research at the library to search out articles about Sudan and its people. The students found an article by Julie Wheelwright, "Holes in the Veil," in *New Statesman and Society* (March 27, 1992, vol. 5, p. 24) and an article by James Wilde, "Starvation in a Fruitful Land," in *Time* (December 5, 1988, vol. 123, no. 23, pp. 43-44). Those articles were read and shared and provided many points of discussion. A month or so later another student was reading about hunger in the world and noted an 800 number that could be called to find out about efforts being taken to alleviate hunger in the world. That number (1-800-2HUNGRY) was listed as the number for an organization called Food for the

Hungry. Several students volunteered to organize some questions, and eventually they called and spoke with one of the representatives of the organization. They shared their information with the class, and soon they were wondering what they could do to help hungry people in our area. Reading the local newspaper brought information about local problems, and soon several of the students (fifth-graders) were volunteering to help at a soup kitchen and at a local agency that boxed food supplies for the needy.

Another class had just finished reading *Little House on the Prairie* by Laura Ingalls Wilder (Harper, 1935; 1953) when an article appeared in the local paper quoting a newly discovered letter of Laura Ingalls Wilder to her daughter, Rose Wilder Lane (Wilder's only daughter). The letter seemed to suggest that Lane might have rewritten some of Wilder's books. That article was brought in by a student and read aloud to the class. The quotes attributed to Wilder and reprinted in the article included some mild profanity, and because of that language, students got an image of a less genteel Wilder than they had had previously. The student had brought the article in spontaneously because it contained information in it that she was interested in and that she thought others might be interested in too. Because the teacher had often brought articles of interest into the classroom, it was not unusual for the students to spot an article and to think to bring it in as well. None of the students felt they had to wait for "current events" time or for an assignment to bring in a news article to share.

2. *Talk about books you read.*

At home: Few of us hesitate to discuss or recommend a good movie we have seen. We need to be more conscious of doing the same for books we have read. In my own household, books by Louis L'Amour, David Morrell, and Piers Anthony are regularly discussed (and exchanged) among the four young men and their dad. The two older children share a passion for science fiction, so that genre is often a subject of conversation when they get together. The older children often recommend titles for their younger sister to read.

At school: We must encourage "book talk" in the classroom, in the library media center, and even in the art room, music room, playground, etc. The adults at school can assist with this by consciously seeking opportunities to mention books and talking about them whenever the opportunity arises. If opportunities do not arise, create them. During an art period in which collage pictures are being made, use books by Ezra Jack Keats and Leo Lionni to focus on examples of art in books. In music class use Irving Burgie's *Caribbean Carnival: Songs of the West Indies* (Tambourine/Morrow, 1992) during a focus on the music from that region of the world. In addition to informal "book talks," set up opportunities for readers to formally share their books. One technique for doing this is to set aside a literary talk time. Each child who has a book to discuss is encouraged to sign up for a triad group. Groups of three sit around a table and discuss their books. It isn't a round-robin "you tell about your book and then I'll tell about my book," but rather an informal discussion of the best parts of their books, what the book reminds them of, and selected readings from it. The discussions are patterned after the type of discussion three friends might have about good movies they have seen. Sometimes it helps to set the stage for this type of discussion by allowing students to write the name of a good movie they have seen recently. Allow them to spend some time discussing those movies in a triad situation. Those discussions are usually animated, spontaneous, and filled with examples of good parts, funny dialogue, and exciting events. Later suggest that the students use this same type of interactive discussion to discuss their books.

3. *Keep books and magazines around the home and classrooms.*

At home: Magazines in the home can encourage reading for information and can promote lifelong learning. Families that include golfers will find *Golf Magazine* interesting reading. Those interested in sports will enjoy *Sports Illustrated.* There is no end to magazines that focus on special topics or special audiences. If the outlay for a subscription seems too much, try to pick up a magazine or two from the grocery store magazine rack.

At school: Solicit donations of magazines. If families subscribe to *Newsweek* or any other suitable title, perhaps the family would consider donating it in a timely manner, after they've read it, to the classroom. The information would be a little less current but still valuable reading material. For classrooms of younger children, perhaps issues of *Cricket* or *Highlights* would be available; back issues of those magazines might be donated by families that subscribe.

But just having the magazines available is not enough. Make a special effort to read an article or two from various magazines to whet student appetites for more reading. I'll never forget the kindergartner who came into the IMC/library one day and stood beside me while I finished a literature session with first-graders. It appeared as if he had something urgent that needed my attention so I turned my attention to him and said, "Romas, do you need to ask me something?" He replied, "No, but I have something to show you." Before I could react he had flipped open his copy of *Ebony, Jr.* and was showing me (and the class, which was literally a captive audience) the double-page spread showing the African-Americans who were being honored on postage stamps in Africa. He mentioned some information about each of the people that he felt was significant and then posed the question about when we thought the United States would honor people like Martin Luther King, Jr. The first-grade audience clapped at the end of his presentation and wanted to know where he had learned all of the information. He responded that he and his dad read this magazine together and that it contained a lot of information. The first-graders were in awe. Later I invited Romas back to give his presentation to some fourth-graders who were reading about the civil rights movement. They too were in awe of his ability to present new information to them.

4. *Give books and magazine subscriptions as gifts.*

At home: If you want your child to be a reader make sure that reading is valued as much as games and other activities. Before holidays or gift-giving occasions, ask children for a list of books that they might like to receive. At our extended family gift exchanges, books are a common gift. One year a 14-year-old received Graeme Base's *The Eleventh Hour: A Curious Mystery* (Abrams, 1989). Many of the teenagers there wanted to read the picture book.

That same year an uncle received a book by Piers Anthony from his teenage nephew. Another cousin received a subscription to *Runner's World* and Grandma, a history buff, received a book about the Civil War. All of the gifts were hits and much appreciated.

At school: Books can serve as prizes for classroom/library contests, for contingency management, or as birthday gifts. Many inexpensive paperbacks are available from the book clubs that regularly send out fliers. The various Scholastic book clubs and the Trumpet book clubs are among the best. They offer classic titles, as well as contemporary favorites, and offer bonus points through which the classroom can earn free books (or other prizes). Bonus points can be used to obtain books for the classroom or as prizes for special occasions. One of my colleagues saves the books the class earns each year so that at the end of the year she can send each child off with one or two books for summer reading. Another teacher puts a new book in the classroom on each child's birthday—in his or her honor. He asks each child who reads the book to put his or her signature (and date) on the inside cover of the book. Sometimes sheets need to be added to the inside cover. Students frequently find the names of older brothers and sisters, or friends, in a book. Students are encouraged to donate a book to the IMC/library or to the classroom in honor of their own birthday or as a special remembrance of a teacher's birthday.

5. *Encourage children to obtain a library card.*

At home: No single library can have all of the material that a reader might wish to have. So, in addition to the school IMC/library, children should be encouraged to borrow material from the public library too. Library cards in most communities are free.

At school: Encouraging parents/guardians to help their child obtain a library card is one way school personnel can assist in reaching this goal. Sometimes families are not aware of the benefits available to them at the public library. A visit to the public library can be a valuable educational field trip. Many times advance arrangements can be made to obtain library card applications for the students who will be visiting the library. Permission from the parents/guardians should be requested and the application signed by the parent/guardian. If the school is willing to verify addresses and other pertinent information, the library will often allow the library card requests to come in from the school rather than individually. Then, on the day of the field trip, those children who do not have library cards can obtain one. A library card is a free pass to the world of reading.

6. *Make regular visits to the IMC/library.*

At home: Families who actually schedule public library visits are more likely to visit frequently. Once or twice a month is not too often. Getting into a regular routine can encourage readers to read frequently. Parents/guardians who read books to their children and remind their children to return books and to check out new books to read are also encouraging frequent visits to the school's IMC/library.

At school: Classroom teachers can help establish frequent visits to the school IMC/library by encouraging their students to visit the IMC/library whenever they need or want information or new reading material. Library media specialists can help by maintaining an open access library—a place where children can come with questions about what a wolf chases or what sound a penguin makes, or just to find a good book to read. Kindergartners will want to go to the IMC/library each day to get some new books to read with parents while intermediate students will visit every few days to get some new novels or research material for their classroom activities. Teachers should encourage students to visit the IMC/library whenever they have a need. In addition, teachers/librarians should, when the situation arises, encourage children to visit the public library. Often when an author is being discussed or promoted, the books by that author are in high demand and difficult to get. A suggestion that the public library would likely have some of the same titles will help alleviate the overload on the school's IMC/library collection.

7. *Help a child compile and illustrate a book.*
At home: Recognize that reading and writing go hand in hand. Children can compile a book of favorite recipes for snacks, a book of family stories, or simply make a book from their own favorite stories written at school. Gifts for grandparents can be a family book made by putting together pages from each child. Each child's page could feature a picture of the child and a simple message to the grandparent. Bind the pages together, make a cover, give the book a title, and the book will be ready.

At school: Making books can easily be an outgrowth of the writing workshop sessions. Innovations on favorite books can be written as a class activity and compiled into a book. The stories written on large pieces of paper can be used as a bulletin board display and later bound into a book for the children to read and share. Some teachers manage to make as many books as they have students in their classrooms. At the end of the year each child is given one of the classroom books to take home as a remembrance of their school year.

8. *Reread a book you loved as a child, then share it with a child.*
At home: In addition to selecting books from *The Latest and Greatest Read-Alouds* to share with children, old favorites from one's own childhood should be located and read with youngsters in the home. If the books seem too out-of-date, consider sharing a love of a special category of books. For example, I remember reading over and over the stories in a two-volume set of fairy tales. One volume contained the stories of Hans Christian Andersen and the other contained the stories collected by the Brothers Grimm. As a consequence, I enjoy all types of fairy tales. I often share the memories of those stories with my own children and frequently share with them a new or special version of either Andersen's or the Brothers Grimm stories. Of course, it does not necessarily need to be a parent/guardian who shares books with younger children in the household. Our older son, Michael, had many books as a child but especially liked the books of Laura Ingalls Wilder. He often told his brothers and sisters how good those books were and encouraged them to read

the books—but "just remember they're mine." Although he left them at home for his siblings to read, he retained "ownership" of his paperback copies until he had completed his special forces training in the U.S. Army. He came home on leave one year and inscribed them as a gift to his younger sister, who had already read through them twice. Wilder's books have been read by all six children, but none with more joy and delight than when they were read by the oldest child and the youngest child—creating a bond that no other read-aloud or gift could match. One day our oldest daughter was telling of a task at which she had been especially successful. During her dialogue about this accomplishment she commented that she "was *terrific*." One of her teenage brothers asked, "Isn't that what Charlotte said to Wilbur?" The shared memories of E. B. White's *Charlotte's Web* brought smiles to both their faces—but he took off running (just in case).

Sometimes memories of a story can help bridge a child's experiences with reading at home with experiences at school. During this past school year one parent brought an autographed copy of Wilson Rawls's *Where the Red Fern Grows* (Bantam, 1961) to share with her child's class. The mother told about reading the book as a child and of meeting with the author to get his autograph. She told them how much she enjoyed the book and read an excerpt to them. The IMC/library's copy of that book did not stay on the shelf for the rest of the year.

At school: As a library media specialist I can always tell the favorite books of teachers who read aloud to their students. The children in Mrs. Benda's third-grade class always liked the stories of Clifford Hick and his books about Alvin Fernald. Those students in Mrs. Bock's class enjoyed stories by Cynthia Rylant and those by Patricia Polacco. Mrs. Myers's class absolutely clamored to get to the Boxcar Children Mystery titles. There is no doubt in my mind that the third-graders in that class wanted to read those books so much because Mrs. Myers liked the books very, very much. She had read them as a child and shared them with her own two sons—a fact she readily shared with her students. She really succeeded in turning her students on to books, and later they reached out to read other mysteries.

It only makes sense to choose the books you like and to share those books. Each teacher should begin with a basic list of books suggested as read-alouds, then infuse their own choices from that list with books (or types of books) they remember from childhood and with books they like that have been published less recently. By the time the three categories are melded together, the list of literature to be shared in one classroom will look quite different than the list generated for another classroom.

9. *Make reading a regular family or classroom event.*

At home: Reading aloud and sharing books needs to be a regular activity that children can count on. The most traditional way to do this in the home is to make a bedtime story a nightly routine. In the early years the read-aloud might be a picture book or two; later, as the child or children grow older, the read-aloud might take the form of a chapter or two from a favorite book. Over a period of time the whole book will be completed. Reading aloud during a trip to visit relatives or friends will help children occupy the time spent in the car. If you are unable to read in a moving vehicle, consider making or buying cassette tapes of books; equip the child or children with a small cassette player and earphones and they can still enjoy books during the trip. Read aloud articles from the newspaper or a magazine while dinner is cooking or read aloud after dinner instead of watching television.

At school: Read-alouds should be much more frequent. Now the trend is to make sure that a read-aloud session occurs no less than three times a day. One of those times should be a continuing read, that is, a book that is read over a period of several days. The other times might feature a picture book that is read just for fun or as an introduction or culmination to a unit of study. For example, *The Butter Battle Book* by Dr. Seuss (Random, 1984), could be used as an introduction to the arms race or a discussion of the arms reduction agreements being negotiated by countries around the world. At the beginning of a practice session with division, read Pat Hutchins's *The Doorbell Rang* (Greenwillow, 1986). The third time might feature a poem, short story, newspaper article, or any other reading that fits into the day's activities. The frequent modeling of good reading does much to motivate reading.

10. *Visit a bookstore with a child.*

At home: The ownership of books is a valuable motivator and is an important part of making children readers. Visits to bookstores can acquaint parents/guardians with the new titles that are available and can serve as a reminder of the great value children do receive when they are able to borrow many books from the library. It is important that children do have some books of their own. When my own family was very young we did not have much money to purchase books or toys, but because ownership of books was important to us, we set up criteria for buying them. Those criteria included the number of times a book had been read. If a child had liked a book enough to have checked it out of the library and to have read the title four or five times, then we tried to make available the money to buy the book for the child's library. Matthew's first chosen book was *The Gingerbread Boy* by Paul Galdone (Clarion, 1975). At the age of four, he often asked for that book and then walked up and down the neighborhood begging our neighbors to read it to him. Steven's first favorite book was a retelling of "Jack and the Beanstalk." He begged his older sister and brothers to act out that story time after time.

At school: School book fairs and school book clubs (such as Scholastic or Trumpet) provide an inexpensive opportunity for children to own their own books. Books that a child is able to own have special meaning for that child, especially if the circumstances surrounding the book are special. Books hold more than the memories between the pages.

11. *Help a child set up a personal library.*

At home: The books that children do own can be dignified with a special place—their own library. In the home the books can be put on a special bookshelf in the child's bedroom or on an accessible shelf in the family room. One 10-year-old I know has organized her library by author. A six-year-old in another family has arranged her books by the color of the binding. Both enjoy reading their own books. The books in a personal library can be organized in several different ways: by author, subject, size, or whatever designation a child wishes to use.

At school: In the classroom, a reading center should be established with a special shelf or in a corner of the room for the creation of a library of sorts. Frequent visits to the school library to select books for the reading center should encourage an ever-changing selection of books in the reading center. At times students may wish to select books by a specific author or illustrator for their book corner; at other times they may wish to select books in a certain category: Caldecott books, mysteries, stories about friendship, etc. In addition to the books available in the reading center, each child should be encouraged to frequently check out books from the library for his or her own personal reading at school and at home.

12. *Help children choose books they want to read.*

At home: Talking about books will help children decide which books they want to read. Guidance should be given, but the choice of reading material should ultimately be left to the child doing the reading. Because there are, it would seem, fewer constraints on what could be read at home, the choices available to children are almost limitless. Frequent visits to libraries in the community can help to expand the choices of reading material that children have available to them.

At school: In the classroom, we must sometimes ask children to make choices among the choices being offered. But if there is no real reason to limit the choice of books being read, then the choice should be entirely the child's. No book should be declared too easy or too hard. Artificial criteria as to which books should be read should be eliminated. One of the most abused criteria is number of pages. One of my colleagues who prided herself on exposing children to the best of literature limited her fifth-grade students to reading books that were at least 100 pages long. That dictate eliminated Patricia MacLachlan's *Sarah, Plain and Tall* (Harper, 1984)—the 1985 Newbery Award book, a superb book that should not be missed.

13. *Use television and radio to encourage reading.*

At home: Most households today have a television, often more than one. Although television can interfere with time for reading, it can also be a stimulus to motivate interest in a topic and to stimulate more reading. For example, the book *Sarah, Plain and Tall* was made into a "Hallmark Hall of Fame" television movie. Students who were fortunate enough to see that production would benefit from reading the book and discussing the different perspective from which the story was presented in each medium. One network aired a special on the horses of Chincoteague Island. Such a program would be a natural lead-in to the classic title by Marguerite Henry, *Misty of Chincoteague* (Macmillan, 1975). A special on Australia might motivate the children to read Mem Fox's *Koala Lou* (Harcourt, 1988) or *Possum Magic* (Harcourt, 1983). Use the subject of television programs to stimulate related reading.

At school: Guidelines for using recordings of commercial television programs in the classroom do limit their use in the schools. However, there are provisions in the copyright law for "fair use." Sometimes the best use of commercial television involves communicating with parents (and directly with the children) about the airing of a program that has potential for use in school. If children can view the program at home, you can follow up on the material in the classroom by suggesting additional reading material to those who were interested in the program.

14. *Talk about local events reported by the media.*

At home: Discussing current events around the dinner table can become a regular part of the family mealtime. The successful implementation of this routine in the home centers on the family's basic level of communication. But in addition to helping children become more aware of what is going on around them, an awareness of the need to read the newspaper and actually listen to news on the radio or television creates an added awareness of the value of communication within the family.

At school: Many teachers encourage the reading of newspapers and magazines by having regular "current events" sessions in their classrooms. This activity dovetails with other activities being undertaken to develop readers. Reading an article from a newspaper or magazine will help students to become more aware of current events and will often stimulate their reading on the same topic. Encourage children to find articles on the same event from various news sources and to compare the perspectives. Use the articles as a stimulus for discussions and more reading.

15. *Encourage children to write—stories, a diary, letters to friends.*

At home: When the family takes a vacation, get postcards from the places you visit and have the children write short messages and send them to grandparents, friends, and classmates. Use a diary to write a short entry recording the day's weather, temperature, or other bits of information.

At school: In the classroom, thank-you notes can be written to a variety of individuals, from guest visitors to the principal to the cafeteria cooks; invitations can be written to special individuals asking them to visit the classroom to read or to share a special program. Letters requesting information can be sent to embassies, museums, and chambers of commerce. Children in your classroom may establish a pen pal connection with a similar classroom in another city or state. One second-grade class established a pen pal relationship with the teacher's sister's second-grade class across town. During the last month of the school year, the classes met in a park for an end-of-the-year picnic. Many of the children continued their individual relationships for several years, and the two teachers have continued to link their students through letter writing.

16. *Plan a summer reading program.*

At home: Many public libraries promote reading during the summer by establishing a summer reading program. Families can help promote reading by making their children's participation in the program possible. Those families who live in communities without a planned program can establish goals and incentives for themselves. Help your child set goals for reading and then hold a special event when those goals are reached. Several intermediate steps before reaching the final goal help keep the momentum going. Companion activities to encourage reading might include having a "literary lunch." If lunch includes a bread-and-jam sandwich read *Bread and Jam for Frances* by Russell Hoban (Harper, 1964). Make doughnuts and read Robert McCloskey's "The Doughnuts" from *Homer Price* (Viking, 1943).

At school: Before school lets out for the summer, plan goals for summer reading. Make a list of books to read and discuss the best of the books on the list. Make summer reading folders or arrange some other method for children to keep track of the books that are read during the summer.

17. *Set family/classroom reading goals.*

At home: As a family set goals for reading. Read a novel a month, read a book on the way to Grandmother's, or read one or two books each night. Setting and achieving goals help recording become a regular activity.

At school: Classrooms can assist in promoting family reading by establishing "family reading challenges" or activities that encourage family reading. One school asked families to bring their favorite family book to the school's open house and offered to take a family picture—showing the family reading. The pictures were then offered at a minimum price; because of the timing of the open house, several of the families were able to use the photo on holiday greeting cards. Whenever those family pictures are displayed or sent to someone, a subtle message promoting family reading is also sent. Goals similar to those for the family could be set for classroom reading.

18. *Give favorite books to other children.*

At home: Ownership of books is the ultimate motivator for many children. That ownership is even more important if the gift is perceived as something special. When someone gifts a special book *of their own* to another, it carries a special message to the receiver. Sometimes the gift can be made special by the nature of the title chosen. One of my sons shares a birthday with Beatrix Potter (July 28) and his name is Thomas. So I am always searching for books or memorabilia that are representative of *The Tale of Tom Kitten.* I have purchased almost every edition of the book that is available—cloth books, board books, regular editions, oversized editions—as well as decorator tins and stuffed animals, all telling the story of Tom Kitten or with a Tom Kitten motif. I also often buy him other books with "Tom" in the title. Those gifts create a special tie to books and reading—a tie he has passed on to his daughter. Younger students who attend birthday parties might be encouraged to give, as a birthday gift, a favorite book of their choosing.

At school: In the classroom, teachers can bring in books that they enjoyed reading as youngsters to read and share with today's youngsters. Writing about a favorite book they would choose for a special friend helps children to think about books as gifts. Sharing books and reading memories help children become involved in the reading activities themselves. Classroom book exchanges might be organized for children to exchange paperback books that they have read.

19. *Pack books for family trips.*

At home: When planning for a vacation, be sure to visit the library to gather reading material for the trip. If reading in the car or on the plane is a problem, plan to take some books on cassette tape. Outfit each child with a headset and cassette player. Put the reading material in a special "reading box" or "reading bag" so that borrowed material stays together and does not get left behind in a motel room or at a relative's home. Make it a practice to return the reading material to the box or bag after finishing reading each day. Try to continue the same reading program that has been established for the family. If bedtime stories are read at home, continue the practice on the road. It may be a good time to enlist the participation of guest readers. If the family is visiting grandparents, perhaps one of them would be willing to be a "celebrity reader" and to read the nightly story or chapter.

At school: If the family trip takes place during the school year, children can be encouraged to check materials out of the school library to take on the trip or to read during any break in the school schedule. If possible, send along with the child a packet of stamped postcards that he or she might write and send back to the class. It will help encourage the vacationing child's writing, but will also allow the other children to read about the child's trip. They can plot the child's travels on a map and look for other sights that the family might be seeing.

Toward the close of the school year, children might be asked to generate a list of books that they might like to take on vacation with them during the summer and to set up a program for continuing to read during those months.

20. *Read together about travel destinations.*

At home: Travel brochures, magazine articles, and books about a specific location can add much to the planning of a trip together. Reading before embarking on a trip has brought our family many special memories. Before beginning a trip to the Black Hills, we learned of the Mine and Technology School in South Dakota. The visit to the school was free and one of the most interesting places we visited that summer. Also realizing that the National Park Service at Mount Rushmore had its own program telling about the construction of the faces and the people involved gave us an alternative to the commercial programs offered by business enterprises.

At school: In the classroom, students could write letters requesting information about destinations and could plan the route and special sites to visit. A class booklet highlighting destinations within the state for weekend visits during the summer could be compiled, duplicated, and sent home with each child to suggest potential family getaway mini-vacations.

21. *Visit a literary landmark.*

At home: Enroute to the Black Hills from Iowa, we made a side trip off the interstate highway and visited DeSmet, South Dakota, the setting in five books written by Laura Ingalls Wilder. The visit to the family homestead site, the surveyor's house, and the Ingalls home and museum remain a highlight of that trip. The sites don't always have to be planned locations. We've pulled off the road to find a pebble as a remembrance of *Sylvester and the Magic*

Pebble by William Steig (Windmill, 1968), and we've stopped to visit a farm with a pig and marvel at the spider web "just like Charlotte's." We've visited the Heard Museum in Phoenix, Arizona, where we learned more about the storyteller figures made by the Pueblo Indians that we had read about in Diane Hoyt-Goldsmith's *Pueblo Storyteller* (Holiday House, 1991), and we've marveled at the hand-painted eggs in the Czech museum in Cedar Rapids, Iowa—eggs that reminded us of the painstakingly decorated ones in *Rechenka's Eggs* by Patricia Polacco (Putnam/Philomel, 1988).

At school: In the classroom, students could help one another locate possible places to visit to extend the joy of a book read. A thorough knowledge of books will assist in fleshing out possibilities for locations to visit. Some will be obvious. A visit to the Appalachian Mountain region will connect with many of Cynthia Rylant's books or the collected tales of Richard Chase. Gerald McDermott's *Arrow to the Sun* (Viking, 1973) takes place in a Pueblo village, similar to many still located in Arizona. Those visiting in northern Florida may wish to locate Cottondale (in the Panama City, Florida, area) that is the setting for Donald Crews's *Bigmama's* (Greenwillow, 1991). Other sites will be more elusive, such as finding the museum with decorated eggs, but if information is shared many sites will be identified.

CONCLUSION

Reading aloud to children is the first most important step in helping children learn to read and to love reading. Going beyond reading aloud and building on that love of reading will bring many more enriching experiences to readers and will help them extend their knowledge beyond what they read to make connections with other facets of their lives. Making reading a priority will help to build a family or classroom of readers—on the way to building a nation of readers.

NOTES

[1] R. C. Anderson, E. H. Hiebert, J. A. Scott, and I. A. Wilkinson, *Becoming a Nation of Readers: The Report of the Commission on Reading* (Washington, D.C.: The National Institute of Education, 1985).

[2] Theo LeSieg, a pseudonym used by the late Theodor Seuss Geisel, who was better known by his most common pseudonym, Dr. Seuss.

Photograph Credits

Title Page
   Heather Hansel, Stephanie Struve, Brittanie Franklin, Stacey Struve, Jack McElmeel, Aubrey McElmeel, and April Hansel. (Photograph by Sharron L. McElmeel)

Introduction
   E. J. McElmeel and Aubrey McElmeel. (Photograph by Sharron L. McElmeel)

Chapter 1
   Jade McElmeel and Michael J. McElmeel. (Photograph by Nick Leadley)

Chapter End
   Members of Grant Wood Drum and Bugle Corp. (Photograph by Sharron L. McElmeel)

Chapter 2
   Josh Franklin, Cassie Franklin, Barb Franklin, and Brittanie Franklin. (Photograph by Sharron L. McElmeel)

Chapter 3
   Brittanie Franklin and Robert Franklin. (Photograph by Sharron L. McElmeel)

Author, Illustrator, Title Index

Featured entries for authors and titles listed in chapters 1 and 2 are indicated by the use of bold-faced type for the page numbers of that entry.

Subject Index

Numbers refer to page numbers.

About the Author

As a young reader in Mason-ville, Iowa, Sharron L. McElmeel enjoyed the stories of the Brothers Grimm, Hans Christian Andersen, and O. Henry. Now she enjoys reading hundreds of books each year—books that she shares with elementary students. For several years her book critiques were aired over a local public radio affiliate. Her book reviews have appeared in national and local periodicals and newspapers. Through *The Latest and Greatest Read-Alouds*, she is able to share information about some of the best read-alouds published in the last five years with readers nationwide.

Sharron McElmeel is a full-time educator, consultant, and author who still lives in the Iowa countryside where horses graze beside her house, tractors hum in the fields nearby, and the bookshelves in her house are filled with wonderful books to read and share.